W9-AVA-185

GIVING USA™ 2009

Information about revisions to prior years, and other additions to *Giving USA 2009* are online at www.givingusa.org/downloads2009.

User id: givingusa

Password: givingusa2009

GIVING USA™ 2009

The Annual Report on Philanthropy for the Year 2008

54th Annual Issue

Researched and Written at

The Center on Philanthropy
AT INDIANA UNIVERSITY
INDIANA UNIVERSITY–PURDUE UNIVERSITY INDIANAPOLIS

Publisher

GIVINGUSA
F O U N D A T I O N

Photo credits and information

Front cover:

Empowered: Three participants in the Breast Cancer 3-Day express their empowerment after completing the last mile of a three-day, 60-mile walk in Boston for the fight against breast cancer.
Organization represented: Breast Cancer 3-Day (www.The3Day.org), Philadelphia
Photographer: Rex Wilder, Los Angeles

Back cover:

Paulina Pie: As the economic crisis affects families around the world, sponsorship becomes even more important by providing crucial benefits for children like 5-year-old Paulina Pie and her family of the area around Santo Domingo, Dominican Republic, who have been sponsored through Children International.
Organization represented: Children International (www.children.org), Kansas City, MO
Photographer: Erenia Mesa Linares, Kansas City

Giving USA is a public outreach initiative of Giving USA Foundation. The Foundation, established in 1985 by what is now the Giving Institute: Leading Consultants to Non-Profits, endeavors to advance philanthropy through research and education.

ISSN: 0436-0257
ISBN: 978-0-9786199-4-7

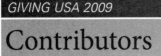

Contributors

We are grateful for the generous gifts to Giving USA Foundation™ for *Giving USA* and wish to recognize in particular the substantial support from the following contributors.

Philanthropy Circle
$15,000
The Center on Philanthropy at Indiana University

Foundation Circle
$10,000–$14,999
CCS Fund Raising
IDC
Marts & Lundy, Inc.

Benefactor
$7,500–$9,999
Grenzebach Glier & Associates, Inc.

Patron
$5,000–$7,499
The Alford Group Inc.
Alexander Haas
Blackbaud, Inc./eTapestry
Campbell & Company
Ketchum, a Pursuant Company
The Sharpe Group

Partner
$2,500–$4,999
Advantage Consulting
Alexander Macnab & Company
Jimmie R. Alford & Maree G. Bullock
Benevon
Claude H. Grizzard
Raybin Associates, Inc.
Ruotolo Associates Inc.
Smith Beers Yunker & Company, Inc.

Developer
$2,000–$2,499
Arnoult & Associates Inc.
The Clements Group
The Curtis Group
The EHL Consulting Group, Inc.
Jeffrey Byrne & Associates, Inc.

Builder
$1,000–$1,999

A.L. Brourman Associates, Inc.
American City Bureau, Inc.
L. Pendleton Armistead, Ed.D.
Bentz Whaley Flessner
Bradley and Teresa Carlson
Gregg and Sharon Carlson
Kristina Carlson, CFRE, ePMT
Carlton & Company
The Collins Group
The Covenant Group, Inc.
Crescendo Interactive, Inc.
Durkin Associates
Jennifer Furla
Global Advancement, LLC
Hodge, Cramer & Associates, Inc.

Jaques & Company, Inc.
Joyaux Associates
The Kellogg Organization, Inc.
Lisa M. Dietlin & Associates, Inc.
Del Martin, CFRE
The Mesaros Family
Miller Group Worldwide, LLC
The Oram Group
The Robert B. Sharp Company of Colorado, Inc.
Semple Bixel Associates, Inc.
Schwab Charitable Fund
StaleyRobeson®
Woodburn, Kyle & Company

Sponsorship
$500–$999

Marilyn Bancel
Blackburn Associates, Inc.
Cardaronella Stirling Associates
Carol O'Brien Associates, Inc.
Compton Fundraising Consultants, Ltd.
DataFund Services, Inc.
Meg Delor
Edith H. Falk
Donald M. Fellows
Peter J. Fissinger, CFRE
Fund Inc®
Kimberly Hawkins
Jeanne Sigler & Associates, Inc.
Richard T. Jolly
Sandy Macnab, FAHP, CFRE
Paulette V. Maehara, CAE, CFRE
Nancy Raybin
Patrick M. Rooney, Ph.D.
George C. Ruotolo, Jr., CFRE
Paul G. Schervish, Ph.D.
Steve & Michelle Verrone
Dawn & Jim Yunker

Friends
Up to $499

Rita Fuerst Adams, CFRE
David Bergeson, Ph.D., CAE
Melissa S. Brown
Clay Buck
Sandi Campione
Clinton C. Crow
Randee Dalzell
Danforth Development
Nick Floratos
Matt Frazier
Clark and Marilynn Gafke
David Garamella
Marc Hilton
Marilyn Hoyt
Jennifer Kelley, SPHR
Thomas Kovach
Elizabeth Lowell
Lynda McKay
Amee Mangkol
Bruce Matthews
Al Seminsky
Colin Ware
Sarah Wagner
Bruce J. Wenger

Contents

Foreword

We estimate that American individuals, corporations, and foundations donated $307.65 billion to charitable causes in 2008. This is a drop of 2 percent in current dollars (-5.7 percent adjusted for inflation), compared to 2007. That is the biggest drop since *Giving USA* began recording the data in the 1950s.

Despite the decline, charitable contributions were an estimated 2.2 percent of Gross Domestic Product. Giving was 2.3 percent of GDP in 2007, when donations soared to an estimated $314.07 (current dollars) billion, as revised in this edition.

This isn't the first time that Americans faced a challenging economic year and saw giving decline. The recession that began in December 2007 included all of 2008. This compares to the recession that began in November 1973, which subsequently included all of 1974. There are other similarities between 1974 and 2008. To help us understand charitable giving, the factors to compare are the indicators most closely associated with giving: changes in the stock market, personal income, corporate profits, and gross domestic product. These are shown in the table below.

The similarity in the economic environments in 1974 and 2008 helps us to understand the similarities in the inflation-adjusted change in charitable giving in those two years. Knowing that changes in the economy and changes in giving are closely linked, we can hope for improvements in 2009 and beyond.

What is a charitable organization to do so that it can survive and even thrive in uncertain times? Here are the most important steps you can take:

- Tell your story honestly and positively. Let your donors and prospective donors know the power of their gifts and what they can accomplish. Avoid a desperate recitation of all the terrible things that will happen if they don't give.

- Stay in touch with your donors. Investigate inexpensive ways to communicate. Show and tell that your organization knows that belts are tightening everywhere and that you are doing your part. Step up public awareness campaigns using

Changes in	1973–1974	2007–2008
Dow Jones Industrial Average	-33 percent	-37 percent
Personal income	-0.2 percent	-0.8 percent
Corporate profits	-16 percent	-18 percent
Gross Domestic Product	-0.5 percent	1.1 percent
Level of Unemployment	7.2 percent	7.2 percent
Estimated change in giving	-5.4 percent	-5.7 percent

social media tools such as blogs, Facebook and Twitter.

- Say thank you. Say it again. Invest a few minutes and 44 cents in a hand-written note. Drop your donor a brief email. Better yet, pick up the phone for an even more personal touch. Make it a conversation about the donor's interests; not every contact should be a solicitation.

- Engage your board members in very practical ways. Make sure they under-stand their role in the fundraising process for your organization and are committed to it. Have them make some of those thank you calls.

- Keep a positive attitude about your mission, vision, and purpose. If you haven't reviewed those in a while, maybe it's time for a refresher so you can recharge your batteries and maintain your role as a key contri-butor to your organization's success.

- Use the practical tips and advice throughout this *Giving USA* report as touchstones of how to raise philanthropic dollars. And don't just read the section that pertains to your sector. Between these covers, you will find a wealth of sound ideas to help you move your fundraising programs forward successfully.

If you work in the development field, take heart. While it's not easy to raise dollars, Americans still care and want to help. Or, if you're reading this because you donate to causes and organizations dear to your heart, thank you. It's your contributions that make philanthropy a worthwhile field.

It enriches all of us and speaks well of the United States as a whole that we continue to be supportive of charitable groups in good times and down times.

Del Martin, CFRE
Chair, Giving USA Foundation™, publisher of *Giving USA*

Nancy L. Raybin
Chair, Giving Institute: Leading Consultants to Non-Profits

Patrick M. Rooney, Ph.D.
Executive Director, The Center on Philanthropy at Indiana University

Giving USA began 54 years ago. As you read these pages, please thank the many donors now and from the past who have made *Giving USA* possible.

As editor, I'd also like to thank researchers who developed the estimating procedures and the many whose findings are included in this year's edition.

In addition, with deep appreciation, thanks go to Del Martin, chair of Giving USA Foundation™, and Nancy Raybin, chair of Giving Institute: Leading Consultants to Non-Profits; James Yunker, chair of the *Giving USA* Editorial Review Board and of the *Giving USA* Advisory Council on Methodology; Edith Falk and Leo Arnoult, co-chairs of the *Giving USA* resource development committee; and Leslie Biggins Mollsen, chair of the photo contest committee. Members of the boards and committees are named beginning on page 233. These many very busy people volunteer hours of time and years of experience to ensure *Giving USA*'s continuation as the yearbook of philanthropy. Members of Giving Institute offer counsel and ask questions that influence what appears in *Giving USA*. One recent addition, showing giving graphed with the Standard & Poor's 500 Index, arose because of inquiries from David King of Alexander Haas.

At the Center on Philanthropy at Indiana University, with gratitude, I thank Patrick M. Rooney, Ph.D., newly appointed as executive director, and Una O. Osili, Ph.D., interim director of research, plus every member of the research department and many other Center colleagues, some of whom pitched in with very little advance notice. Doctoral or master's degree candidates in philanthropy programs at Indiana University-Purdue University Indianapolis wrote many of the chapters, and I am grateful for their fresh perspectives. They are credited in full on page 238.

The physical production of the book relies on the talents of Rich Metter of Rich Metter Graphics (New York City), J. Heidi Newman of Mark My Word! (Indianapolis), Miriam Lezak (Acton, MA), and the printing team at IPC, St. Joseph, MI. Their professionalism and focus make it possible for readers to see and hold a completed text.

My family, as ever, deserves the highest praise for their many (unsung and often unknown) contributions to this work. To my husband, children, and this year, my mother who visited in May and took on duties that I would normally do, I can only say, thank you.

Melissa S. Brown
Managing Editor, *Giving USA 2009*

1 Key findings

Overall charitable giving in the U.S. decreased an estimated 2 percent (-5.7 percent adjusted for inflation) in 2008, to $307.65 billion, down from a revised estimate of $314.07 billion for 2007.

Individual giving is estimated to be $229.28 billion, a drop of 2.7 percent (-6.3 percent adjusted for inflation). Individual giving is 75 percent of total estimated giving.

Charitable bequests are estimated to be $22.66 billion, a decrease of 2.8 percent (-6.4 percent adjusted for inflation) compared with the revised estimate of $23.31 billion for 2007. Charitable bequests are 7 percent of total estimated giving.

Foundation grantmaking is estimated by the Foundation Center to be $41.21 billion in 2008, a 3 percent increase (but a drop of 0.8 percent adjusted for inflation). Foundation giving is 13 percent of total estimated giving.

Corporate giving is estimated to be $14.5 billion, a decline of 4.5 percent (-8.0 percent adjusted for inflation). Corporate giving is 5 percent of total estimated giving.

Contributions to religious organizations reached an estimated $106.89 billion in 2008. This is growth of 5.5 percent (1.6 percent adjusted for inflation) compared with 2007. Giving to religious organizations is 35 percent of total estimated giving for 2008.

Gifts to educational organizations are estimated to be $40.94 billion in 2008. This is a drop of 5.5 percent (-9 percent adjusted for inflation) compared with 2007. The education sector received 13 percent of total estimated giving.

The Council for Aid to Education (CAE) reported growth in the 2007–2008 fiscal year of 6.2 percent in higher education giving (2.3 percent adjusted for inflation). Nearly one-half of that growth was attributed to 20 of the largest educational institutions. The decline estimated by *Giving USA* reflects changes estimated for the last half of 2008 based on stock market changes.

Gifts to foundations dropped to $32.65 billion in 2008. This is a decrease of 19.2 percent (-22.2 percent adjusted for inflation). Gifts to foundations are 11 percent of total estimated giving.

The estimate does not include payments by Warren Buffett on his pledge to the Gates Foundation. Those gifts will be distributed within a few years to recipient agencies and will be reported as grants made. In recent years, gifts to foundations have been 13 percent of the sum of individual and charitable bequest giving. The estimate for 2008 reflects that pattern.

Gifts to human services organizations are estimated to be $25.88 billion in 2008. This is a drop of 12.7 percent (-15.9 percent adjusted for inflation). Human services giving is reported at 9 percent of total estimated giving.

Gifts to health organizations dropped to an estimated $21.64 billion in 2008. This is a decrease of 6.5 percent (-10 percent adjusted for inflation). Health giving is 7 percent of total estimated giving.

Gifts to public-society benefit organizations reached an estimated $23.88 billion in 2008. This reflects an increase of 5.4 percent (1.5 percent adjusted for inflation). Public-society benefit giving is 8 percent of total estimated giving.

Contributions to many public-society benefit charities are distributed to human services organizations in allocations made through United Ways, Jewish federations, and free-standing donor-advised funds.

The arts, culture, and humanities subsector received an estimated $12.79 billion in contributions in 2008. This is a drop of 6.4 percent (-9.9 percent adjusted for inflation). Arts, culture, and humanities giving is 4 percent of total estimated giving.

International affairs organizations received an estimated $13.3 billion in 2008. This is an increase of 0.6 percent (but a decrease of 3.1 percent adjusted for inflation) compared with 2007. International affairs giving is 4 percent of total estimated giving.

Donations to environment/animals organizations fell to an estimated $6.58 billion in 2008. This is a decline of 5.5 percent (-9 percent adjusted for inflation). This subsector is 2 percent of total estimated giving.

Deductions carried forward and unallocated contributions are estimated to be $19.39 billion, or 6 percent of total estimated giving.

Unallocated giving includes gifts to newly formed organizations; individual and corporate deductions expected to be claimed in 2008 for gifts made in prior years (carried over); amounts that donors deduct at a value different from what the nonprofit reports as revenue (e.g., corporate deductions at cost and nonprofit receipt at fair market value); gifts and grants to government entities claimed by donors but not reported as received at a 501(c)(3) charity; gifts to organizations treated legally as foundations, but not making grants or qualifying as operating foundations; and foundation grants to organizations located in another country. The Foundation Center reports for 2007 that $1.9 billion was granted to organizations in other nations.[1]

---

1   S. Lawrence and R. Mukai, *Foundation Giving Trends: Update on Funding Priorities*, March 2009, The Foundation Center, www.foundationcenter.org.

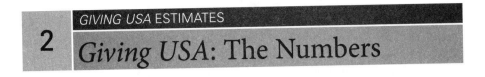
Giving USA: The Numbers

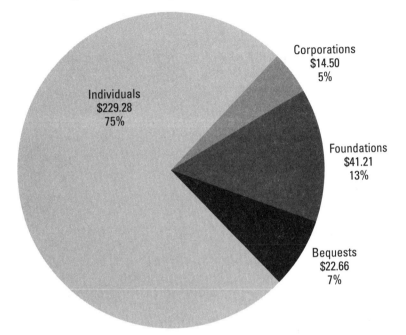

2008 contributions: $307.65 billion by source of contributions
($ in billions – All figures are rounded)

Corporations
$14.50
5%

Individuals
$229.28
75%

Foundations
$41.21
13%

Bequests
$22.66
7%

- Total giving for 2008 is estimated to be $307.65 billion. This is a decrease of 2.0 percent (-5.7 percent adjusted for inflation) compared with the revised estimate of $314.07 billion for 2007.
- This is the first decline in giving since 1987 and the second since *Giving USA* began in 1956.
- Individual giving, at $229.28 billion, includes estimated charitable deductions on tax returns filed for 2008 and an estimate of charitable giving by taxpayers who do not itemize deductions.
- The charitable bequest estimate of $22.66 billion reflects estimates for charitable deductions on estate tax returns filed in 2008 and giving by estates not filing federal estate tax returns.
- Individual giving and charitable bequests combined are estimated to be $251.94 billion (82 percent of the total).
- Foundation grantmaking reached an estimated $41.21 billion. Of that, about $18.5 billion is likely to be from family foundations, based on the percentage of family foundation grants in 2007 reported by the Foundation Center. Grantmaking by corporate foundations is in the estimate of corporate giving.
- Individual, bequest, and estimated family foundation giving combined are approximately $270 billion, or 88 percent of the total. Individual giving and family foundation giving added together are about $248 billion, which is approximately 81 percent of the total.
- Corporate giving is estimated to be $14.50 billion. This includes estimated grants made by corporate foundations.

2008 contributions: $307.65 billion by type of recipient organization
($ in billions – All figures are rounded)

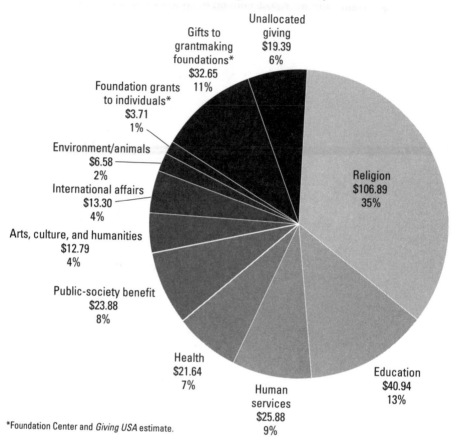

Unallocated giving $19.39 6%

Gifts to grantmaking foundations* $32.65 11%

Foundation grants to individuals* $3.71 1%

Environment/animals $6.58 2%

International affairs $13.30 4%

Arts, culture, and humanities $12.79 4%

Public-society benefit $23.88 8%

Health $21.64 7%

Human services $25.88 9%

Education $40.94 13%

Religion $106.89 35%

*Foundation Center and *Giving USA* estimate.

- Total charitable giving reached an estimated $307.65 billion. This includes contributions to nine types of charitable organizations, using nonprofit definitions from the National Taxonomy of Exempt Entities. It also includes grants awarded to individuals, which are reported here for the first time in *Giving USA*, as well as a portion of giving that could not be allocated to a recipient type.

- The estimated $106.89 billion to religion is 35 percent of the total giving. This is a slight increase from the share reported in 2008 for giving in 2007, when giving to religion was 33 percent of the total.

- Giving to education, estimated to be $40.94 billion and 13 percent of the total, is down from 14 percent reported in 2008 for giving in 2007.

- Human services charities received an estimated $25.88 billion in contributions in 2008, which is less than was estimated for 2007. The 2008 amount is rounded at 9 percent of total giving, down from nearly 10 percent reported in 2008 for giving in 2007.

- Health organizations also realized an estimated decline in giving to $21.64 billion in 2008. This puts giving to the health subsector at 7 percent of total giving, which is a decrease from nearly 8 percent reported in 2008 for giving in 2007.

- Giving to public-society benefit organizations is estimated to have grown in 2008, to $23.88 billion. This puts this subsector at 8 percent of total giving, up from 7 percent reported in 2008 for giving in 2007.

- Arts, culture, and humanities organizations reported a difficult year in 2008, and the estimate shows a drop in charitable giving to $12.79 billion. This subsector is now 4 percent of total giving, down from 5 percent reported in 2008 for giving in 2007.

- International affairs organizations saw large contributions in 2005, a decline in contributions in 2006, followed by growth in giving in 2007. The estimate for this year is $13.30 billion. This subsector remains at 4 percent of the total.

- Organizations in the environment/animals subsector received an estimated $6.58 billion in 2008, which reflects a drop in giving from 2007. This subsector received an estimated 2 percent of total giving, as it did in 2007.

- The Foundation Center tracks foundation grants made to individuals. This includes products distributed by operating foundations created by pharmaceutical companies, scholarships paid to individuals, and grants to artists. These grants are estimated to be $3.71 billion in 2008, which is 1 percent of the total.

- Gifts to grantmaking foundations (independent, community, and operating foundations) are estimated to be $32.65 billion, which is 11 percent of the total.

- A portion of giving is unallocated. This includes deductions carried over multiple tax years, gifts to new organizations and government agencies, and foundation grants to international recipients. The Foundation Center reports for 2007 that $1.9 billion was granted to organizations in other nations. It also includes donations to charitable trusts and differences in fiscal year and calendar year reporting. For 2008, this is estimated to be $19.39 billion or 6 percent of the total.

Changes in giving by source, 2006–2007 and 2007–2008, and 2006–2008 cumulative
(In current dollars)

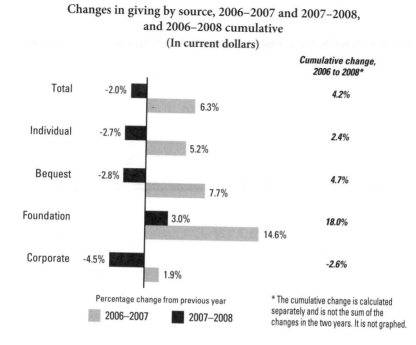

Cumulative change, 2006 to 2008*

	2007–2008	2006–2007	Cumulative change, 2006 to 2008*
Total	-2.0%	6.3%	4.2%
Individual	-2.7%	5.2%	2.4%
Bequest	-2.8%	7.7%	4.7%
Foundation	3.0%	14.6%	18.0%
Corporate	-4.5%	1.9%	-2.6%

Percentage change from previous year
2006–2007   2007–2008

* The cumulative change is calculated separately and is not the sum of the changes in the two years. It is not graphed.

- Total giving decreased in current-dollar terms for the first time since 1987. The drop is 2 percent and is attributable to economic concerns. The decline in 1987 occurred in a year that followed tax law changes in 1986 that inspired "pre-giving" to maximize the deductibility of gifts prior to limits that took place in 1987. The cumulative change from 2006 to 2008 is 4.2 percent.

- Individual giving in 2008 fell an estimated 2.7 percent compared with 2007. This is the first decline since 1987. This drop follows growth of 5.2 percent estimated for 2007. The cumulative change from 2006 to 2008 is 2.4 percent.

- Charitable bequests (which include realized planned gifts) fell an estimated 2.8 percent in 2008 compared with 2007. The cumulative change from 2006 to 2008 is growth in charitable bequests of 4.7 percent, which reflects an increase of 7.7 percent in 2007.

- Foundation grantmaking increased an estimated 3.0 percent in 2008 and a confirmed 14.6 percent in 2007. This is the fastest growing source of charitable donations, with a cumulative change of 18.0 percent from 2006 to 2008.

- Corporate giving declined an estimated 4.5 percent in 2008. The cumulative change from 2006 to 2008 is a decline of 2.6 percent, with an estimated increase of 1.9 percent in 2006 to 2007. Corporate giving rose in 2005 as companies gave exceptional amounts for disaster relief. Corporate giving has gradually been slowing or declining since 2005, but remains above the 2004 amount of $11.36 billion.

Changes in giving by source, 2006–2007 and 2007–2008, and 2006–2008 cumulative
(Adjusted for inflation)

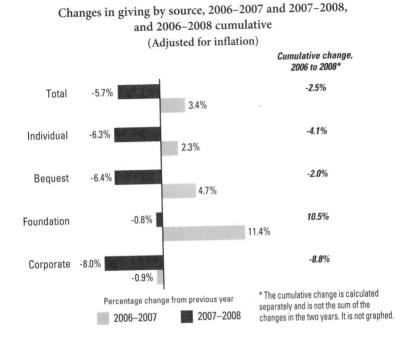

Cumulative change, 2006 to 2008*

Source	2007–2008	2006–2007	Cumulative change, 2006 to 2008*
Total	-5.7%	3.4%	*-2.5%*
Individual	-6.3%	2.3%	*-4.1%*
Bequest	-6.4%	4.7%	*-2.0%*
Foundation	-0.8%	11.4%	*10.5%*
Corporate	-8.0%	-0.9%	*-8.8%*

Percentage change from previous year

☐ 2006–2007   ■ 2007–2008

* The cumulative change is calculated separately and is not the sum of the changes in the two years. It is not graphed.

- Total giving in 2008 fell an estimated 5.7 percent, adjusted for inflation, compared with growth of 3.4 percent in 2007. Cumulatively, since 2006, giving has fallen an estimated 2.5 percent.

- Individual giving declined 6.3 percent in 2008, after adjusting for inflation. It increased 2.3 percent in 2007. The cumulative change from 2006 to 2008 is a decline of 4.1 percent.

- Estimated charitable bequests declined 6.4 percent, adjusted for inflation, in 2008. Charitable bequests increased an estimated 4.7 percent in 2007. The cumulative change from 2006 to 2008 is a drop of 2.0 percent, adjusted for inflation.

- Grantmaking by independent, community, and operating foundations fell 0.8 percent, adjusted for inflation, in 2008. In 2007, foundation grantmaking rose by 11.4 percent, and the cumulative change from 2006 to 2008 was 10.5 percent.

- Corporate giving fell an estimated 8.0 percent in 2008, adjusted for inflation, reflecting a difficult year for profit-making in most industry sectors. Corporate giving declined an estimated 0.9 percent in 2007. The cumulative change from 2006 to 2008 was a decline of 8.8 percent. Nonetheless, corporate giving in 2008 remains above the level it reached in 2004, prior to the natural disasters that inspired high levels of corporate giving in 2005.

Changes in giving by type of recipient organization, 2006–2007 and 2007–2008, and 2006–2008 cumulative
(In current dollars)

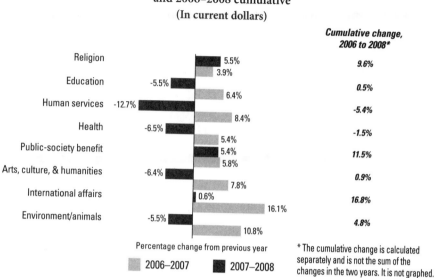

Cumulative change, 2006 to 2008*

Recipient	2006–2007	2007–2008	Cumulative change, 2006 to 2008*
Religion	5.5%	3.9%	9.6%
Education	6.4%	-5.5%	0.5%
Human services	8.4%	-12.7%	-5.4%
Health	5.4%	-6.5%	-1.5%
Public-society benefit	5.8%	5.4%	11.5%
Arts, culture, & humanities	7.8%	-6.4%	0.9%
International affairs	16.1%	0.6%	16.8%
Environment/animals	10.8%	-5.5%	4.8%

Percentage change from previous year

☐ 2006–2007   ■ 2007–2008

* The cumulative change is calculated separately and is not the sum of the changes in the two years. It is not graphed.

■ Three subsectors saw estimated growth in giving in 2008: religion, public-society benefit, and international affairs. The other subsectors saw decreases, as did giving to foundations, which is not shown in this graph.

■ Except for giving to religion, estimates for 2007 and 2008 are based on the historical relationships between changes in household income (personal income), the Standard & Poor's 500 Index, giving to each type of charity, and total giving. These estimates will be revised when data are available from IRS Forms 990 filed by charities with revenue of $25,000 or more.

■ The estimated change in giving to religion is based on data from the National Council of Churches of Christ, the Evangelical Council for Financial Accountability, and surveys of Catholic parishes from 2002 through 2006.

■ *Giving USA* projects that giving to religion increased by 5.5 percent in 2008, compared with growth of 3.9 percent in 2007. The cumulative change from 2006 to 2008 is an increase of 9.6 percent.

■ Gifts to education are estimated to have decreased 5.5 percent in 2008, following growth of 6.4 percent in 2007. The change from 2006 to 2008 is a cumulative increase of 0.5 percent.

■ Giving to human services organizations is estimated to have dropped 12.7 percent in 2008, following an increase of 8.4 percent in 2007. The cumulative change from 2006 to 2008 is a decline of 5.4 percent.

■ Giving to health organizations fell an estimated 6.5 percent in 2008, after increasing an estimated 5.4 percent in 2007. The cumulative change from 2006 to 2008 is a decline of 1.5 percent.

■ Giving to public-society benefit organizations rose an estimated 5.4 percent in 2008 and by an estimated 5.8 percent in 2007. The cumulative change is 11.5 percent from 2006 to 2008.

■ Giving to arts, culture, and humanities organizations declined an estimated 6.4 percent in 2008 and rose by an estimated 7.8 percent in 2007. The cumulative change is 0.9 percent growth from 2006 to 2008.

■ Giving to organizations working in the areas of international relations, international affairs, and international development rose an estimated 0.6 percent in 2008 and an estimated 16.1 percent in 2007. The cumulative change is growth of 16.8 percent from 2006 to 2008.

■ Giving to organizations in the environment/animals subsector declined an estimated 5.5 percent in 2008 after increasing an estimated 10.8 percent in 2007. The change from 2006 to 2008 is cumulative growth of 4.8 percent.

■ This graph does not show other types of recipients, including foundations (estimated decline of 19.2 percent) and grants made to individuals (estimated increase of 10 percent).

Changes in giving by type of recipient organization, 2006–2007 and 2007–2008, and 2006–2008 cumulative
(Adjusted for inflation)

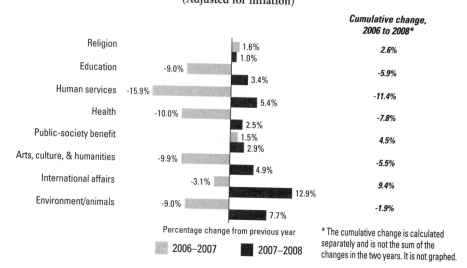

Cumulative change, 2006 to 2008*

Recipient	2006–2007	2007–2008	Cumulative change, 2006 to 2008*
Religion	1.6%	1.0%	2.6%
Education	-9.0%	3.4%	-5.9%
Human services	-15.9%	5.4%	-11.4%
Health	-10.0%	2.5%	-7.8%
Public-society benefit	1.5%	2.9%	4.5%
Arts, culture, & humanities	-9.9%	4.9%	-5.5%
International affairs	-3.1%	12.9%	9.4%
Environment/animals	-9.0%	7.7%	-1.9%

Percentage change from previous year

2006–2007   2007–2008

* The cumulative change is calculated separately and is not the sum of the changes in the two years. It is not graphed.

- Giving to religion and public-society benefit increased, adjusted for inflation. All other subsectors are estimated to have had a decline in giving, with sharp declines (9 percent or more) in five types of organizations. These are the most drastic declines in giving to these subsectors in the past 40 years.

- This is the first year since 1987 (when all subsectors above began to be tracked and when the series based on IRS Forms 990 began) that six of the eight tracked subsectors have been estimated to decline. The prior worst year was 2002, when total giving fell an inflation-adjusted 1.1 percent and five of the eight subsectors showed a drop in charitable contributions.

- Adjusted for inflation, giving to religion increased 1.6 percent. This includes donations to houses of worship in all faith groups, including non-denominational churches. It also includes media ministries, missionary societies, and other entities organized to teach or promote religious faith and practice.

- Stock market changes are associated with changes in giving to the education, human services, and health subsectors.
  — Giving to education declined an estimated 9.0 percent.
  — Giving to human services declined an estimated 15.9 percent.
  — Giving to health dropped an estimated 10.0 percent.

- Giving to organizations in the public-society benefit subsector rose an estimated 1.5 percent, adjusted for inflation, in 2008. This subsector includes United Ways, Jewish federations, economic and community development programs, civil rights groups, and freestanding donor-advised funds.

■ Giving to organizations in the arts, culture, and humanities subsector dropped an estimated 9.9 percent in 2008.

■ The international subsector saw an estimated 3.1 percent decline in contributions received in 2008 compared with 2007. International disasters in 2008 included a winter weather crisis in China, a cyclone in Myanmar, and a May earthquake in China. U.S. companies and households responded to all of these with donations of aid.

■ Organizations engaged in the environment/animals subsector received an estimated 9.0 percent less in 2008 compared to 2007.

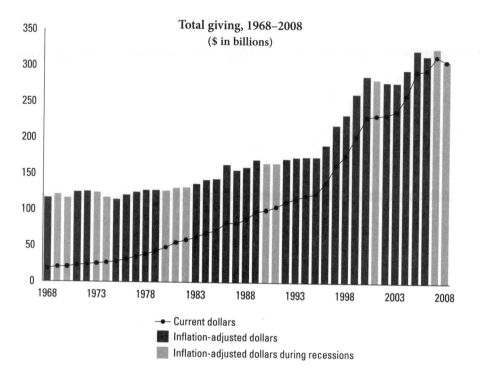

Total giving, 1968–2008
($ in billions)

- Current dollars
- Inflation-adjusted dollars
- Inflation-adjusted dollars during recessions

- Total giving has increased in current dollars in every year but two: 1987 and 2008.

- Adjusted for inflation, giving typically increases in non-recession years and falls in recession years.

- Not shown on the graph is giving during the Great Depression (1929 to 1933). In 1930, itemized individual giving fell 7.6 percent. It rose in 1931 and fell 20 percent between 1931 and 1932. In 1933, it fell another 5.3 percent. During the Great Depression, Gross Domestic Product fell 25 percent; unemployment reached as high as 38 percent; and the Dow Jones Industrial Average fell 85 percent from its pre-Depression high to the lowest value during the Depression (1932).

- The 1973–1975 recession, the longest on record between 1933 and 2007, saw a cumulative drop in total giving of 9.2 percent. The worst single-year decline between the Depression and 2007 was in 1974 when total giving fell 5.4 percent, adjusted for inflation.

- In 1987, total giving fell 4.7 percent, following an unusual increase (14 percent) in 1986. The increase followed a well-publicized tax law change. In 1987, the law limited tax deductions for charitable contributions. Many people "pre-gave" in 1986 to maximize their tax deductions.

- In 2008, total giving fell an estimated 5.7 percent, adjusted for inflation. The recession that began in December 2007 continued into 2009, and many charity leaders are planning for the possibility that giving in the second year will be even lower than in the first year of the downturn.

Giving by individuals, 1968–2008
($ in billions)

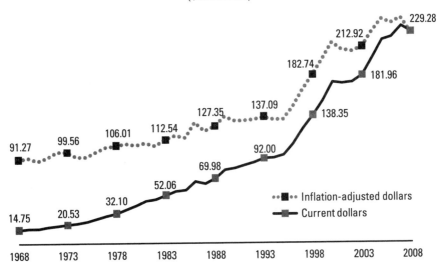

- Individual giving in 2008 is estimated at $229.28 billion, which is the lowest value since inflation-adjusted giving increased from its 2003 level of $212.92 billion.

- Individual giving includes everything that would qualify under tax law as a charitable contribution. This includes gifts of money and donations of household items to an entity like Goodwill.

- In 1988, the inflation-adjusted amount given by individuals ($127.35 billion) divided by the number of American households (91.12 million, using Current Population Survey data from the Census Bureau) results in an estimate of giving of $1,398 (adjusted for inflation) per household.

- In a similar calculation, by 1998 the number of households reached 102.53 million and the per household average gift rose to $1,782. For 2008, with estimated giving by individuals of $229.28 billion and approximately 116.78 million households, the average donation is $1,963 per household.

- The calculations "per household" include all households, even those that do not give. This allows for comparison over time.

Giving by bequest, 1968–2008
($ in billions)

- Charitable bequests reached an estimated $22.66 billion in 2008.

- The estimate for 2008 includes an estimated $19.70 billion in charitable bequests from estates filing federal estate tax returns in 2008 and an estimated $2.96 billion from estates that do not file federal returns.

- Among all decedents, an estimated 120,000 estates leave a charitable bequest each year. The vast majority of the amount in the estimate (about 85 percent) is from about 8,000 estates that file estate tax returns and claim charitable deductions.

- Since at least 2001, an average of 45 percent of the amount contributed according to estate tax returns has gone to foundations. The balance is divided among all other types of charities. Assuming this pattern held true for 2008, an estimated $12.5 billion in 2008 was bequeathed to charities other than foundations, based on the estimated charitable bequests from estates that do and do not file estate tax returns.

Giving by foundations, 1968–2008
($ in billions)

Source: The Foundation Center. Excludes giving by corporate foundations, which is in giving by corporations.

- Grantmaking by independent, community, and operating foundations reached an estimated $41.21 billion in 2008, according to a survey by the Foundation Center. This is an increase of 3.0 percent (a drop of 0.8 percent adjusted for inflation) from the revised foundation grantmaking total of $40.0 billion released by the Foundation Center in spring 2009. The final number for 2007 is based on IRS Forms 990 and 990-PF filed by foundations.

- Despite a recession and a stock market decline, foundation grantmaking in 2008 is estimated by the Foundation Center to have surpassed all prior records. Grants made in 2008 include distributions from the Bill & Melinda Gates Foundation in the amount of $2.8 billion as well as grantmaking by other private, community, and operating foundations.

- The continued growth of foundation grantmaking in 2008 reflects strong foundation asset growth in 2006 and 2007.

- While overall grantmaking increased among the foundations surveyed for 2008 giving estimates, the Foundation Center found that nearly half (46.9 percent) reduced their giving in the year.

- According to the Foundation Center, about 90 percent of foundations surveyed make grants from investment earnings. Grantmaking is considered "new money" for philanthropy. This may change as more donors arrange for their gifts to foundations to be "spent down" rather than invested in perpetuity.

- The Foundation Center cautioned that grantmaking is expected to decline in 2009, although the reduction will likely be far less than market losses might suggest.

Giving by corporations, 1968–2008
($ in billions)

- Corporate contributions, which include distributions from corporate foundations, reached an estimated $14.50 billion in 2008.

- The estimate shows a drop in giving during 2008, reflecting lowered corporate profits. The decline in corporate profits reported by the federal Bureau of Economic Analysis includes the closure, merger, and losses reported by firms in the financial and insurance sector in 2008.

- Estimated contributions by corporate foundations are approximately 30 percent of the estimated total for 2008. In 2006, the most recent year for which there are complete data, corporate foundation giving was 27.5 percent of the total amount contributed by companies. From 2001 through 2006, corporate foundation grantmaking averaged 29 percent of corporate giving.

Total giving by source by five-year spans in inflation-adjusted dollars, 1969–2008
($ in billions)

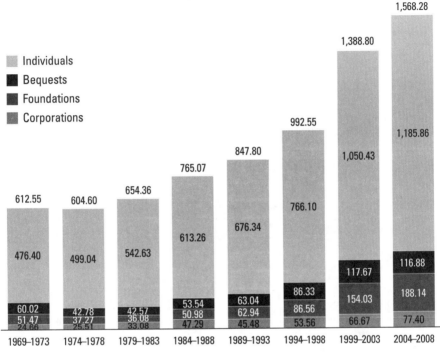

Individuals
Bequests
Foundations
Corporations

	1969–1973	1974–1978	1979–1983	1984–1988	1989–1993	1994–1998	1999–2003	2004–2008
Total	612.55	604.60	654.36	765.07	847.80	992.55	1,388.80	1,568.28
Individuals	476.40	499.04	542.63	613.26	676.34	766.10	1,050.43	1,185.86
Bequests	60.02	42.78	42.57	53.54	63.04	86.33	117.67	116.88
Foundations	51.47	37.27	36.08	50.98	62.94	86.56	154.03	188.14
Corporations	24.66	25.51	33.08	47.29	45.48	53.56	66.67	77.40

Giving USA uses the Consumer Price Index (CPI) to adjust for inflation.

- After two decades of comparatively slow growth from 1969 through 1988, giving shows a steep increase, adjusted for inflation, from 1989 through 2008.

- The amount given from corporations, foundations, and individuals has steadily risen since 1994. Bequests increased in amount from 1994–1998 to the 1999–2003 period and have held at approximately the same level in the past five years.

Giving by source: Percentage of the total by five-year spans, 1968–2008

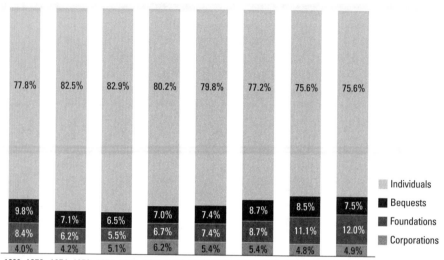

1969–1973 1974–1978 1979–1983 1984–1988 1989–1993 1994–1998 1999–2003 2004–2008

- As giving has increased over the past 40 years, foundations have been giving a larger share of the total and individuals have been giving a smaller share of the total. This reflects the growth in the number and assets of family foundations. The Foundation Center estimated that in 2007, family foundations distributed about 56 percent of all grants made by independent foundations.

- Bequest contributions, at 9.8 percent of the total from 1969 through 1973, have been a less significant part of the total since then. Giving in life has become increasingly important. This is especially noticeable in giving to foundations, as the Gates family, the Moore family, the Broad family, and many others have done in recent years.

Total giving as a percentage of gross domestic product, 1968–2008

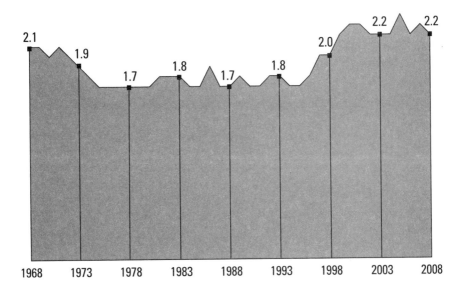

- Gross domestic product (GDP) increased from 2007 to 2008 by 3.3 percent in current terms and by 1.1 percent, adjusted for inflation, according to the Bureau of Economic Analysis of the federal government, which adjusts for inflation differently than *Giving USA* does.

- Giving is estimated to be 2.2 percent of GDP. This level is a slight decline from an estimated 2.3 percent in 2007. For the period from 1998 to 2007, giving averaged 2.2 percent of GDP. In that time, it ranged from a low of 2.0 percent (1998) to a high of 2.4 percent (in 2005).

- The 2.2 percent average from 1998 to 2007 is the highest 10-year average in the 40-year history tracked in this edition of *Giving USA*. For the period from 1968 to 1977, giving averaged 1.9 percent of GDP. For the two successive periods of 1978 to 1987 and 1988 to 1997, giving was, on average, 1.8 percent of GDP.

Total charitable giving graphed with the Standard & Poor's 500 Index, 1968–2008
(Adjusted for inflation)

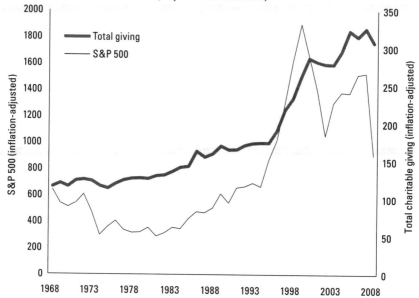

- Three sources of contributions are linked with stock market values:
  - Individuals: because higher wealth means more assets to contribute and a greater sense of financial security;
  - Foundations: because most foundation assets are invested in stocks; and
  - Bequests: because many—although not all—estate assets are securities or are otherwise linked to stock market values (mutual funds, for example).

- This graph shows that changes in giving are associated with changes in the Standard & Poor's 500 Index. Giving, however, does not necessarily change as dramatically as the stock market does in any one year. The stock market values used are for the last trading day of the year.

- From 1972 to 1974, when the market fell from above 600 to around 300 (adjusted for inflation) or 51 percent, total giving fell 7 percent.

- Similarly, from 2000 through 2002, the market fell from above 1650 to just over 1052 (a drop of 36 percent), and giving declined just 3 percent.

- The same trend appears in 2008. The stock market dropped precipitously (-40 percent for the Standard & Poor's 500 Index and a drop of 37 percent for the Dow Jones Industrial Average), and giving declined an estimated 5.7 percent adjusted for inflation.

**Trends in giving as a share of selected types of personal outlays
and as a share of disposable personal income, 1968–2008**
(2007 is most recent data on expenditure types)

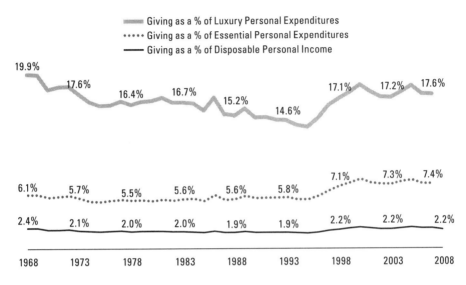

- Charitable giving by households is a form of personal consumption. Gifts can be made from income, wealth, or both. This graph examines giving as a share of disposable personal income—the income that remains after taxes are paid—and as a share of essential and luxury expenditures.

- Charitable giving was 2.4 percent of disposable (after-tax) personal income (DPI) in 1968. It fell to 1.9 percent of DPI in 1988 and rose to 2.2 percent (its current level) by 1998.

- From disposable income, households must pay for shelter, food, clothing, utilities, and gasoline. Giving was just over 6 percent in 1968 of these essential expenditures and declined to 5.6 percent by 1988. It rose to 7.1 percent by 1998 and was an estimated 7.4 percent in 2007 (the most recent year for expenditure data). Essential expenditures were one-third (33 percent) of total personal consumption expenditures for 2007.

- Households also choose other expenses. These include restaurant meals, travel, jewelry, tobacco and alcohol, and recreation (spectator sports, movies, amusement parks, and more). Giving was 19.9 percent of these "luxury" expenditures in 1968 and was 17.6 percent in 2007 (most recent expenditure data). Expenditures coded as "luxury" for this analysis were less than one-seventh (14 percent) of total household spending in 2007.

Corporate giving as a percentage of corporate pretax profits, 1968–2008

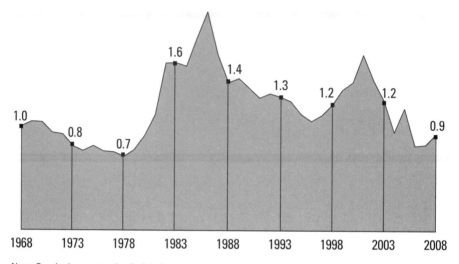

Note: Graph shows actual calculated percentages. In text, percentages are rounded to the nearest 1/10 of one percent.

- Corporate giving has averaged around 1 percent of corporate profits for at least the last four decades, with variations year-to-year as profits and giving programs change.

- Years where giving is a low percentage of corporate profits can reflect either very high profit levels or lower than usual giving levels.

- The recent dip in giving as a share of corporate profits (2006 to 2007) actually reflects increased profits.

- Corporate profits declined in 2008, however, giving did not fall at the same rate. Therefore, giving as a share of corporate profits is estimated to have increased slightly in 2008 to 0.9 percent.

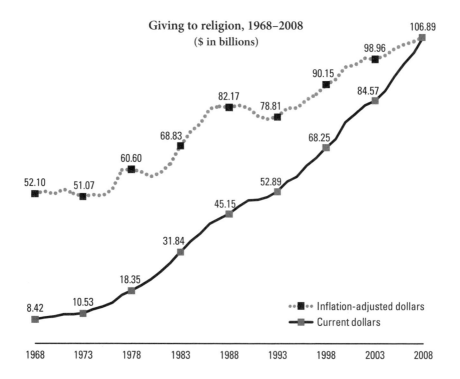

Giving to religion, 1968–2008
($ in billions)

- Giving to religion in current dollars has increased steadily over 40 years. Adjusted for inflation, it has stagnated periodically with the last such period in the mid-1980s to mid-1990s.

- Since 1995, giving to religion, adjusted for inflation, has shown nearly annual increases.

- In 1988, the inflation-adjusted amount given to religion ($82.17 billion) divided by the number of American households (91.12 million, using Current Population Survey data from the Census Bureau) results in an estimate of giving to religion of $901 (adjusted for inflation) per household.

- In a similar calculation including giving from all donor types, by 1998, the number of households had grown to 102.53 million and the per household average gift to religion fell to $879. For 2008, with estimated giving to religion of $106.89 billion and approximately 116.78 million households, donations to religion averaged $915 per household.

- The calculations "per household" include all households, even those that do not give to religion. They also include all giving to religion, including that from corporations, foundations, and through charitable bequests. This allows for comparison over time and across subsectors.

Giving to education, 1968–2008
($ in billions)

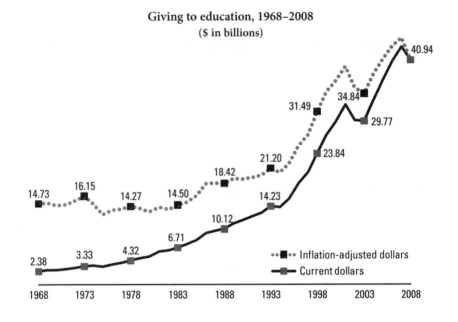

- Giving to education has increased a great deal, particularly since the mid-1990s.

- In 1988, the inflation-adjusted total amount given to education ($18.42 billion) divided by the number of American households (91.12 million, using Current Population Survey data from the Census Bureau) results in an estimate of giving to education of $202 (adjusted for inflation) per household.

- In a similar calculation, by 1998, the number of households had grown to 102.53 million and the per household average gift to education rose to $307. For 2008, with estimated giving to education of $40.94 billion and approximately 116.78 million households, donations to education averaged $351 per household.

- The calculations "per household" include all households, even those that do not give to education. They also include all giving to education, including that from corporations, foundations, and through charitable bequests. This allows for comparison over time and across subsectors.

Giving to foundations, 1968–2008
($ in billions)

Gifts to foundations began to be reported in 1978.
Data: The Foundation Center.
Excludes gifts to corporate foundations and an estimate of the amount given by Warren Buffett
to the Gates Foundation.

- The Foundation Center and *Giving USA* estimate giving to foundations of $32.65 billion. This is a decline of 19.2 percent (-22.2 percent adjusted for inflation) from the revised value of $40.43 billion for 2007, which is based on IRS Forms 990 and 990-PF as analyzed by the Foundation Center minus an estimate of the amount Warren Buffett gave to the Bill & Melinda Gates Foundation.

- In 1988, the inflation-adjusted total amount given to foundations ($7.15 billion) divided by the number of American households (91.12 million, using Current Population Survey data from the Census Bureau) results in an estimate of giving to independent, operating, and community foundations of $78 (adjusted for inflation) per household.

- In a similar calculation, by 1998, the number of households had grown to 102.53 million and the per household average gift to independent, operating, and community foundations rose to $257. For 2008, with estimated giving to foundations at $32.65 billion and approximately 116.78 million households, donations to foundations averaged $280 per household.

- The calculations "per household" include all households, even those that do not give to foundations. They also include all giving to independent, operating, and community foundations, including that from corporations and through charitable bequests. This allows for comparison over time and across subsectors.

Giving to human services, 1968–2008
(\$ in billions)

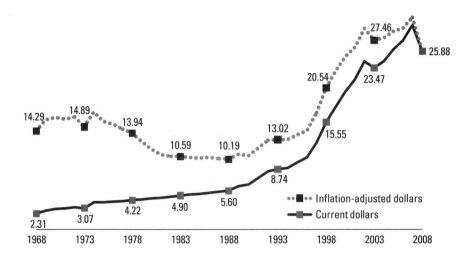

- Giving to human services has increased a great deal, particularly since the mid-1990s.

- In 1988, the inflation-adjusted amount given to human services (\$10.19 billion) divided by the number of American households (91.12 million, using Current Population Survey data from the Census Bureau) results in an estimate of giving to human services of \$112 (adjusted for inflation) per household.

- In a similar calculation including giving from all donor types, by 1998, the number of households had grown to 102.53 million and the per household average gift to human services had risen to \$200. For 2008, with total estimated giving from all sources to human services of \$25.88 billion and approximately 116.78 million households, donations to human services have increased to an average \$222 per household.

- The calculations for "per household" giving to human services include all households, even those that do not give to human services. They also include all human services giving, including that from corporations, foundations, and through charitable bequests. This allows for comparison over time and across subsectors.

Giving to health, 1968–2008
($ in billions)

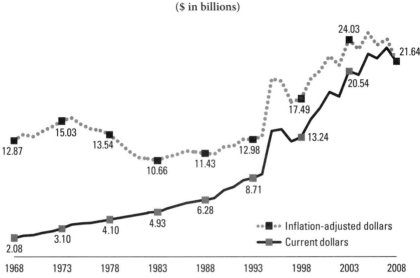

- Giving to health has increased a great deal, particularly since the mid-1990s.

- In 1988, the inflation-adjusted amount given to health ($11.43 billion) divided by the number of American households (91.12 million, using Current Population Survey data from the Census Bureau) results in an estimate of giving to health of $125 (adjusted for inflation) per household.

- In a similar calculation including giving from all donor types, by 1998, the number of households had grown to 102.53 million and the per household average gift to health had risen to $171. For 2008, with total estimated giving from all sources to health of $21.64 billion and approximately 116.78 million households, donations to health increased slightly to an average $185 per household.

- The calculations for "per household" giving include all households, even those that do not give to health. They also include all health giving, including that from corporations, foundations, and through charitable bequests. This allows for comparison over time and across subsectors.

Giving to public-society benefit, 1968–2008
($ in billions)

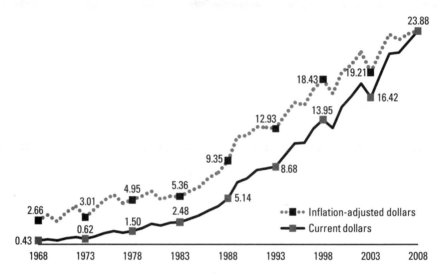

- Giving to public-society benefit has increased steadily since the 1960s.

- In 1988, the inflation-adjusted amount given to public-society benefit ($9.35 billion) divided by the number of American households (91.12 million, using Current Population Survey data from the Census Bureau) results in an estimate of giving to public-society benefit of $103 (adjusted for inflation) per household.

- In a similar calculation including giving from all donor types, by 1998, the number of households had grown to 102.53 million and the per household average gift to public-society benefit had risen to $180. For 2008, with total estimated giving from all sources to public-society benefit of $23.88 billion and approximately 116.78 million households, donations to public-society benefit increased to an average of $204 per household.

- The calculations for giving "per household" include all households, even those that do not give to public-society benefit. They also include all public-society benefit giving, including that from corporations, foundations, and through charitable bequests. This allows for comparison over time and across subsectors.

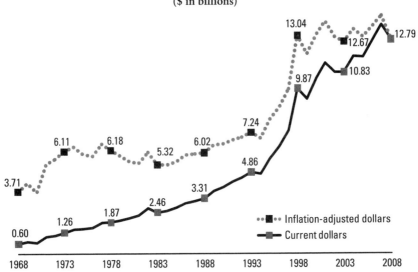

Giving to arts, culture, and humanities, 1968–2008
($ in billions)

- Giving to arts, culture, and humanities has increased steadily since the 1960s.

- In 1988, the inflation-adjusted amount given to arts, culture, and humanities ($6.02 billion) divided by the number of American households (91.12 million, using Current Population Survey data from the Census Bureau) results in an estimate of giving to arts, culture, and humanities of $66 (adjusted for inflation) per household.

- In a similar calculation including giving from all donor types, by 1998, the number of households had grown to 102.53 million and the per household average gift to arts, culture, and humanities had nearly doubled, to an average of $127. For 2008, with total estimated giving from all sources to arts, culture and humanities of $12.79 billion and approximately 116.78 million households, donations to arts, culture and humanities declined to an average of $110 per household.

- The calculations of giving "per household" include all households, even those that do not give to arts, culture, and humanities. They also include all arts, culture, and humanities giving, including that from corporations, foundations, and through charitable bequests. This allows for comparison over time and across subsectors.

Giving to international affairs, 1968–2008
($ in billions)

Giving to the international affairs subsector began to be tracked separately in 1987.

- Giving to international affairs has increased steadily from 1988 to 2004. Since 2004, it has fluctuated considerably.

- In 1988, the inflation-adjusted amount given to international affairs ($1.62 billion) divided by the number of American households (91.12 million, using Current Population Survey data from the Census Bureau) results in an estimate of giving to international affairs of $18 (adjusted for inflation) per household.

- In a similar calculation including giving from all donor types, by 1998, the number of households had grown to 102.53 million and the per household average gift to international affairs had nearly quadrupled to $65. For 2008, with total estimated giving from all sources to international affairs of $13.3 billion and approximately 116.78 million households, donations to international affairs increased to an average of $114 per household.

- The calculations of giving "per household" include all households, even those that do not give to international affairs. They also include all international affairs giving, including that from corporations, foundations, and through charitable bequests. This allows for comparison over time and across subsectors.

Giving to environment/animals, 1968–2008
($ in billions)

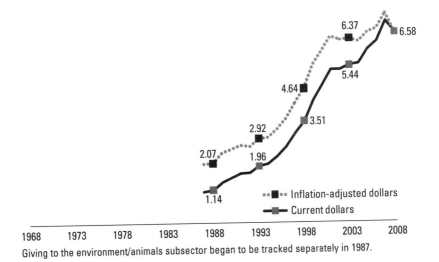

Giving to the environment/animals subsector began to be tracked separately in 1987.

- Giving to environment/animals has increased steadily from 1988 to 2007. It is estimated to have dipped slightly in 2008.

- In 1988, the inflation-adjusted amount given to environment/animals ($2.07 billion) divided by the number of American households (91.12 million, using Current Population Survey data from the Census Bureau) results in an estimate of giving to environment/ animals of $23 (adjusted for inflation) per household.

- In a similar calculation including giving from all donor types, by 1998, the number of households had grown to 102.53 million and the per household average gift to environment/animals had risen to $45. For 2008, with total estimated giving from all sources to environment/animals of $6.58 billion and approximately 116.78 million households, donations to environment/animals increased to an average of $56 per household.

- The calculations of giving "per household" include all households, even those that do not give to environment/animals. They also include all environment/animals giving, including that from corporations, foundations, and through charitable bequests. This allows for comparison over time and across subsectors.

Giving by type of recipients, five-year spans (adjusted for inflation), 1969–2008
($ in billions)

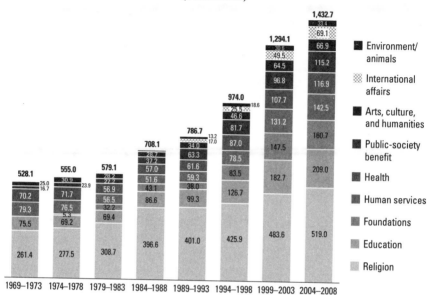

- Giving to all subsectors has increased over time. Growth rates nearly always exceed the rate of inflation in all subsectors. This is most noticeable with the growth in giving to all subsectors since 1999. The period from 1999 through 2003 saw double-digit rates of growth in giving in every subsector when compared with the prior period (1994 to 1998).

- One consistent exception to growth in the early years was in contributions to human services. These declined consistently from the 1969–1973 period through the 1989–1993 period. They have climbed, however, since the 1994–1998 period.

- Many of the charities that provide human services are also funded through allocations from other charities, such as United Way, Jewish federations, and freestanding donor-advised funds like Fidelity Charitable Gift Fund or National Christian Foundation. These combined purpose funds are in the public-society benefit subsector, which has one of the highest rates of growth in giving in the past decade (1999 through 2008).

- In the most recent five-year span (2004 to 2008), charitable contributions increased by 7 to 10 percent (adjusted for inflation) for religion, foundations, human services, health, and environment. One subsector saw a much lower rate of change: arts, culture, and humanities (4 percent increase in 2004–2008 compared with 1999–2003). Three saw faster rates of change from the 1999–2003 period to the 2004–2008 period. These are: Education (14 percent increase); public-society benefit (19 percent increase); and international affairs (40 percent increase).

Giving by type of recipient as a percentage of total giving, 1969–2008
(Five-year spans; does not include "unallocated")

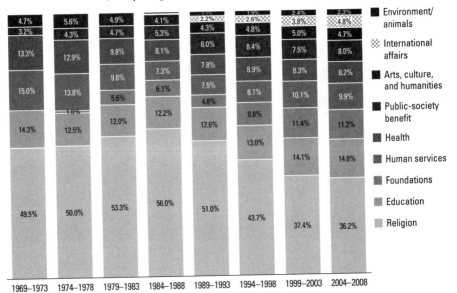

- Each subsector has increased in dollar amounts, yet the allocation or percentage share for each type of recipient has shifted to reflect different giving patterns and preferences, especially of households and foundations.

- Giving to religion dropped to less than 40 percent of the total in the 1999–2003 period. In that same period, giving to foundations rose to 11 percent of the total (from less than 9 percent previously).

- Education, which was 14 percent of the total in the 1969–1973 period, returned to that level in the 1999–2003 period after decades at less than 13 percent.

- Human services declined in total contributions, and as a share of the total, from the 1969–1973 period through the 1984–1988 period. Giving to this subsector began to increase in amount and as a proportion of the total in the 1989–1999 period and has remained near 10 percent since the 1999–2003 period.

- Health has gradually declined as a share of the total from more than 13 percent in the 1969–1973 period to just 8.2 percent in the 2004–2008 period. It was a lower percentage of the total in the period from 1984 through 1993, but has been bolstered recently by grants made by the Bill & Melinda Gates Foundation and in gifts to major hospitals and children's hospitals (see *Giving USA 2008*).

- The public-society benefit subsector jumped as a share of the total in the early 1990s from 5.3 percent (1984–1988) to 8.0 percent (1989–1993). It has remained between 7.5 percent and 8.5 percent since then.

- The arts, culture, and humanities subsector has been between 4 and 5 percent of the total in all periods except 1974 to 1978, when it reached 5.6 percent of the total. It is 4.7 percent of the total for the 2004–2008 period.

- The international affairs and environment/animal subsectors have become larger shares of the total since they began to be tracked in the late 1980s.

The number of 501(c)(3) organizations, 1999–2008

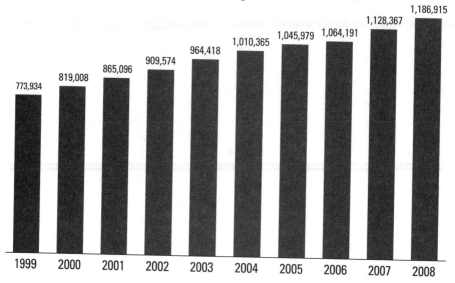

- The number of registered charities has increased steadily, averaging growth of 5 percent per year in the past decade.

- The number of active charities is not fully represented by the number of registered organizations. Houses of worship are not required to register, although some do. Small organizations, with very little income, are not required to register at the federal level. A study by Kirsten Grønbjerg of Indiana University found as many as one-third more active charities than appeared on official registration lists.

- The number of registered charities increased by 53 percent between 1999 and 2008. In that same period, according to the Current Population Survey conducted annually by the Census Bureau, the number of households increased 12 percent and inflation-adjusted total giving rose 17 percent. Household (individual) giving rose 15 percent. Foundation giving rose 55 percent.

Registered 501(c)(3) charities per 100,000 households, 1999–2008

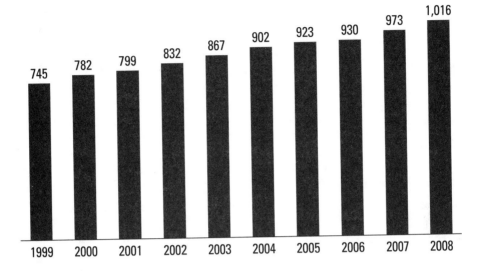

- Tracking growth in the number of registered charities is one way to assess the size and impact of the nonprofit sector. Another is to look at trends in the ratio of nonprofit organizations to households. A common measure is the number of nonprofit organizations per 100,000 households.

- The Current Population Survey, which is conducted by the U.S. Bureau of the Census, reports an annual number of households. For 2008, it is 116.78 million. There are 1.186 million registered charities under section 501(c)(3) of the Internal Revenue Code. This comes to 1,016 registered charities for every 100,000 households for 2008.

- This is an increase of 36 percent in the past decade. The nonprofit sector has grown faster than the household sector. There were 745 registered charities for each 100,000 households in 1999. By 2008, that ratio climbed to 1,016 registered 501(c)(3) charities for every 100,000 households.

- This does not necessarily mean that all households are served by more charities, nor does it mean that all households receive requests for support from more charities than they did a decade ago. Nonprofit formation is not uniformly distributed in the nation, so that there are some areas with a high density of charities (New York, Atlanta, and Washington, D.C. would be some examples) and some areas with low density. In addition, it is important to remember that registered charities are not all active, nor are all active charities registered.

Giving by individuals

- Giving by individuals reached an estimated $229.28 billion in 2008. This is the lowest value (adjusted for inflation) for giving by individuals since 2003 when individual giving was $212.92 billion.

- This is a decline of 2.7 percent (-6.3 percent adjusted for inflation) from the revised estimate of $235.58 billion for 2007.

- Individual giving estimated for 2008 is 75 percent of total estimated giving.

- Individual giving includes everything that qualifies under tax law as a charitable contribution. Gifts range from a small donation of household articles to an entity like Goodwill to the largest amounts given to foundations or other charitable organizations.

Giving USA findings

In 2006, the most recent year with final IRS data, 30 percent of individual tax returns itemized charitable contributions. These account for roughly 83 percent of total individual giving in 2006.[1]

The *Giving USA* estimate uses the historical record of itemized contributions from 1948 to 2006 from the Internal Revenue Service. The estimated change in itemized giving from 2007 to 2008 is developed using the historical relationship between changes in giving and the variance in personal income, the stock market, and the itemized deductions that taxpayers take for charitable gifts in a given year.[2] For 2008:

- The change in giving based on the Standard & Poor's 500 Index, which fell 40 percent adjusted for inflation in 2008, would be a decline of more than $9 billion, if the stock market were the only driver of charitable contributions.

- However, personal income and recent giving history are also associated with giving. The negative impact from the stock market was counteracted by a small increase in personal income this year and by recent growth in contributions.[3]

- Taking all of the factors into account, the estimated change in itemized contributions is a drop of $7.69 billion.

- None of the estimates reflect changes in tax rates because there are no differences in tax rates for 2008 compared with 2007.

After the itemized giving amount is estimated, we add an estimate of giving by non-itemizing households using data from the Center on Philanthropy Panel Study (COPPS), which is a module of the Panel Study of Income Dynamics. The estimate of charitable contributions for 2008 includes an increase of $1.39 billion in donations from households that do not itemize contributions on tax returns. This estimate includes a projection that more households in 2008, compared with 2007, will choose the standard deduction instead of itemizing deductions when they complete their tax returns.

- An estimated 65 percent of non-itemizing households contribute to charity (compared with 90 percent of itemizers). Among these donor households, the average gift is estimated to be about $1,025.

- The total estimate for approximately 64 million non-itemizing households is $42.58 billion.

None of the announced gifts on the Center on Philanthropy Million Dollar List or on the Slate 60 list for 2008 was large enough to alter the rate of change by more than one half of one percentage point. With no single gifts at that level, the estimate for 2008 does not include a supplement for "mega-gifts." The last year to contain such a supplement was 2006. The amount originally estimated for 2006 is now known and reported in this edition.

Individual giving during and following recessions

Individual (also called household) charitable giving is linked to income and wealth. In general, during years that are part of a recession, individual giving has declined an average of 1.5 percent.[4] The range of change in individual giving during recession years (adjusted for inflation) varied from a drop of 5.3 percent in 1974 to an increase of 2.4 percent in 1981.

In addition to the change in giving during recessions, the historical record from *Giving USA* shows how long it has taken giving to attain pre-recession levels.

- In 1974, the middle year of the long recession of 1973–1975, the stock market fell 33 percent and personal income dropped 0.2 percent. In that year, giving by individuals declined 5.3 percent. Once the 1973–1975 recession ended, individual giving returned to its pre-recession level in 1977 (All figures are adjusted for inflation).

- In the recessions of 1980 and 1981–1982, unemployment rates reached more than 10 percent and interest rates for home loans were 15 percent or more. Following that recession, inflation-adjusted indi-vidual giving reached pre-recession levels by 1983.

- After the recession of 1990–1991, individual giving stayed fairly constant between $134 billion and $137 billion until the stock market began lifting assets around 1996.

- There was a leveling off period in individual giving from 1999 through 2003, when inflation-adjusted individual giving ranged from $200 to $218 billion. Growth began again in 2004, as wealth grew in both markets—stock and real estate—and as incomes began to rise.

Some individuals giving through family foundations

At least some family foundation grant-making can be considered individual giving. The Foundation Center found for 2007 that $18.5 billion was granted by family foundations.[5] If this total was added to individual and household giving, total contributions directed by living donors would be about $248 billion or 81 percent of total estimated giving.

The largest gifts in 2008

Charitable contributions from the nation's wealthiest households play an important role in total giving from individuals. The Internal Revenue Service reported, for example, that the top 0.0003 percent of tax returns (the 400 tax returns with the highest income) in 2006 accounted for 1.31

percent of total adjusted gross income that year, and 5.3 percent of total itemized deductions for charitable donations. About 326,000 tax returns with income of $1 million or more (about 0.2 percent of tax returns) claimed 26 percent of all itemized contributions for 2006.

The largest gifts in the U.S. have been tracked for more than a decade by *The Chronicle of Philanthropy* and Slate.com. Since 2000, the Center on Philanthropy at Indiana University has published the Million Dollar List, which monitors gifts of $1 million or more that are announced publicly and covered by the media.

Table 1
Living donors of $100 million or more in 2008

Donor(s)	Principal source of wealth	Donation total	Recipient(s)
Peter G. Peterson and Joan Ganz Cooney	Finance	$1 billion	Peter G. Peterson Foundation, Peter G. Peterson Institute for International Economics, and Sesame Workshop
David G. and Suzanne Deal Booth	Finance	300 million	University of Chicago Booth School of Business
Michael R. Bloomberg	Media and entertainment	235 million	1,200 nonprofit groups focused on the arts, education, health care, and social services
Helen L. Kimmel	Real estate	156.5 million	New York University Langone Medical Center
H.F. (Gerry) and Marguerite B. Lenfest	Media and entertainment	139.9 million	Philadelphia Museum of Art, Curtis Institute of Music, Williamson Free School of Mechanical Trades, Washington and Lee University, Barnes Foundation, and Columbia University School of Law
David Rockefeller	Family wealth, Finance	137.8 million	Harvard University, Stone Barns Center for Food and Agriculture, Mayor's Fund to Advance New York City, American Museum of Natural History, Southwest Research Station, New York Botanical Garden, and Museum for African Art
Jeffrey S. Skoll	Technology	110.8 million	Skoll Foundation
Stephen A. Schwarzman	Investments	105 million	New York Public Library, Inner-City Scholarship Fund

Data: Slate 60 and *The Chronicle of Philanthropy*

For 2008, the total recorded on the Slate 60 list reached $15.78 billion, up from more than $7.79 billion in 2007.[6] The largest gifts on the list in 2008 were bequests or pledges. The threshold gift amount to be listed was $25 million, down from $30 million in 2007.

Business Week continued its list of the 50 "most generous" givers, based on estimated giving, including pledges, from 2004 through 2008.[7] Of the people on the list, at least four contributed amounts that exceed current net worth:

- Veronica Atkins (widow of Robert Atkins of the Atkins diet);
- Bernard Osher (a banker, art collector, and businessman);
- Ted and Veda Stanley (he founded The Danbury Mint, which grew to become MBI); and
- Shelby White (widow of investor Leon Levy).

Eleven on the list (22 percent) had contributed 10 percent or less of their net worth, according to publicly available information. These include:

- The Walton Family (net worth at $93 billion; donations at 2 percent of net worth from 2004–2008);
- John Kluge (net worth of $9 billion; donations at 8 percent from 2004–2008); and
- Dan Duncan and family (net worth of $7.6 billion; donations at 4 percent from 2004–2008).

Women Moving Millions raises millions

An initiative launched publicly in late 2007, Women Moving Millions challenged women donors to commit $1 million each to a network of causes linked through the Women's Funding Network. Founders Helen LaKelly Hunt and Swanee Hunt made a joint gift of $10 million, and by mid-2008, the effort reported $105 million raised toward its $150-million goal.[8] Donations to the initiative went to members of the Women's Funding Network (WFN), which comprise more than 145 women's foundations on six continents, or directly to the WFN. The goal to raise $150 million was set in part to help propel the collection of women's funds to total $1 billion or more.[9]

Philanthropic Giving Index tracks success of fundraising techniques; most fundraising tools decline in 2008

The Philanthropic Giving Index, conducted by the Center on Philanthropy at Indiana University, surveys a panel of senior fundraising executives every six months and assesses their fundraising confidence. In December 2008, respondents reported lower levels of success in the fundraising vehicles most often used in their organizations compared to other years. These fundraising tools include: Major gifts, planned giving, foundation grants, and direct mail.[10] Figure 1 shows the year-end success levels for these four fundraising techniques, as averaged for the 250 or so regular respondents to the Philanthropic Giving Index.

The figure shows that, generally, 2008 had the most pronounced drops in fundraising success since 2002. The steepest drops were in major gifts

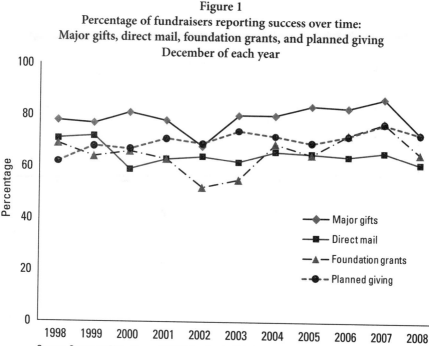

Figure 1
Percentage of fundraisers reporting success over time:
Major gifts, direct mail, foundation grants, and planned giving
December of each year

Source: Center on Philanthropy, 2008 Philanthropic Giving Index

(from 87 percent in December 2007 to 73 percent in December 2008) and foundation grants (from 77 percent successful in December 2007 to 65 percent in 2008).

Several other fundraising strategies are used by a smaller share of the PGI participants, including telephone appeals, online fundraising, email solicitations, special events, and corporate gifts. Figure 2 shows the year-end success level of these fundraising vehicles. Among these approaches, most showed declines in success rates in 2008.

In this group, corporate gifts declined the most (from 54 percent success rate in December 2007 to 42 percent

in 2008). Telephone appeals are the only vehicle that rose in success, up by nearly 7 points from December 2007 to December 2008.

AFP survey finds majority of respondents reporting declines in 2008 by all fundraising vehicles except online appeals

In its survey of members, the Association of Fundraising Professionals found that 54 percent saw total giving either stay at 2007 levels or decline in 2008; just 46 percent saw an increase.[11] This is the lowest percentage reporting growth since 2001. In a typical year, AFP says, 60 percent or more of its survey respondents report growth in charitable revenue.

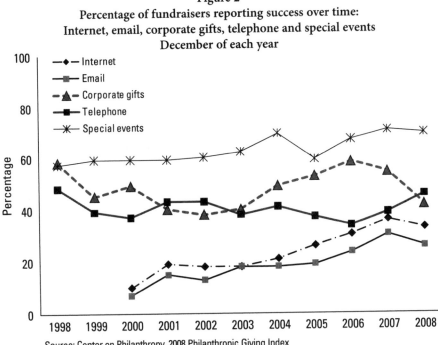

Figure 2
Percentage of fundraisers reporting success over time:
Internet, email, corporate gifts, telephone and special events
December of each year

Source: Center on Philanthropy, 2008 Philanthropic Giving Index

The survey also showed that the percentage of organizations raising more money using major gifts, traditionally one of the strongest and most resilient methods of fundraising, fell from 63 percent in 2007 to 43 percent in 2008. Every fundraising technique but one that was measured (direct mail, telemarketing, major gifts, planned giving, special events, and corporate/foundation grants) saw significant decreases compared to 2007. Direct mail success was reported by 38 percent of the organizations, down from 51 percent in 2007.

The only type of fundraising where a majority of respondents reported raising more funds in 2008 compared to 2007 was online solicitations. However,

online fundraising typically accounts for a very small percentage of overall charitable revenue, so this outcome had a very minor impact on total fundraising.

Studies examine 2008 results for direct marketing and online fundraising

Two providers of fundraising and analysis services issue annual reports based on fundraising results among their clients. The Target Analytics study compared direct response mail and Internet fundraising for some of the nation's largest charities, and the Convio study looked at online giving for a mix of organizations using its web-hosting and gift processing services. Key findings from each study for 2008 are summarized.

Target Analytics sees revenue decline among 60 percent of participants

Target Analytics, a Blackbaud Company, released a twelve-month study of giving to 75 client organizations in 2008, comparing these organizations with their 2007 direct marketing fundraising results.[12] The Target Analytics' organizations raise the majority of their revenue in direct response marketing. In 2008, participants in the Target Analytics study raised over $2 billion through direct response fundraising from 36 million donors.

Among the charitable organizations in the Target Analytics data set, 60 percent saw declines in donors and in revenue from 2007 to 2008. Median revenue per donor was $61 for 2008. The median retention rate for organizations participating in the index was just under 50 percent.

The largest revenue declines occurred in the fourth quarter of 2008, when the median revenue received fell by 8 percent compared with the fourth quarter in 2007. The general trend throughout the year was downward, both in terms of revenue and measured by the number of donors. Rates of donor acquisition were significantly lower in 2008 than in the prior two years.

Target Analytics added an index for online giving for 59 of its 75 organizations. In this group, the median share raised online was 7 percent and the median for direct mail was 77 percent of the total total raised. The balance was through other channels, such as telemarketing and events. While the amount raised from gifts made through the Internet was comparatively low; at a median of 7 percent, it rose to that level from a median of 3 percent in 2004.

Convio reports declines in the 4th quarter of 2008 in average gift and other metrics

Convio, a provider of constituent relationship management software and services, analyzed 2008 online giving results for 204 of its clients that had data for both 2007 and 2008.[13] In its study, Convio found that donors continued to give, even in the fourth quarter, but the average gift amount declined in the last few months of the year for many organizations. The average gift in the fourth quarter of 2008 was $84.51, compared with an average of $90.32 in 2007. This

GOOD TO KNOW

Just fewer than 20 percent of the 700 respondents to the *2008 Bank of America Study of High Net-Worth Philanthropy* said that their gifts make a major impact on the charities they support. This is a surprisingly low percentage given that 67 percent said their gifts are motivated, at least in part, by the fact that a gift can make an immediate difference.

In a separate study based on 33 interviews with high-net-worth donors, University of Pennsylvania researchers found that impact information was difficult for donors to obtain.

The personal connection for high-net-worth donors is extremely important. The *2008 Bank of America Study of High Net-Worth Philanthropy* found that 58 percent gave to causes or issues that affected them personally or affected someone they know. Additionally, people volunteering for charity gave more than people who were not volunteering.

University of Pennsylvania researchers found that at least some people make a practice of NOT giving to organizations that request funds impersonally, such as in email or letters.

It may be that too many nonprofit organizations look at someone's wealth or ability to give rather than focusing on strengthening the relationship with a prospective donor so that the donor is personally linked to the organization and its work.

is a drop of 6 percent. Additionally, organizations in the Convio study saw total online giving increase slightly, by 3 percent.

Studies of giving by wealthy donors show common results

A survey conducted in 2008 of high-net-worth households for the Bank of America by the Center on Philanthropy at Indiana University found that nearly all (98 percent) contributed to charity and that on average, these households gave more than $56,600 in direct contributions (from family resources).[14] In addition, 30 percent also made gifts through a foundation or fund, which could be a donor-advised fund at a community foundation or another charity. On average, those foundation or fund contributions were just over $119,350 (excluding outliers). In this study, high-net-worth was defined as annual income of $200,000 or more or net worth of $1 million or more.

Compared with data from a similar survey conducted for Bank of America

in 2006 about giving in 2005, average and median charitable donations from high-net-worth households had declined in 2007. However, nearly the entire decline occurred in households with income (not wealth) of $5 million or more. The amounts increased in other income categories.

High-net-worth donors motivated to give back; prefer personal appeals

The *2008 Bank of America Study of High Net-Worth Philanthropy* reported that more than 80 percent of nearly 700 respondents reported making charitable contributions because they want to give back to the community. More than two-thirds (66.9 percent) said they gave to make an immediate difference on the world around them. A majority (57.5 percent) said they gave because an issue or cause affected them personally or was important to someone they were close to.

In interviews with donors who gave, on average, $1.5 million each, Kathleen Noonan and Katherina Rosqueta from the Center for High-Impact Philanthropy at the University of Pennsylvania found that 26 of the 33 respondents rated it "important" or "very important" to learn about a group from a peer before making a gift.[15]

Paul Schervish, writing in *The Routledge Companion to Nonprofit Sector Marketing*, summarized motivations for high-net-worth donors based on his research as the director of the Center on Wealth and Philanthropy at Boston College. He found, based on 250 or more interviews, donors tend to find these factors important:

- Identification with the cause, issue, or program;

- "Giving back," especially as a formal expression of gratitude for benefits or blessings received earlier;

- A sense of financial security, defined as the ability to provide at the level one desires for self and family;

- Passing along enough, but not too much, to heirs. The act of giving is also a way to provide important lessons for children; and

- "Philia," which is caring about and for others in communal or societal relationships.

These motivations and the resources to act on them combine among the donors Schervish interviewed so that "the ability … to change the world becomes an especially strong motivation for philanthropy (p. 176)."

Review of publicly announced gifts of $1 million or more finds different giving preferences associated with different sources of wealth

Developed through the 2008 William B. Hanrahan CCS Fellowship at the Center on Philanthropy at Indiana University, *An Analysis of Million Dollar Gifts (2000–2007)* examined publicly announced gifts of $1 million or more in the United States. Data come from the Million Dollar List™ at the Center on Philanthropy at Indiana University.[16] Among the findings:

- Entrepreneurs were less likely than all other donors to give to environment or religion. They are more likely to give to a foundation or to international aid and human services organizations.

- Investors were more likely to give to education, environment, foundations, and religion.

- Donors with wealth from real estate were more likely than other donors to give to campus-wide initiatives and to "service-related" fields. They were less likely to give to science or technology organizations, and no gifts were reported to libraries.

■ Investors and entrepreneurs who tended to give to foundations were less likely to give to education than were donors whose wealth came from other sources.

Research focusing on differences in giving by generation

Work appeared in 2008 reporting differences in giving by people in different generations and in motivations for giving. This section summarizes findings from two of these studies.

Motivations identified for charitable giving vary for Millennials (born since 1981)

In a study conducted for Campbell & Co., the Center on Philanthropy at Indiana University analyzed differences in motivations for giving by people of different generations.[17] Among the key findings (age ranges noted in the figure):

■ The probability of giving to secular causes varied by generation. The Silent generation was more likely to give to secular causes than younger generations. For Boomers and later generations, there were no statistically significant differences in the probability of giving to religion or to secular causes, once controlling for income, age, marital status, frequency of attendance at worship services, and education level.

■ Millennial donors were most likely to be motivated by a desire to make the world a better place.

■ Millennials were less likely than earlier generations to identify the

desire to control how their money is spent as a motivation for giving.

In looking at the total giving reported by donors in each generation, the report found that Millennials gave slightly less than 60 percent of their total to religion. In contrast, nearly 22 percent of this generation's giving went to "umbrella" causes (United Way, Salvation Army, and other organizations providing a multiplicity of services). Millennials gave a larger share of total giving to international affairs organizations and a lower share to helping meet people's basic needs than did earlier generations. Figure 3 shows the allocation of all dollars contributed by type of recipient by generation.

Among Millennials, the nearly 22 percent of dollars going to "umbrella charities" is a result of a high average gift ($404) for that type of recipient. Millennials gave comparatively less than earlier generations to most other types of charities; this is a combination of lower participation rates and lower average gifts. However, in international giving, Millennials contributed a larger share (2.8 percent) than did donors in other generations.

One report hypothesizes that Boomers' concern for financial security undermines their giving

In research unrelated to the study for Campbell & Company, direct marketing experts Roger Craver and Tom Belford found that in 2007–2008, Boomers gave an average of $1,081, compared with average gifts of $1,542 from people in earlier generations and $1,205 from later generations.[18] Mr. Craver and

Figure 3
Share of giving to type of recipient by generation, 2006*

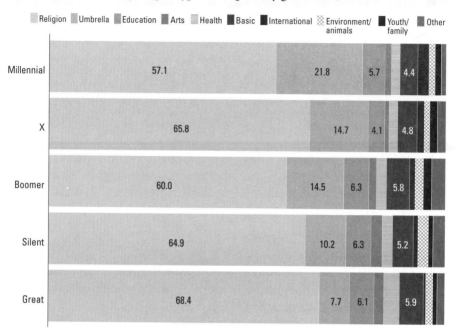

*Excludes outlier amounts by subsector, 3 sd above mean for subsector for all ages of donors.

Great = born before 1929; Silent = born 1929–1945; Boomer = born 1946–1963; X = born 1964–1981; Millennial = born since 1981 and over 18 at the time of the study (Spring 2007).

Source: The Center on Philanthropy, *Generational differences in charitable giving and in motivations for giving*, prepared for Campbell & Company, 2008.

Mr. Belford said that, in their opinion, the Baby Boom generation gave less because of concerns about household finances and future economic prospects. In their Donor Trends white paper series, using data from regular surveys they conducted, these consultants reported that:

- The percentage of Boomers who give, as well as their average gifts, have decreased.

- The strongest growth in giving since 2006 has occurred among people born after 1964.[19]

Attention on the "hybrid model" of financing global change

In case studies of the six founders of four technology firms (Microsoft, AOL, Google, and e-Bay), author Lewis Solomon (George Washington University Law School) examines philanthropic goals and methods that, he argues, distinguish these donors and create new forms of distributing resources in addressing major social and global concerns.[20] Among the shared traits that these donors have are:

While the Boomer generation has long been touted as the largest and wealthiest, people born since 1964 are growing in importance as donors as they enter their peak earning years (typically 45 to 65) and as their interests increasingly shape debate about what is important. Compared with those born before 1964, younger donors tend to favor international causes and education over health and arts, for example.

- Valuing the importance of making social investments during their lifetimes;

- Emphasis on personal engagement and on organizational effectiveness and efficiency;

- A global vision of solving "problems of human suffering"(p. 3); and

- Use of a "hybrid model" that blends gifts (under tax law definitions) with investment in for-profit businesses and other approaches to distributing resources.

The cases profiled were Bill and Melinda Gates; Pierre Omidyar (e-Bay); Jeffrey Skoll (e-Bay); Stephen Case (AOL); and Larry Page and Sergey Brin (Google).

In *Philanthrocapitalism*, Matthew Bishop (of *The Economist* magazine) and Michael Green (a professional economist) also explore new models (and some old ones) of sharing wealth.[21] They interviewed a number of current prominent donors, including Bono,

Bill Clinton, Bill Gates, Angelina Jolie, George Soros, and Ted Turner, among many others.

In an interview with *The Chronicle of Philanthropy*, Mr. Bishop and Mr. Green said that they want their book to "spark a public debate about the role of well-heeled donors in fighting social ills."[22]

Even before it appeared, commentators debated the work's premises and conclusions. Among these were Michael Edwards, a program officer at the Ford Foundation, who wrote, "...what separates the good and bad performers is not whether they come from business or civil society...but whether they have a clear focus to their work, strong learning and accountability mechanisms... and the ability to motivate their staff members or volunteers..."[23] Phil Buchanan of the Center for Effective Philanthropy wrote, "The biggest mistake [in this book] comes in equating... 'impact' and 'strategic philanthropy' with 'business' and 'capitalism.'" He

Heightened awareness of philanthropic terms, such as "impact philanthropy," and similar concepts, is likely to lead many donors to adopt concerns and trends reported in the media about charitable giving. Nonprofit organizations that can show how their operations are effective and efficient will be well-placed to attract contributions from donors who seek to maximize the social change that they can bring about with their dollars.

added, "Many…nonprofit groups in this country are models of effectiveness—and they were not all founded in the last decade by the protagonists of Mr. Bishop and Mr. Green's book."

Research about what influences charitable giving

Scholarly research about charitable giving has become an important topic for sociologists, economists, marketers, and others, especially in the past decade. During 2008, articles appeared covering motivations for giving; the impact of changes in income or changes in tax rates on charitable giving; and the potential role of family in teaching children to give. Four studies reporting on these topics in 2008 are summarized here.

Creating empathy leads to giving more in experimental situations

Fundraisers know the importance of having a strong connection between the organization's work and the people asked to support that work. Two studies published in the *Journal of Consumer Research*'s special October 2008 issue on consumer welfare used scientific methods to explore the psychology that underlies this link.

- In a series of experiments conducted with undergraduate students, Deborah Small and Uri Simohnson of the University of Pennsylvania demonstrated that both sympathy and donations are greater when the person knows someone affected by the circumstance to be addressed by the money raised.[24] The "knowledge" of someone else in the experiments was based on a simple series of conversations among people seated near one another.

- In a series of experiments, Wendy Liu (University of California, Los Angeles) and Jennifer Aaker (University of California, Berkeley) tested whether people gave more based on whether they were asked first, "How much time would you like to volunteer?", or "How much money would you like to donate?" They found that asking first about time led participants to feel a higher emotional connection to the cause and to give more.[25]

Both studies reached undergraduate participants and discovered a phenomenon similar to that found by Professor Schervish among older, high-net-worth individuals. People in their late teens

GOOD TO KNOW

Give your prospective donors a chance to meet people who benefit from your work (or those who have already benefited). Even short conversations can build a rapport that seems to be associated with higher giving, based on research reported here.

Ask prospective donors to give some time to your cause before you ask them for money. Research released in 2008 shows that the act of asking people to consider donating time is associated with higher giving.

GOOD TO KNOW

Tax benefits for charitable giving are linked with current giving—the higher the available deduction, the more likely a donor will give a larger amount. When donors can anticipate a change in tax rates, they will time their gifts to maximize their tax deduction. Thus, if the amount that can be deducted declines, donors will "pre-give." Over time, the giving rate and amount will return to prior levels, but it could take at least a few years for donors to adjust.

The tax benefit of charitable giving is also a topic that parents may use to teach their children about giving, which may increase the probability that young people will practice philanthropy when they have their own incomes.

and early 20s responded with financial donations (with money they earned by participating in the experiment) when given the opportunity to develop a personal or emotional connection to the cause, either by getting to know someone, even just a little, or by being asked to volunteer before being asked for money. Drs. Liu and Aaker tested why asking for volunteer time was associated with higher contributions. They concluded, "Considering time appears to activate goals of emotional well-being and beliefs involving personal happiness. Such a mind-set leads to greater willingness to make an actual donation (p. 552)."

Giving is sensitive to changes in permanent income and in tax rates

Jon Bakija (Williams College) and Bradley Heim (now at the U.S. Treasury) examined multiple years of data for a large file of tax returns.[26] Among other findings, they confirm earlier work (Randolph, 1995) that reveals changes in giving are larger when income changes permanently (e.g., a salary raise) than when there are transitory income shifts (such as a bonus or tax

rebate check). They also find that for every 1 percentage point drop in a household's tax rate (e.g., from 35 percent to 34 percent), a household can be predicted to give 0.7 percent less (giving does not fall as far as the tax rate drops, but giving does fall when the tax deduction benefit is lower). Further, when a tax-rate change that lowers the amount households can deduct for contributions is publicized in advance, people will increase their charitable giving before the rate change. This is especially true for high-income households.

Stability of income matters in giving

Patricia Hughes and William Luksetich (both affiliated with St. Cloud University, Minnesota) find that a high level of variability in annual income negatively affects contributions.[27] These authors suggest that nonprofit organizations should recognize the importance of income stability and create channels for stable donations. Arrange for payroll deductions, automatic transfers from a checking account, or pre-approved monthly charges on a credit card.

Parents' giving associated with giving behaviors of offspring

Mark Wilhelm (Indiana University-Purdue University Indianapolis-IUPUI), Eleanor Brown (Pomona College), Patrick Rooney (IUPUI), and Richard Steinberg (IUPUI) reported strong connections in the amount given to religion by parents and their adult children.[28] That is, the giving of adult children is closely related to how much their parents give to religion. There is also a relationship between parental giving to religion and their children's giving to non-religious (secular) causes, but it is not as strong. The authors also argue that tax policies that promote more giving will be more likely to help younger generations learn about generosity and giving than will tax policies that reduce giving.

Key findings from annual studies

Table 1 presents three years of data from studies released regularly about giving by individuals. Web site addresses are provided so readers may access complete reports.

Table 2
Key findings from studies of giving

Percentage who give and volunteer in an ongoing study of a nationally representative sample of the general population Center on Philanthropy Panel Study A module of the Panel Study of Income Dynamics			
	2000	2002	2004 (most recent available)
Percentage who give	66.8	68.5	70.2
Average donation amount (2008 dollars)	$2,368	$2,248	$2,333
Percentage of heads of household who volunteer (does not include all volunteers, only heads of household interviewed)	25.3	26.7	28.1
Percentage of heads of household who give and volunteer	22.1	23.4	24.9

Percentage reporting success by fundraising tactic Philanthropic Giving Index (selected tactics)			
	2006	2007	2008
Direct mail	64	66	61
Major gifts	83	87	73
Special events	67	70	69
Internet	30	36	33
Telephone	34	39	46

Internal Revenue Service Average amount itemized in charitable deductions Inflation adjusted to 2008 dollars			
	2004	2005	2006 (most recent available)
Percentage of individual tax returns with itemized deductions for charitable gifts	30	31	30
All itemizers who claim charitable gift(s)	$4,573	$4,838	$4,702
Households with income > $100,000 who claim charitable gift(s)	$9,458	$10,002	$9,149
Households with income > $200,000 who claim charitable gift(s)	$24,216	$25,689	$22,608

1 Internal Revenue Service data for individual tax returns filed in 2006, analyzed by the Center on Philanthropy at Indiana University. There were 41.44 million returns with itemized charitable deductions of a total of 138.39 million individual tax returns filed.

2 P. Deb et al., 2003. Estimating charitable giving in *Giving USA. Nonprofit and Voluntary Sector Quarterly*, December 2003.

3 Data are for the last trading day of the year and are obtained from StandardandPoors.com. Adjustment for inflation is done by *Giving USA* using the Consumer Price Index.

4 Giving during recessions, *Giving USA Spotlight*, Issue #3, 2008.

5 S. Lawrence and R. Mukai, *Key Facts on Family Foundations*, The Foundation Center, January 2009, www.foundationcenter.org.

6 R. Larimore, The 2008 Slate 60, January 23, 2009, www.slate.com.

7 The 50 top American philanthropists, *Business Week*, Nov. 25, 2008, www.businessweek.com.

8 J. Lapham, Wealthy women give to women, *Christian Science Monitor*, July 30, 2008, www.csmonitor.com.

9 Women's Funding Network, Women Moving Millions, June 8, 2009, www.womensfundingnetwork.org.

10 The Center on Philanthropy, Philanthropic Giving Index, December 2008, www.philanthropy.iupui.edu.

11 AFP Survey results, Press release, March 31, 2009, www.afpnet.org.

12 Target Analytics Group, Index of National Fundraising Performance, Q4 2008, released April 2009, www.blackbaud.com/targetanalytics.

13 Q. Donovan, V. Bhagat, and B. Hauf, *The Convio Online Marketing Nonprofit Benchmark Index™ Study*, March 2009, www.convio.com.

14 The Center on Philanthropy at Indiana University, *Bank of America Study of High Net-Worth Philanthropy*, 2008, www.philanthropy.iupui.edu.

15 K. Noonan and K. Rosqueta, *"I'm not Rockefeller": 33 High Net Worth Philanthropists Discuss Their Approach to Giving*, September 2008, www.impact.upenn.edu/UPenn_CHIP_HNWP_Study.pdf.

16 The Million Dollar List, because it is based on media reports, is not a scientific sample of gifts nor does it include all gifts of $1 million or more. It is estimated that the

gifts on the Million Dollar List represent one-quarter of all donations of $1 million or more. It almost certainly under-reports major gifts to religion.

17 The Center on Philanthropy, *Generational differences in charitable giving and in motivations for giving*, prepared for Campbell & Company, 2008. Available for download at www.campbellcompany.com or at www.philanthropy.iupui.edu.

18 H. Hall, Baby Boomers blamed for fundraising drops, *Philanthropy Today*, an online daily summary of news issued by *The Chronicle of Philanthropy*, June 27, 2008.

19 New Agitator Paper: Giving Across Generations, downloaded April 3, 2009 from http://www.theagitator.net/research/new-agitator-paper-giving-across-generations/.

20 L. Solomon, *Tech Billionaires: Reshaping Philanthropy in a Quest for a Better World*, 2008, Piscataway NJ: Transaction Publishers.

21 M. Bishop and M. Green, *Philanthrocapitalism: How the Rich Can Save the World*, 2008, London: Bloomsbury Press.

22 I. Wilhelm, New hope or hype: "Philanthrocapitalists examined in just-released book, *The Chronicle of Philanthropy*, October 2, 2008, www.philanthropy.com.

23 M. Edwards, Has 'philanthrocapitalism' met its promise?, *The Chronicle of Philanthropy*, May 21, 2008, www.philanthropy.com.

24 D. Small and U. Simonsohn, Friends of victims: Personal experience and prosocial behavior, *Journal of Consumer Research*, October 2008, http://www.journals.uchicago.edu/toc/jcr/2008/35/3.

25 W. Liu and J. Aaker, The happiness of giving: The Time-ask effect, *Journal of Consumer Research*, October 2008, http://www.journals.uchicago.edu/toc/jcr/2008/35/3.

26 J. Bakija and B. Heim, How does charitable giving respond to incentives and income? Dynamic panel estimates accounting for predictable changes in taxation, National Bureau of Economics, August 2008, Working Paper 14237, www.nber.org.

27 P. Hughes and W. Luksetich, Income volatility and wealth: The effect on charitable giving, *Nonprofit and Voluntary Sector Quarterly*, June 2008, http://nvs.sagepub.com.

28 M. O. Wilhelm, E. Brown, P. Rooney, and R. Steinberg, The intergenerational transmission of generosity, *Journal of Public Economics*, October 2008, Volume 92, No. 10, pages 2146–2156.

4 Giving by bequest

- Charitable bequests are estimated to be $22.66 billion in 2008, a decrease of 2.8 percent (-6.4 percent adjusted for inflation) compared to the revised 2007 estimate of $23.31 billion, which is based on IRS information released in 2008 about charitable bequests in 2007.

- Charitable bequests for 2008 are estimated to be 7 percent of total estimated giving.

- The estimate for bequests includes gifts eligible to be claimed as charitable deductions when an estate files an estate tax return. This includes funds from trusts and other realized planned gifts.

Findings about charitable bequests, 2008

Giving USA is no longer annually surveying a national sample of charitable organizations in the process of estimating bequest totals.

The estimate for charitable bequests in 2008 includes an estimated $19.70 billion in charitable bequests from estates filing federal estate tax returns in 2008 and an estimated $2.96 billion from estates that do not file federal returns.

Among all deaths in the United States, an estimated 120,000 leave a charitable bequest each year.[1] The vast majority of the total estimated bequest amount (about 85 percent) is from approximately 8,000 estates that file estate tax returns and claim charitable deductions.

Since at least 2001, according to estate tax returns, on average 45 percent of the amount contributed by bequests has gone to foundations. The balance is divided among all other types of charities. If the percentage of bequest dollars going to foundations holds for 2008, then approximately $12.5 billion

in 2008 was bequeathed to charities other than foundations.

Charitable bequests fluctuate dramatically from year to year depending on the estates closed within a particular time. Peaks tend to represent a few very large estates filing an estate tax return in a given year.

The amount in charitable bequests has generally been lower since 2001 than it was in the 1990s. This might be the result of the 2001 Economic Growth and Tax Relief Reconciliation Act of 2001. This legislation initiated gradual estate tax reductions over the course of nine years, which will culminate in a total repeal of the estate tax in 2010. This analysis, however, is insufficient to draw the conclusion that the drop in bequests is caused by the changes in estate tax legislation, as a number of other factors have also shifted since 2001. These factors include increasing longevity (which reduces assets at the time of death), changes in the market values for assets, and a shift among high-net-worth donors who have said they prefer to give during their lifetimes.

Estate gifts announced in 2008 are not reflected in values

In 2008, some exceptionally large bequests were announced. These bequests are not included in the estimates, however, because it typically takes two years before an estate is settled and the tax return is filed. Thus, these gifts will be captured in the tax data in 2010 or later. The 2008 estates announcing bequests include the following:

- $4.5 billion from inventor and Utah businessman James LeVoy Sorenson, to the Sorenson Legacy Foundation[2];

- $360 million from Harold Alfond (founder of Dexter Shoe Company) to the Harold Alfond Foundation in Maine[3];

- $272 million from Frank Doble, founder of an engineering company, to two universities in Massachusetts: Lesley University and Tufts University[4];

- $225 million from Dorothy Patterson, whose family included founders of the *Chicago Tribune* and the *New York Daily News*, to the Patterson Foundation in Florida.[5]

Other entities released information about bequests

Other organizations study the amount received in bequests by members or specific types of organizations. These include the following:

- The Council for Aid to Education (CAE) announced that bequests from responding institutions of higher education in fiscal year 2007–2008 totaled $2.64 billion. This is an increase of 7.5 percent compared with 2006–2007, but a slower rate of growth than the 13.0 percent reported in 2005–2006 and in 2006–2007. Note, however, that the CAE receives information about bequests from a variety of higher education institutions, but does not receive consistent year-to-year responses from the same institutions.

- United Way of America reported bequests, endowment gifts, and other realized planned gifts of $72.4 million in 2007–2008 and will release information about 2008–2009 in fall 2009.

- United Jewish Communities (UJC) reported $2.6 billion in contributions to endowment funds held by the UJC/Jewish Federation system. Many of these contributions are from planned gifts (includes instruments other than bequests), according to the UJC annual report for 2007–2008.[6] In the report for 2006–2007, the UJC reported that its member federations received $1.3 billion through their planned gift and endowment programs.

GOOD TO KNOW

A will is a legal document that enables donors to make a significant legacy gift without reducing the assets available during their life. Before naming a charity in a will, most individuals will want to arrange to transfer assets to their family members.

Distribution of bequests, 2007

In 2007, data show that 7,672 estates claimed charitable deductions totaling $19.70 billion. More than 51 percent of deducted dollars for charitable bequests ($10.08 billion) were directed to "philanthropy and voluntarism," the subsector for private foundations.

Bequests made to educational institutions accounted for 13.9 percent ($2.73 billion) of claimed deductions for charitable bequests, making it the second most common destination. Figure 1 shows the distribution of dollars claimed as deductions for charitable bequests on estate tax returns.

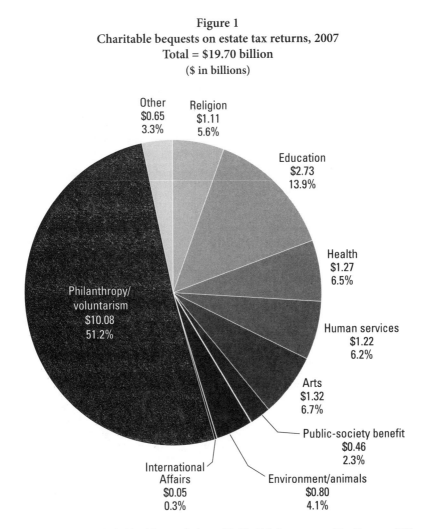

Figure 1
Charitable bequests on estate tax returns, 2007
Total = $19.70 billion
($ in billions)

Other
$0.65
3.3%

Religion
$1.11
5.6%

Education
$2.73
13.9%

Health
$1.27
6.5%

Human services
$1.22
6.2%

Philanthropy/
voluntarism
$10.08
51.2%

Arts
$1.32
6.7%

Public-society benefit
$0.46
2.3%

International
Affairs
$0.05
0.3%

Environment/animals
$0.80
4.1%

Data: Brief facts about charitable giving, analysis provided by U.S. Department of the Treasury, 2009.

Religious organizations received charitable bequests, from 20 percent of estates claiming charitable deductions. Educational organizations received the second-highest percentage of charitable bequests with 18 percent of estates with a charitable deduction making a gift to education. Figure 2 compares the percentage of estates that claimed a charitable deduction to the percentage of total dollars bequeathed by type of recipient organization.

Internal Revenue Service shows data for estate tax returns filed in 2004

Dr. Brian Raub, an economist at the Statistics of Income division of the Internal Revenue Service, analyzed estate tax returns filed by 42,239 individuals who died in 2004 and

had gross estates of $1.5 million or more. These individuals were subject to an estate tax under the threshold in force for that year.[7] Men outnumbered women, making up 56.2 percent of the filers, and held 59.3 percent of the value of assets reported on the returns. On average, a man's estate came to a total asset value of $4.65 million. Women's estates had an average of $4.09 million in assets. The majority of the women (61.4 percent) were widows.

People whose estates are large enough to be subject to the estate tax live longer than do people in the general population. Hence, wealth is associated with longevity. Men whose estates filed returns in 2004 had an average age of 77.2 at death, compared with an average of 75.2 for men in the general

Figure 2
Percentage of estates with a charitable bequest by type of recipient organization

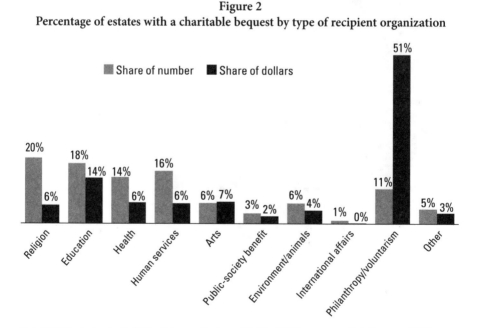

Data: Brief facts about charitable giving, analysis provided by U.S. Department of the Treasury, 2009.

population. Women whose estates filed returns in 2004 also lived about 2 years longer, dying at an average age of 82.0, compared to 80.4 for women in the U.S. overall.

For these returns, which are based on the year of death (not year of tax filing, which is how *Giving USA* does its estimates), 20.6 percent of estates included a charitable deduction. Total charitable bequests came to $17.8 billion, or 9.6 percent of the gross estate value for all of the returns filed (not just for those leaving a charitable bequest).

Estates with gross estate value of $20 million or more left an average of 20.1 percent to charity (including non-bequesters) and accounted for 56.2 percent of all charitable bequest dollars.

Watch for changes in *Giving USA* Methods

This past year, Russell N. James, III, of the University of Georgia, undertook an analysis for *Giving USA*, conducting

a longitudinal study using a nationally representative sample of people aged 50 and over. This study, named the "1995–2006 Health and Retirement Study," captured data of 6,000 research participants over the course of these years. When someone in the study died, a survivor was interviewed about the disposition of the estate. James then used the data from this survey to develop a method of estimating giving through charitable bequests by estates that were below the federal estate tax filing threshold. In the spring of 2009, this bequest estimation model was provided to the Giving USA Advisory Council and may result in the adoption of an alternative procedure (and a revision to historical data) in *Giving USA 2010*.

Reports appearing annually, summarized

Table 1 presents three years of data from studies released annually about bequests. Web site addresses are provided so readers can access the full reports.

Table 1
Key findings from studies of bequests and deferred giving

Charitable remainder annuity trust Tax returns filed Data available at www.irs.gov			
	2005	2006	2007
Number	21,667	21,296	20,187
Assets (book value, in billions)	$9.39	$8.87	$9.08

Charitable lead trusts Tax returns filed Data available at www.irs.gov			
	2005	2006	2007
Number	6,168	6,298	6,377
Assets (book value, in billions)	$15.10	$15.99	$18.09

Charitable remainder unitrust Tax returns filed Data available at www.irs.gov			
	2005	2006	2007
Number	94,779	94,767	95,567
Assets (per Form 5227, book value, in billions)	$79.84	$79.93	$86.74
Assets (year-end, estimated fair market value, in billions)	$95.05	$95.84	$106.43

Internal Revenue Service Estate tax returns filed, data available at www.irs.gov			
	2005	2006	2007
Federal estate tax filing threshold (Based on death date, not return date)	$1.5 million	$2.0 million	$2.0 million
Total number of estate tax returns filed	45,070	49,050	38,031
Number with charitable deduction (from analysis by U.S. Department of the Treasury)	8,074	9,222	7,672
Charitable deductions itemized on returns (from analysis by U.S. Department of the Treasury), in billions	$19.56	$17.59	$19.70
Percentage of estates filing estate tax return claiming a charitable deduction	20.5%	19.4%	20.2%
Percentage of gross estate value from all estate tax returns claimed in charitable deductions	11.0%	8.3%	9.7%

1   Russell N. James III estimates that 5.3 percent of decedents over age 50 leave a charitable bequest. (R.N. James, The Myth of the Coming Charitable Estate Windfall, *The American Review of Public Administration*; published edition forthcoming). Using recent data (2006) about adult deaths by age range released by the Centers for Disease Control, the estimate would be approximately 121,900 estates with charitable bequests for 2006.

2   *Philanthropy News Digest*, Feb. 6, 2008, www.foundationcenter.org.

3   *The Chronicle of Philanthropy*, June 26, 2008, www.philanthropy.com (need a Chronicle account to access).

4   Lesley University, Press release, April 8, 2008, www.lesley.edu and Tufts University, April 9, 2008, Feature story, www.tufts.edu.

5   Gift puts Sarasota charity in big leagues, *Sarasota Herald Tribune*, July 29, 2008, www.heraldtribune.com.

6   *UJC Annual Report*, United Jewish Communities, 2008, www.ujc.org.

7   B. Raub, Federal Estate Tax Returns Filed for 2004 Decedents, Statistics of Income Bulletin, Spring 2008.

5 Giving by foundations

- Grantmaking by independent, community, and operating foundations reached an estimated $41.21 billion in 2008, according to a survey by the Foundation Center. This is an increase of 3.0 percent (decline of 0.8 percent adjusted for inflation) from the revised foundation grantmaking total for 2007 of $40.0 billion, which the Foundation Center released in March 2009. The final number for 2007 is based on IRS Forms 990 and 990-PF filed by foundations.[1]

- Despite a recession and a stock market decline, the Foundation Center estimated that foundation grantmaking in 2008 surpassed all prior records. Grants made in 2008 include distributions from the Bill & Melinda Gates Foundation in the amount of $2.8 billion,[2] as well as grantmaking by other private, community, and operating foundations.

- The continued growth of foundation grantmaking in 2008 reflects strong foundation asset growth in 2006 and 2007.[3]

- While overall grantmaking increased among the foundations surveyed for 2008 giving estimates, the Foundation Center reported that nearly half (46.9 percent) reduced their giving during the year.[4]

- According to the Foundation Center, about 90 percent of foundations surveyed in 2009 reported making grants from investment earnings.[5] Because grants are issued from investment earnings, grantmaking is considered "new money" for philanthropy.

- The Foundation Center cautioned that grantmaking is expected to decline in 2009, although the reduction is estimated to be far less than market losses might suggest.

Giving USA findings

Giving USA reports the Foundation Center's estimates of foundation grant-making for the year just concluded.[6] *Giving USA* adjusted the Foundation Center's figure of $45.64 billion to remove $4.43 billion of corporate foundation grantmaking and added it to the corporate giving estimate for *Giving USA*. The estimate provided here for 2008 includes only grant-making by independent, community, and operating foundations.

The Foundation Center attributes the 3.0 percent growth (decline of 0.8 percent adjusted for inflation) in grantmaking by independent, community, and operating foundations to:

- Two years of double-digit gains in foundation assets (2006 and 2007), which are included in the rolling averages used to determine grantmaking levels at many of the top funders.

- Establishment of new foundations in recent years and major contributions totaling $40.43 billion in 2007 to existing and new foundations, excluding corporate foundations.

- A 40 percent increase in giving by the Gates Foundation, from $2.0 billion in 2007 to $2.8 billion in 2008. This alone accounted for a change in total grantmaking of 1.9 percent. Without the Gates Foundation included, the shift in 2008 grantmaking was 1.1 percent (a drop of 2.9 percent adjusted for inflation) for all other independent, community, and operating foundations.

- A stronger rate of growth in community foundation grantmaking, at 6.7 percent, compared to independent foundation grantmaking, which increased giving by 2.5 percent. Community foundations awarded a record $4.6 billion in 2008. This stems, at least in part, from the growth of foundation assets during the years 2003 through 2007 (including new gifts).

For 2009, the Foundation Center, based on a survey it conducted early in the year, predicts a decline in grantmaking. This decline is attributed to both the economic downturn and a sharp decline of 21.9 percent in foundation assets in 2008. Nevertheless, the Foundation Center estimates that grantmaking will fall less steeply than the decline in asset values because foundation payout rates are determined, at least in part, by a multi-year rolling average of asset values and the continued effect of the growth in foundation assets between 2006 and 2007.[7] The Foundation

Center predicts that the impact of the economic recession on foundation assets will continue to be felt until at least 2010, but it remains to be seen how the wavering economy will ultimately affect foundation grantmaking.

The largest grants announced in 2008

In 2008, seven grants of $200 million or more were announced, the same number as in 2007. Three of the seven were from the Bill & Melinda Gates Foundation, which was the same number of grants of this size announced by this foundation in 2007. The grants announced in 2008 totaled $1.439 billion, more than the $985 million of the top seven grants announced in 2007. Table 1 summarizes the seven largest 2008 grants.

Impact of the recession on foundation endowments and grantmaking

Although grantmaking increased 3.3 percent in 2008, that modest growth reflected the recession's impact on asset values held by foundations. The recession, which began in December 2007[8] and is predicted to run until at least mid-2009[9], has reduced endowments among many of the largest foundations. The Foundation Center reported, for example, that 46.9 percent of foundations it surveyed in early 2009 reduced their giving in 2008. This is nearly twice the 29 percent of foundations that reported in an early 2008 survey that they planned to reduce their grantmaking during the year.[10]

Early in 2009, the Foundation Center established an interactive Web site

Table 1
Top seven announced foundation grants, 2008
($ in millions)

Donor	Amount	Recipient
Eli and Edythe Broad Foundation	$400	Broad Institute of Harvard and MIT
Bloomberg Philanthropies	$250	Various organizations and governments
Robert W. Woodruff Foundation	$200	Grady Memorial Hospital
Bill & Melinda Gates Foundation	$169	PATH (Program for Appropriate Technology in Health)
Bill & Melinda Gates Foundation	$165	Alliance for a Green Revolution in Africa (AGRA)
American Contemporary Art Foundation	$131	Whitney Museum of American Art
Bill & Melinda Gates Foundation	$125	Various organizations and governments
Total	$1,440	

related to foundation giving during the economic crisis.[11] That site provides information about grants made, anticipated changes in grantmaking, and suggestions from foundations for nonprofits. Some of the site's information, current as of March 2009, is summarized here along with information provided by other organizations working with foundations.

Declining assets at the nation's top funds show reductions planned in 2009

The Standard & Poor's 500 Index fell nearly 40 percent (adjusted for inflation) in 2008. The Foundation Center estimated a drop of 21.9 percent in asset values at foundations, which included investment results as well as the value of new gifts received in 2008.

The Foundation Center surveyed the nation's top funders in early 2009[12] and found:

- 67 percent planned to decrease giving in 2009;

- 22 percent planned to increase their giving in 2009; and

- 11 percent anticipated making no change in their giving.

The authors of the Foundation Center study wrote:

The outlook beyond 2009 remains unclear, and much depends on when and how strongly the economy and stock market recover.... Even if a solid economic recovery begins in 2010, foundations that establish their grants budgets based on a rolling average of asset values... will be forced to factor in the dismal 2008 investment performance (p. 3).

Foundations with few or no staff also adjusting grantmaking

An informal September 2008 survey of members of the Association of Small

Thirty-one percent of foundations surveyed by the Council on Foundations in mid-2008 planned to increase grantmaking that assists families or aids low-income populations whether directly or indirectly.[17]

The Chronicle of Philanthropy noted in November 2008 that many foundations—particularly community foundations—began rolling out new programs to stabilize charities that provide basic human services.[18]

Foundations, a membership association for foundations with few or no staff, indicated that about two-thirds planned to maintain or increase their total grantmaking in 2009, though nearly a quarter said that they would be reducing grantmaking through the rest of the year.[13]

Grantmaking to alleviate recession-related impact announced

The Foundation Center noted that foundations making grants in direct response to the recession directed most of their grant dollars to soften the recession's impact in their own communities.[14] Examples include the following[15]:

- The MacArthur Foundation committed $38 million to mitigate the impact of foreclosures in the Chicago area;

- A range of foundations—particularly community foundations—committed local grants to cover the cost of emergency assistance and meeting basic needs such as food, utility service, and housing;

- Several foundations funded efforts to examine the root causes of the crisis and develop mechanisms to prevent such a crisis in the future; and

- Others funded efforts to educate broad segments of the public regarding economics and finance.

Some shift in focus expected in grantmaking priorities

The Foundation Center found that giving priorities did not shift markedly during the most recent periods of economic distress. They noted, however, that grant support intended to address "the crisis at hand" (September 11 in 2001 and the freeze of the credit markets in 2008) was substantial.[16]

Funding pressures may lead to mergers and collaborative projects

Paul Brest at the William and Flora Hewlett Foundation said that the recession might create pressure for mergers both between nonprofits providing duplicate services in a single market and between foundations serving the same geographic or program area.[19] The Association of Small Foundations included a recommendation that foundations, "collaborate with other funders and encourage collaboration among grantees" as one strategy for tough economic times.[20] At least one foundation, the Fairfield (CT) County Community Foundation, considered making grants to support efforts of local charities that were considering mergers.[21]

Implications for philanthropy concerning the Madoff crisis

The full impact of the alleged Ponzi scheme promulgated by Bernie Madoff was not completely clear at press time for *Giving USA 2009*. Early estimates (as of mid-December 2008) of losses totaled as much as $50 billion for all investors affected.[22] The known effects were severe for a range of foundations and their grantees. Particularly affected were Jewish charities and foundations, in addition to several foundations in New York and Florida, which lost an estimated sum of $2.5 billion.[23] The financial impact on foundations and other charities have generated substantial (and not necessarily negative) attention to foundation investment policies, including a review of appropriate tolerances for investment risk and responsibility for portfolio oversight.[24] While scrutiny of foundations from state attorneys general is likely as a direct or indirect result of the Madoff case,[25] the scope and scale of that attention remains to be seen.

Studies examine how funders support organizations seeking social change

Grantmaking to organizations that engage in advocacy received significant attention in 2008. Atlantic Philanthropies explored the efforts of 10 foundations

(including itself) to support advocacy efforts in various forms, including[26]:

- Research and dissemination;
- Increasing public awareness;
- Community organizing;
- Grassroots lobbying;
- Building capacity at advocacy organizations;
- Policy development;
- Direct lobbying;
- Litigation; and
- Electoral activity.

While noting that most U.S.-based foundations are limited to the support of 501(c)(3) public charities, the report stressed both the potential benefits and the necessary considerations of risk that foundations must examine in funding advocacy efforts, such as[27]:

- Foundations and grantees must be clear on the limits of acceptable action, both for 501(c)(3) public charities and 501(c)(4) social welfare organizations.

- Foundations must determine how specifically they will provide grant funds to advocacy organizations by answering these key questions: Do they fund nonprofits that promote advocacy activities directly or indirectly? Further, in funding

GOOD TO KNOW

As the economy shifts and foundations determine what they can and should do, nonprofit organization applicants should monitor announcements and changes. To provide this information, the Foundation Center launched a tracking system that invites foundations to share their policies and to record distributed grants in order to help charities as they respond to the economic crisis.

advocacy activities, do they fund these organizations directly, through an intermediary, or via a "consortium of funders?"

Jodi Sandfort of the University of Minnesota examined the unique challenges of foundation support for social change, noting the state of the field and the various tools that foundations use. [28] These include:

- Grants to cover general operating expenses;

- Grants to address issues—such as information technology systems or facilities upkeep—that are generally not captured by either general operating support grants or program-specific grants;

- Non-grant support, including loan guarantees and access to facilities;

- Efforts to convene stakeholders to address strategic issues related to the area of interest;

- Communications to influence public opinion on an issue;

- Research to document the existence and extent of social problems of interest to grantees; and

- Building networks to mobilize responses.

Mission-related investing guidelines and summaries issued

An issue discussed in the 2008 edition of *Giving USA* continued to receive substantial attention in 2008: Mission-related investing. Also known as "responsible investment," or as "ESG (Environmental, Social, and Governance) analysis," mission-related investing generated considerable interest in 2008 both among members of the public and among investors.[29]

Publications in 2008 by Rockefeller Philanthropy Advisors[30] and the Boston College Center for Corporate Citizenship[31] developed guidelines to facilitate mission-related investing on the part of both individuals and institutions, including foundations. Others issued guidebooks on the law of mission-related investing for foundations,[32] as well as summaries of guidance issued by the U.S. Internal Revenue Service and the American Bar Association regarding acceptable practice and boundaries of mission-related investing.[33]

One-third of community foundation assets held in donor-advised funds

A report from the Council on Foundations, based on a summer

GOOD TO KNOW

Efforts to align a foundation's investment portfolio with its social or strategic goals may slow because foundations will be under more pressure than usual to generate returns on investments.[34] Other efforts, including approaches that channel investment capital into projects that will benefit the local economy, may well accelerate.[35] This trend warrants continued attention in 2009. Organizations might consider proposing "program-related investments" to foundations as one way to help the foundations achieve their social mission and improve the community at the same time.

2008 survey, found approximately $16.5 billion was held by about 49,000 separate donor-advised funds established at community foundations.[36] The donor-advised fund assets were about one-third of the money invested by the community foundations.

Grants paid by donor-advised funds constituted 62 percent of community foundation grantmaking. One reason the donor-advised funds accounted for such a large share of grantmaking is that the payout rates averaged 16.4 percent for funds versus 5 percent for other foundation assets. It should be noted, however, that more than half of the participating foundations reported payout rates below 10 percent for their donor-advised funds. The largest community foundations ($1 billion or more in assets) had comparatively high payout rates, averaging 18.5 percent, for their donor-advised funds.

Diversity among foundation staff, boards, and grantees examined

In February 2008, the California General Assembly introduced legislation that would have required large foundations to disclose data on the ethnicity, gender, and sexual orientation of their staff and boards. Foundations also would have been required to disclose the same information regarding their grantees and contractors.[37] This legislation, inspired in part by a Greenlining Institute study, generated attention to the issue of diversity within foundations and their grantees in California and beyond.

Although the legislation was ultimately withdrawn, the issues that it raised continued to resonate in the foundation community. In California, grantmakers formed the Foundation Coalition, which, among other action steps, committed to[38]:

- Increasing grant support to grassroots organizations representing and serving low-income and minority Californians by more than $20 million;

- Developing training and technical assistance programs to increase leadership skills and organizational capacity among such organizations, at a cost of more than $10 million over three years; and

- Conducting research regarding the level and state of minority leadership in California's nonprofit community.

At the national level, the Foundation Center and Rockefeller Philanthropy Advisors solicited responses from foundations regarding the mechanisms they use to collect information on the gender, race, and ethnic identities of their beneficiaries.[39] Their initial report found a range of efforts among foundations to support diversity, including programs to:

- Improve the ability of foundations to take steps toward greater inclusiveness and diversity;

- Encourage diverse donors to increase the scale and impact of their giving to benefit underserved majority-minority communities; and

- Employ and leverage the expertise of non-majority foundation staff to solicit and articulate information about the needs of diverse communities.[40]

Within grantmaker communities, diversity is a topic of increasing concern. Charitable organizations seeking foundation funding should be able to provide statistics about their staff, board membership, and constituencies as foundations seek ways to demonstrate their commitment to inclusiveness. For some foundations, the processes used to include broad engagement from the community are as important, or more important, than counts of people in different groups.[41]

Foundation giving priorities, 2007

In a survey of 1,339 foundations granting $21.65 billion in 2007, the Foundation Center found that foundation support for eight of the ten major subsector areas rose in 2007 compared to 2006.[42] Funding for the category "environment/animals" rose at the fastest rate, up 28.5 percent from the prior year—more than double the 13.2 percent rise in overall grant dollars. Figure 1 shows the 2007 funding priorities. Prior editions of *Giving USA* have comparable graphs for earlier editions of the Foundation Center research.

Other key findings from the study of funding priorities in 2007 include:

- Foundations awarded a record 188 grants of $10 million or more in 2007. Of the ten largest, eight were made by the Gates Foundation, mainly for health-related activities and international development.

- International giving—which cuts across all areas and includes grants awarded directly to overseas recipients and to U.S.-based international programs—reached more than $5 billion, a record 23.4 percent of the dollars granted by the surveyed foundations.

- Among specific populations, the economically disadvantaged benefited from the largest share of grant dollars, rising to a record $5.3 billion, from $4.0 billion in 2006.

Family foundations account for nearly 45 percent of foundation grantmaking
Approximately $18.46 billion of $41.21 billion granted by independent, community, and operating foundations in 2007 came from family foundations,[43] which is 44.8 percent of all grantmaking by these foundations. If all family foundation grant dollars are added to individual giving for 2007, total gifts directed to charities by individuals, families, and family foundations comes to an estimated $254 billion, which is almost 81 percent of total estimated giving for 2007.

One-third of the 37,539 family foundations tracked by the Foundation Center were established between 2000 and 2007. Family foundations accounted for an estimated 56 percent of the assets of independent foundations in 2007. While major foundations, such as the Bill & Melinda Gates Foundation, the Walton Family Foundation, and Annenberg Foundation are considered family foundations, nearly half of family foundations (48 percent) reported less than $50,000 in giving for 2007.

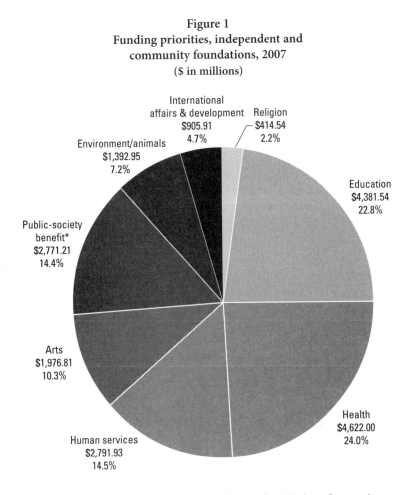

Figure 1
Funding priorities, independent and
community foundations, 2007
($ in millions)

International
affairs & development Religion
$905.91 $414.54
4.7% 2.2%

Environment/animals
$1,392.95
7.2%

Education
$4,381.54
22.8%

Public-society
benefit*
$2,771.21
14.4%

Arts
$1,976.81
10.3%

Health
$4,622.00
24.0%

Human services
$2,791.93
14.5%

*Includes amounts for "science and technology" and for "social science," reported
separately by the Foundation Center.
Data: Foundation Center, *Foundation Giving Trends*, 2009 edition, page 37. Based on a
sample of foundations.

The Foundation Center identifies
family foundations using several
criteria, including the word "family"
or "families" in the name; two or more
trustees with the same surname as
that of a living or deceased donor; or
a foundation that identifies itself as a
family foundation when completing
a Foundation Center survey.

**Analysis of grantmaking and
estimate of return on investment**
Robert Shapiro, chairman of the
consulting firm Sonecon, and Aparna
Mathur of the American Enterprise
Institute, examined extensive literature
about the economic benefits provided to
nonprofits by foundation grantmaking
in order to estimate the economic

value to society of grants made in each of 11 different categories.[44] Where there were a range of economic benefits found in different studies about comparable types of organizations, Drs. Shapiro and Mathur developed a weighted average. In some instances, the values used were assumed or served as a lower bound. For the categories of religion, international affairs, social science research, and "other," the authors conservatively estimated the societal benefit to be equal to the foundation funding (1:1).

Figure 2 shows the estimated value of the direct benefit to the different nonprofit subsectors for every $1 in independent or community foundation support.

Key findings from other studies summarized

Table 2 presents three years of findings from studies released annually about foundations. Web site addresses are provided to help readers attain access to the full report.

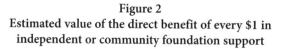

Figure 2
Estimated value of the direct benefit of every $1 in independent or community foundation support

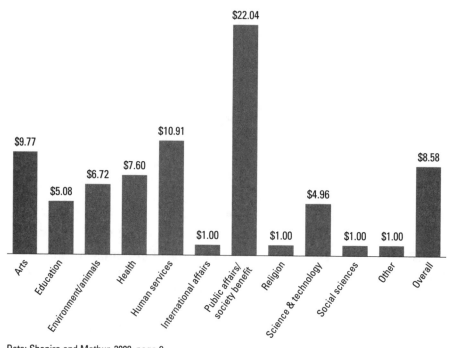

Data: Shapiro and Mathur, 2008, page 9.

Note: The value for Public Affairs/Society Benefit is shaped in large part by just three of the 13 studies used to develop the average. Those three found ratios ranging from 48:1 to 58:1. Eight of the 13 had ratios below 10:1, and the other two had ratios of 15:1 and 18:1 (p. 26).

Table 2
Key findings from other studies about foundation giving

Foundation Yearbook, 2007, 2008 and 2009 editions Foundation Center, www.foundationcenter.org			
	2005	2006	2007
Number of active independent and community grantmaking foundations	63,766	65,122	67,751
Number of all active grantmaking foundations (including corporate and operating)	71,095	72,477	75,187
Assets in independent and community foundations	$500.15 billion	$559.02 billion	$620.90 billion

Foundation Giving Trends, 2007, 2008 and 2009 editions Foundation Center, www.foundationcenter.org			
	2005	2006	2007
Average grant amount, surveyed foundations	$125,442	$136,122	$143,957
Median grant amount, surveyed foundations	$26,000	$25,000	$25,000

1   S. Lawrence and R. Mukai, *Foundation Growth and Giving Estimates*, March 2009, The Foundation Center, www.foundationcenter.org.
2   Bill & Melinda Gates Foundation, *Foundation Fact Sheet*, April 1, 2009, www.gatesfoundation.org/about/Pages/foundation-fact-sheet.aspx.
3   Same as note 1.
4   Same as note 1.
5   S. Lawrence, *Research Advisory: Foundations Address the Impact of the Economic Crisis*, April 2009, figure on page 4, The Foundation Center, www.foundationcenter.org.
6   Same as note 1.
7   Same as note 1, p. 3.
8   L. Levine, *Job Loss and Infrastructure Job Creation during the Recession*, December 2008, Congressional Research Service, p. 1.
9   J. Renier, *National Economic Update*, December 22, 2008, www.dallasfed.org.
10 Same as note 1.
11 L. McGill and S. Lawrence, *Grantmakers*

Describe the Impact of the Economic Crisis on Their Giving, March 2009, The Foundation Center, www.foundationcenter.org.
12 Same as note 1.
13 B. Gose, P. Wasley, and I. Wilhelm, After the Fall: Financial crisis is affecting nonprofit groups in myriad ways, *The Chronicle of Philanthropy*, October 16, 2008, www.philanthropy.com.
14 S. Lawrence, *A First Look at the Foundation and Corporate Response to the Economic Crisis*, January 2009, Foundation Center, www.foundationcenter.org.
15 Same as note 14.
16 S. Lawrence, *Do Foundation Giving Priorities Change in Times of Economic Distress?*, November 2008, The Foundation Center, www.foundationcenter.org.
17 Council on Foundations, *Foundations support families hit by economic downturn*, May 1, 2008, www.cof.org.
18 B. Gose, Extending a helping hand: Foundations retool their grantmaking

plans as the economy declines, *Chronicle of Philanthropy*, November 13, 2008, www.philanthropy.com.

19 M. Nauffts, Newsmakers Paul Brest, President, William and Flora Hewlett Foundation: Smart Philanthropy in Tough Times, *Philanthropy News Digest*, November 20, 2008, The Foundation Center, www.foundationcenter.org.

20 10 strategies for tough economic times, Association of Small Foundations, www.smallfoundations.org.

21 Getting creative in hard times: Rising demand forces area nonprofit agencies to adjust, *Stamford Advocate*, January 29, 2009, www.stamfordadvocate.com.

22 B. Gose, Charities calculate losses in alleged Ponzi scheme, *The Chronicle of Philanthropy*, December 16, 2008, www.philanthropy.com.

23 B. Gose, In scandal's wake: A Ponzi scheme causes major foundations to close and causes losses for scores of charities nationwide, *The Chronicle of Philanthropy*, January 15, 2009, www.philanthropy.com.

24 D. Blum, Charities revamped investment policies in 2008, survey finds, *The Chronicle of Philanthropy*, January 7, 2009, www.philanthropy.com.

25 B. Gose, Trustees could be held liable for decisions in Madoff case, *The Chronicle of Philanthropy*, January 15, 2009, www.philanthropy.com.

26 The Atlantic Philanthropies, *Why Supporting Advocacy Makes Sense for Foundations*, May 2008, The Atlantic Philanthropies, p.3f.

27 Same as note 26, p. 8.

28 J. Sandfort, Using lessons from public affairs to inform strategic philanthropy, *Nonprofit and Voluntary Sector Quarterly*, September 2008, http://nvs.sagepub.com, p. 544ff.

29 Boston College Carroll School of Management Center for Corporate Citizenship, *Handbook on Responsible Investment Across Asset Classes*, 2008, Boston College, p. 2.

30 S. Godeke and D. Bauer, *Philanthropy's New Passing Gear: Mission-Related Investing—A Policy Guide for Foundation Trustees*, Rockefeller Philanthropy Advisors, www.rockpa.org.

31 Same as note 29.

32 M. Kramer and A. Stetson, *A Brief Guide to the Law of Mission Investing for U.S.*

Foundations, October 2008, FSG Social Impact Advisors, www.fsg-impact.org.

33 A. Stetson and M. Kramer, *Risk, Return and Social Impact: Demystifying the Law of Mission Investing by U.S. Foundations*, October 2008, FSG Social Impact Advisors, www.fsg-impact.org.

34 N. Wallace, Invested with purpose: Foundations see growing appeal of mission-related investing, *The Chronicle of Philanthropy*, November 27, 2008, www.philanthropy.com.

35 N. Wallace, Foundations make investments to spur economic growth in regions where they make grants, *The Chronicle of Philanthropy*, November 27, 2008, www.philanthropy.com.

36 S. Nilsen, *Donor Advised Funds Provide Majority of Grant Funds Awarded by Community Foundations*, January 2009 Council on Foundations, www.cof.org.

37 S. Perry, California Assembly votes to make foundations disclose key information on diversity, *The Chronicle of Philanthropy*, February 7, 2008, www.philanthropy.com.

38 The Foundation Coalition, *Strengthening Nonprofit Minority Leadership and the Capacity of Minority-Led and Other Grassroots Community-Based Organizations*, December 2008, www.packard.org.

39 I. Wilhelm, Survey seeks better sense of how much grant makers give to minorities, *The Chronicle of Philanthropy*, September 18, 2008, www.philanthropy.com.

40 J. Chao, J. Parshall, D. Amador, M. Shab, and A. Yañez, *Philanthropy in a Changing Society: Achieving Effectiveness through Diversity*, April 2008, Rockefeller Philanthropy Advisors, p. 3, www.rockpa.org.

41 L. McGill, J. Kroll, and T. Jeavons, Diversity in Philanthropy: What is the Relationship to Effectiveness in Grantmaking? Proceedings from the Second Annual Grantmaker/Researcher Forum, release date Sept. 2009, www.foundationcenter.org and www.cof.org.

42 S. Lawrence, R. Mukai, and J. Atienza, *Foundation Giving Trends*, 2009 Edition, The Foundation Center, www.foundationcenter.org.

43 The Foundation Center, *Key Facts on Family Foundations*, 2009 edition, www.foundationcenter.org.

44 R. Shapiro and A. Mathur, *The Social and Economic Value of Private and Community Foundations*, December 2008, The Philanthropy Collaborative, www.philanthropycollaborative.org.

6 Giving by corporations

- Corporate giving is estimated to be $14.5 billion in 2008.

- This is a decline of 4.5 percent (-8.0 percent adjusted for inflation).

- Corporate giving is 5 percent of total giving.

- Corporate giving includes cash and in-kind donations that corporations take as charitable deductions on their tax returns. However, *Giving USA* removes the donations made to corporate foundations and counts, instead, the amount that corporate foundations donate to charities. For 2008, the corporate foundation estimate is approximately 30 percent of total estimated corporate giving.

Giving USA findings

The U.S. economy entered a recession in December 2007, which persisted throughout 2008 and beyond. The finance and home-building sectors were the most negatively affected by this economic crisis, which was catalyzed by increasing numbers of people who had borrowed money, whether to purchase homes or for other expenses, not being able to meet payments. Several financial firms collapsed in 2008. One example is Lehman Brothers, which, at over $600 billion in debt, was the largest bankruptcy in history, dwarfing the prior record set in 2002 by Enron.

In fall 2008, banks, car manufacturers, and other firms received significant cash support through either transfers or through guarantees from the federal government. However, with reduced new credit for homebuyers and businesses; lower consumer spending; and growing lay-offs, there was a ripple effect throughout the economy. By late 2008, major companies in most key sectors of the economy saw losses instead of profits for the year.[1]

Charitable giving by corporations has historically been linked to corporate profits and to overall national Gross Domestic Product (GDP). In 2008, corporate profits decreased nearly 18 percent, adjusted for inflation, according to the Bureau of Economic Analysis. The change in GDP was 1.1 percent compared with growth of 2.0 percent in 2007 and 2.8 percent in 2006. Not surprisingly, with such a difficult year for corporate profits, charitable giving by most companies stayed flat or fell.[2]

Corporate giving estimates from surveys also show declines

The *Giving USA* estimate is supported by survey results collected independently. In a survey of 345 corporate CFOs, conducted by Financial Executives International and Baruch College's Zicklin School of Business in early December 2008, half of the respondents whose companies have historically given to charity reported a decrease in their charitable giving during 2008, and 33 percent cited a shift in their giving towards strategies that align philanthropy with business goals.[3]

Committee Encouraging Corporate Philanthropy finds growth in non-cash giving

The Committee Encouraging Corporate Philanthropy's (CECP) *Corporate Philanthropy 2008: Data Trends and the Changing Economy* finds 2008 aggregate giving totaled $10.03 billion and is a 7.8 percent drop, adjusted for inflation, from 2007 (-3 percent in current dollars).[4] This rate of change is based on 102 firms that participated in CECP's 2007 and 2008 surveys. Median giving per company fell to $30.8 million, a 7.8 percent drop from a peak in 2007 of $33.2 million. These figures include corporate cash grants, foundation cash grants, and non-cash contributions.

Among all of the firms surveyed, 53 percent increased their giving from 2007 to 2008, despite a drop in corporate profits in 2008 for 68 respondents. Among firms that increased giving, 27 percent said they increased their giving by 10 percent or more compared with 2007. This is about 19 percent of all firms in the survey.

Among the companies that gave more in 2008, non-cash giving increased the most—surging by nearly 35 percent. Companies whose giving declined predominately decreased in cash grants from the corporate side. In comparison, overall corporate foundation giving levels changed only nominally from 2007 to 2008 for both groups of companies.

Companies that increased giving cited various reasons for heightened giving, including: obtaining better data on con-

tributions, particularly on international grant-making and giving conducted by business units, and responding to disasters, such as the Sichuan earthquake in China and the California wildfires. For companies that decreased giving in 2008, the economic downturn and its associated symptoms were referenced most often.

The Conference Board survey finds corporate giving increased moderately in 2007

In its *2008 Corporate Contributions Report*, the Conference Board released findings about 197 companies that it surveyed about their 2007 giving. The respondent corporations are among the largest corporate donors in the country. They reported total contributions of $10.97 billion in 2007, up slightly from $10.21 billion in 2006.[5] A total of $8.62 billion went to U.S.-based charities, and $2.35 billion went to recipients outside the U.S. The pharmaceutical industry continued to make the largest total U.S. donations, at $3.84 billion, and non-cash contributions, at $3.23 billion; while the banking industry was the largest U.S. cash giver with $714.09 million. Figure 1 shows the allocation of corporate giving by type of U.S. recipients in 2007.

Health and human services organizations continued to receive the largest share of corporate support in the U.S., rising to $4.56 billion (compared with $3.8 billion in 2006). This amount includes $3.2 billion, or 70 percent, from in-kind contributions by pharmaceutical companies.

Giving to civic and community organizations increased to $1.1 billion in

Figure 1
Corporate giving, cash and non-cash by type of recipient (n=197)
($ in billions)

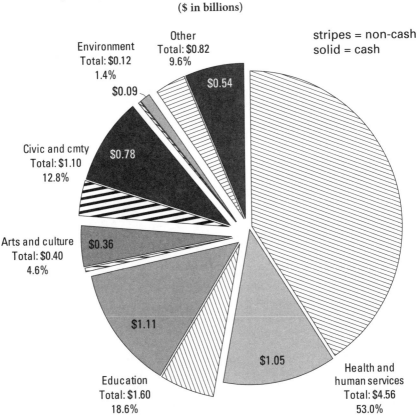

Data: The Conference Board, *The 2008 Corporate Contributions Report,* Tables 19-25

2007, representing 13 percent of total corporate giving reported to the Conference Board. This increase is attributed to a dramatic increase in support by technology firms.

Among the 197 firms participating in both the 2006 and 2007 surveys, total U.S. contributions rose by 13 percent. Giving to civic and community organizations saw the largest increase of 56.5 percent; whereas giving to educational

organizations rose only 0.4 percent from 2006 to 2007.

Median corporate contributions to U.S.-based charities were 1.48 percent of pretax income in 2007, up from 1.16 percent in 2006. Companies with annual giving budgets between $10 million and $20 million, as well as companies with budgets of $50 million or more, had a much higher median rate, at 2.12 percent and 2.21 percent, respectively.[6]

Giving by corporations

Foundation Center estimated corporate foundation giving for 2007

The Foundation Center's survey of foundation giving in 2007 reported that corporate foundation giving totaled approximately $2.1 billion.[7] The largest share of corporate foundation dollars went to education, followed by public-society benefit organizations and human services. Figure 2 shows the distribution of grants by subject area. The report is based on all grants of $10,000 or more awarded by a sample of 1,339 larger foundations.

Company surveys indicate 3 to 5 percent drop in corporate charitable giving for 2009

According to a survey of 76 major U.S. corporations conducted by LBG Research Institute, overall corporate giving is likely to decrease in 2009, but not at a severe level.[8] In the November 2008 survey, the majority of corporations expected their giving to remain flat or increase in 2009. Half of those with

Figure 2
Corporation foundation grantmaking priorities, 2007
($ in billions)

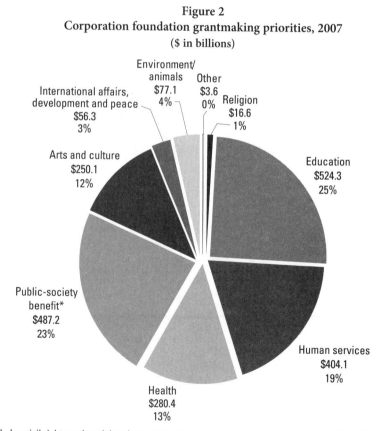

* Includes civil rights and social action; community improvement and development; public affairs; science and technology research; and social science research
Data: Foundation Center, Foundation Giving Trends: Update on Funding Priorities, 2009 edition, page 37.

corporate foundations said the foundation's budget will stay the same in 2009. The aggregate decrease in corporate giving in 2009 is predicted to be 3 to 5 percent, far less than the 7.5 percent drop in the 2001 recession found by *Giving USA*.

The *2009 Outlook Report* released by the Minnesota Council on Foundations was more optimistic: almost 60 percent of 39 corporate foundations and giving programs surveyed expected no changes in the amount of their grantmaking in 2009.[9]

According to the LBG survey, over 80 percent of corporate respondents plann to spend their charitable budgets more strategically in 2009, which means that they plan to align their giving more closely with corporate goals. Hence, organizations that support environmental causes or basic needs may see the largest increase coming from corporate giving. About 23 to 24 percent of respondents expect to increase their giving in one of these two areas. However, only 4 percent said they will increase their support in arts and culture, whereas nearly half of respondents plann to decrease their giving in this area.

In addition, a survey of large U.S. corporations, conducted by *The Chronicle of Philanthropy*, suggests that many businesses will be more selective in the future about building new relationships with charities, and that they will seek to maintain their relationships with the charities they have supported for years.[10]

Philanthropic expectations for companies remain high despite the current economic downturn

The 2008 Cone Cause Evolution Study revealed that consumers continue to have high expectations that companies support social causes.[11] About 52 percent of more than 1,000 respondents felt companies should maintain their level of financial support for social and environmental causes and nonprofit organizations, and 26 percent expected companies to give even more despite the current economic downturn.

Consumers surveyed by Cone reported strong support for cause marketing, with results compared with a study done in the early 1990s. In both 1993 and 2008, 85 percent of respondents said that they had a more positive image of a product or company when it supported a cause they cared about. In 2008, 85 percent felt it was acceptable for companies to involve a cause in their marketing, compared with 66 percent in 1993. These findings are confirmed by the 2008 goodpurpose™ global study of consumer attitudes.[12] Nearly 70 percent of 6,000 consumers in 10 countries, including the U.S., reported that they would stay loyal to a brand during a recession if it supports a good cause.

The 2008 PRWeek/Barkley Public Relations Cause Survey researched companies' involvement with cause marketing programs.[13] Of 113 corporate respondents, 67 percent had an existing cause marketing program; 97 percent of companies with a cause program regarded cause branding as an effective business strategy. When asked about the current economic impact on company involvement with such programs, 72 percent of those with cause programs responded that they will continue their commitment to these programs; 17.3 percent said they have had to decrease their investment in such programs; and 6.7 percent have had to put the programs on hold due to the economy.

Companies are cutting back on matching-gift programs

Matching-gift programs have been popular for years with companies, employees, and nonprofits. However, according to an article in *The Wall Street Journal*, more than a dozen large U.S. companies suspended or greatly reduced their matching programs during 2008. The article cited work by HEP Development Services, which estimated that matching programs accounted for about $860 million, or 10 percent of the total $8.6 billion giving to U.S. organizations tracked by the Conference Board survey for corporate giving in 2007.[14] The recession, as well as mergers of financial and media companies

that have long giving histories, are factors that hurt matching programs. Nevertheless, HEP Development Services estimated that about one in 10 donations to charities can still be matched with a corporate gift.

Education is top issue for business support

The *2008 Corporate Community Investment Study*, sponsored by Business Civic Leadership Center and conducted in part by the Center on Philanthropy at Indiana University, surveyed nearly 470 businesses located in the 100 largest metropolitan areas to understand corporate community investment strategies.[15] The findings are based on responses received, and may not be representative of the general business community. According to the study, approximately 83 percent of company respondents reported cash donations in 2007, and their average giving was $850,245 (median $18,850). Around 52 percent of corporations reported in-kind donations in 2007, with the average amount of $121,899 ($8,700 median). Figure 3 shows the top five issues to which companies made cash donations.

Figure 3
Percentage of respondents reporting that the company made a cash donation in 2007
Top five issues to which businesses make cash donations

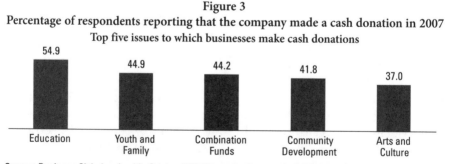

Education	Youth and Family	Combination Funds	Community Development	Arts and Culture
54.9	44.9	44.2	41.8	37.0

Source: Business Civic Leadership Center, *2008 Corporate Community Investment Study*, December 2008. Researched and written by the Center on Philanthropy at Indiana University.

Table 1
Corporate cash donations by size of businesses (donors only)

Size of Corporation	Percentage donating	Average giving	Median giving
Small (revenue < $1 million)	93.8%	$19,311	$3,500
Medium (revenue $1–$10 million)	87.4%	$23,702	$10,000
Large (revenue > $10 million)	77.7%	$1,416,398	$100,000

Source: Business Civic Leadership Center, *2008 Corporate Community Investment Study*, December 2008. Researched and written by the Center on Philanthropy at Indiana University.

The study also finds that corporate cash donations vary by the size of the companies surveyed. As Table 1 shows, large corporations with revenue more than $10 million gave more in cash to charitable organizations ($1.4 million on average); but small companies with revenue under $1 million were more likely overall to make cash donations (nearly 94 percent).

Fortune 100 companies actively support education initiatives

A study by Wendy Erisman and Shannon M. Looney at the Institute for Higher Education Policy examined the extent of corporate support for education among Forbes Fortune 100 companies.[16] Ninety corporations supported education as one of their philanthropic goals, and 68 firms supported college readiness and access programs particularly. Among these 68 companies:

■ Most supported existing programs rather than developing their own;

■ Most programs focused on meeting the company's workforce needs and were located in the same geographic regions;

■ 65 percent supported one to three programs, and 53 companies contributed resources to programs that were supported by more than one corporation; and

■ Nineteen of the 68 corporations also supported education policy or advocacy initiatives, suggesting that relatively few firms aligned their giving with broader educational goals.

The study also identified four kinds of giving strategies that these companies use. These are:

■ Aligning decisions with corporate and industry priorities;

■ Adopting data-driven decision making;

■ Building ongoing and reciprocal partnerships; and

GOOD TO KNOW

With the rise in "strategic philanthropy," which means aligning giving programs to fulfill company marketing, branding, or sales objectives, and with corporate profits suffering, charities will need to develop creative giving opportunities to complement corporate goals. The chapters about giving to the arts and giving to the environment both reveal some examples.

- Seeking sustainability and wider impact, rather than simply providing general support.

55 percent of small businesses support educational organizations

Although small businesses are feeling the negative effects of the economy, 66 percent reported that they donated cash to local nonprofit organizations in 2008, while 55 percent reported supporting education.[17] Chamberlain Research Consultants of Madison, Wisconsin worked with *The Chronicle of Philanthropy* and Advanta Bank Corporation to survey 1,000 small business owners in 2008. Most revealed that they give because of local connections and personal interests, not because of strategic philanthropy objectives. Additionally, most small businesses do not have a plan for philanthropy and do not believe their donations will promote business.

Business-to-consumer companies were found to be more generous

In the 2008 edition of its *Corporate Contributions Report*, the Conference Board released findings on corporate contributions according to business type (B2B vs. B2C vs. "mixed type" companies).[18] It was found that business-to-consumer (B2C) companies gave the largest share of contributions to charities both inside and outside the U.S., with $3.66 billion and $1.52 billion, respectively; whereas business-to-business (B2B) companies gave considerably less, with $1.43 billion in the U.S. and $244.20 million overseas. The high amount of charitable giving from B2C was driven heavily by

in-kind donations, which accounted for 75.5 percent of their U.S. giving and 85.3 percent of their international giving.

Furthermore, B2C companies gave substantially more to health and human services organizations, representing 80 percent of their total support to U.S.-based charities and 60 percent of their contributions internationally. B2B firms gave more of their U.S. contributions to educational organizations (42 percent) and more of their international giving to health and human services organizations (43 percent). Companies that identified themselves as both B2B and B2C divided their support more evenly among three beneficiary types: health and human services, education, and civic and community organizations.

Corporate giving is constrained by economic concerns even after accounting for catastrophic events

Corporations played an important role in disaster relief in recent years. Two recent studies revealed that firms more closely connected to the catastrophic event gave more, on average, than less connected companies. By analyzing donation announcements made by 490 Fortune Global 500 firms, Alan Muller and Gail Whiteman, both in business schools at universities in the Netherlands, found that companies are more likely to donate, and donate more, to disasters if their headquarters, subsidiaries, or business relations are located in the disaster-stricken area.[19]

In a separate study, William Crampton and Dennis Patten of Illinois State University found that differences in giving were positively and significantly

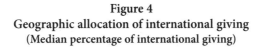

Figure 4
Geographic allocation of international giving
(Median percentage of international giving)

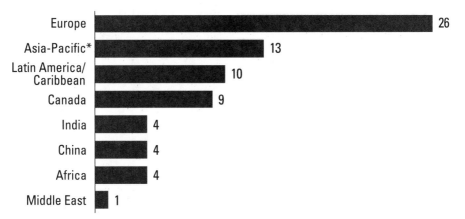

*Other than China and India
Source: The Conference Board, The 2008 Corporate Contributions Report, page 30.

related to the profitability levels of companies after the September 11, 2001 terrorist attacks.[20] Their study suggests that corporate giving is constrained when companies have economic concerns, even when companies face increased social pressure to give right after catastrophic events.

International contributions held steady at $2.35 billion in 2007

The Conference Board reported $2.35 billion in international giving by corporations in 2007, compared with $2.3 billion in 2006.[21] In-kind contributions accounted for 66 percent. Among the 74 companies with international giving programs that participated in both the 2006 and 2007 surveys, total international giving went up by 30 percent. The pharmaceutical industry is the largest donor of both cash and

non-cash donations. Health and human services organizations based outside the U.S. received 43 percent of international corporate support, followed by educational organizations (26 percent) and civic and community organizations (17 percent).

In its studies, the Conference Board found that Europe received the most international funding from respondent companies, with a median percentage of 26 percent. The median percentage of international contributions to the Asia-Pacific area, excluding China and India, was 13 percent, whereas the funding to China, India, and Africa was 4 percent for each. The Middle East received the lowest share of donations. Figure 4 illustrates the geographic allocation of international giving from 86 respondent companies with international giving programs.

The size of the donating company's workforce in the local market and humanitarian needs are the top two criteria that respondent companies considered when allocating their international giving.

Table 2 presents three years of data from studies released annually about corporate giving. Web site addresses are provided so that readers can access the full reports.

Table 2
Key findings from annual studies about corporate giving

Million Dollar List, gifts from corporations $10 million and above (2006–2008) Center on Philanthropy at Indiana University, www.philanthropy.iupui.edu			
	2006	2007	2008
Largest publicized corporate gift	$289 million, in-kind software grant from UGS Corporation to University of Cincinnati	$307 million, in-kind, software from UGS Corporation to three Gulf Coast school districts affected by the 2005 hurricanes	$105 million from Intel to Society for Science & the Public for its science competitions and outreach programs

The Corporate Contributions Report The Conference Board, www.conference-board.org			
	2005	2006	2007
Percent change in total giving over prior year among firms that responded two years in a row to the survey (U.S. firms)	18.3 209 firms	-6.3 146 firms	13.1 139 firms
U.S. contributions as a percentage of U.S. pretax income (median)	1.01 percent	1.16 percent	1.48 percent
U.S. contributions as a percentage of consolidated (U.S. and international operations) pretax income (median)	0.71 percent	0.71 percent	0.71 percent
Donations per employee, worldwide (median)	$434	$449	$542
Share from corporate cash (U.S. contributions)	23.2 percent	24.9 percent	25.3 percent
Share in-kind (U.S. contributions)	52.9 percent	50.4 percent	54.2 percent
Share from foundation grants (U.S. contributions)	23.9 percent	24.7 percent	20.5 percent

Giving by corporations

Foundation Center report about corporate foundations _Foundation Yearbook_, various editions Foundation Center, www.foundationcenter.org			
	2005	2006	2007
Number of corporate foundations	2,607	2,548	2,498
New gifts received	$4.008 billion	$4.370 billion	$4.420 billion
Grants made	$3.996 billion	$4.100 billion	$4.400 billion

Charitable giving at major corporations, August 17, 2006, August 23, 2007, and August 21, 2008 _The Chronicle of Philanthropy_, www.philanthropy.com (Note: 2008 data not available in mid-2009)			
	2005	2006	2007
Corporate donor identified as largest cash donor and amount contributed in cash	Walmart $236.1 million	Walmart $264 million	Walmart $301 million
Company reported with the highest amount in cash and product donations	Pfizer $1.6 billion	Pfizer $1.7 billion	Oracle $2.1 billion

Sponsorships (includes for-profit and nonprofit) IEG Sponsorship Report, www.sponsorship.com $ in billions (% change)			
	2005	2006	2007
Sports	8.94 (7.6)	9.94 (11.2)	11.4 (14.7)
Entertainment	1.38 (17.9)	1.56 (13.3)	1.63 (4.5)
Fairs, events, festivals	0.60 (17.1)	0.70 (14.9)	0.75 (7.1)
Causes	1.30 (17.1)	1.44 (10.4)	1.52 (5.6)
Arts	0.74 (14.5)	0.80 (8.3)	0.83 (3.7)
Associations/membership groups	0.40 (18.5)	0.46 (14.1)	0.48 (4.3)

1   D. Jolly, Worldwide, a bad year only got
    worse, *The New York Times*, June 2, 2009,
    www.nytimes.com and Swann, C., GDP
    and the Economy: Final Estimates for the
    Fourth Quarter of 2008, U.S. Bureau of
    Economic Analysis, April 2009, www.bea.gov.
2   Gross Domestic Product: Fourth Quarter
    2008 (Final), Corporate Profits, Fourth
    Quarter 2008, U.S. Bureau of Economic
    Analysis, March 2009, www.bea.gov.
3   F. Park, CFOs see sweeping business cuts
    to continue into 2009, *PR Newswire*,
    December 19, 2008, www.prnewswire.com.
4   Committee Encouraging Corporate
    Philanthropy, Corporate Philanthropy 2008:
    Data Trends and the Changing Economy.
    June 2, 2009, www.corporatephilanthropy.org.
5   The Conference Board, The 2008 Corporate
    Contributions Report, December 2008,
    www.conference-board.org.
6   Same as Note 5, Chart 2, page 14.
7   S. Lawrence and R. Mukai, *Foundation
    Giving Trends*, 2009, the Foundation Center,
    www.foundationcenter.org.
8   Not all gloom and doom for corporate
    charitable giving in 2009, LBG Research
    Institute, Press release, January 6, 2009,
    www.lbgresearch.org.
9   Minnesota Council on Foundations,
    2009 Outlook Report, January 1, 2009,
    www.mcf.org.
10 N. Barton, and C. Preston, A gloomy giving
    outlook, *The Chronicle of Philanthropy*,
    August 21, 2008, www.philanthropy.com.
11 Cone, LLC, Past. Present. Future. The 25th
    anniversary of cause branding, October 1,
    2008, www.coneinc.com.
12 Edelman, Despite economic crisis,
    consumers value brands' commitment to
    social purpose, November 17, 2008, www.
    goodpurposecommunity.com.
13 Cause Survey 2008: A good time to give, *PR
    Week*, October 27, 2008, www.prweek.com.
14 S. Banjo, Next benefit to face the ax: matching
    gifts, *PR Week, The Wall Street Journal*,
    January 14, 2009, www.online.wsj.com.
15 Business Civic Leadership Center, 2008
    Corporate Community Investment Study,
    December 2008. Researched and written
    by the Center on Philanthropy at Indiana
    University.
16 W. Erisman and S. M. Looney, Corporate
    investments in college readiness and
    access, June 2008, http://www.bhef.com/
    publications/BHEF_IHEP_June08.pdf.
17 C. Preston, Making a Big Difference: Small
    businesses want to offer cash and services
    to charities, *The Chronicle of Philanthropy*,
    October 16, 2008, www.philanthropy.com.
18 Same as Note 5.
19 A. Muller and G. Whiteman, Exploring
    the Geography of corporate philanthropic
    disaster response: A study of Fortune
    Global 500 firms, Journal of Business
    Ethics, 2009.
20 W. Crampton and D. Patten, Social responsive-
    ness, profitability and catastrophic events:
    evidence on the corporate philanthropic
    response to 9/11, *Journal of Business
    Ethics*, 2008.
21 Same as Note 5.

7 Giving to religion

- Giving to religion reached an estimated $106.89 billion in 2008, which was an increase of 5.5 percent (1.6 percent adjusted for inflation) from the estimate for 2007 of $101.32 billion.

- Giving to religion is 35 percent of estimated total giving.

- Charitable contributions for religious organizations generally include donations to houses of worship; to the governing bodies of faith groups; and to ministries, which include broadcast and print initiatives. It does not include "faith-based" charities, such as Jewish federations or agencies offering health care, education, and care for the young or the elderly. It also does not include special offerings or in-kind gifts that religious organizations collect and send to other charities without registering them in their own financial records (e.g. hurricane relief and church-building in other nations).

Giving USA findings about giving to religion, 2008

The 2008 *Giving USA* estimate of giving to religion[1] includes:

- Contributions to religious congregations, including congregations of people of all faiths and denominations.

- Giving to other entities for organized religious practice, including:
  - National or regional offices of faith groups;
  - Missionary societies;
  - Religious media (including print and broadcast); and
  - Other organizations formed for religious fellowship, worship, or evangelism (Youth for Christ, Campus Crusade for Christ, and others).

The estimate does not, however, include contributions made to separately incorporated faith-based organizations (FBOs) that provide education, healthcare, international relief, or other services. Thus, giving to St. Elizabeth's Hospital, the Reform Jewish Academy, or Lutheran Social Services and similar organizations appears in health, education, and human services, respectively.

Trends in giving to religion, 1968–2008

In prior recession years, giving to religious organizations averaged an inflation-adjusted drop of -0.1 percent from prior year percentages, ranging from a decrease of 3.6 percent (1991) to an increase of 5.5 percent (1982). Giving to this subsector increased (adjusted for inflation) in five of the eleven recession years between 1968 and 2006.[2]

Using a standardized measure of giving to religion allows us to compare contributions to this subsector over time. One standard measure is to estimate giving per household. To do this, the sum of contributions from all sources (not just households) is divided by the number of households in the country. Table 1 shows the results for giving to the religious sector per household

Contributions to religion are just over one-third of giving by all sources (individuals, estates, foundations, and corporations). Giving to religious organizations predominantly derives from individuals.

To calculate the share of secular charitable giving that comes from individuals, take $106.89 billion (estimated religious giving) away from the individual giving estimate (as an approximation) in 2008. The result is $122.39 billion, which represents individual giving for nonreligious (secular) causes. That, added to giving from other types of donors (foundations, corporations, and in charitable bequests), results in a total of $200.76 billion (estimated) given to secular causes in 2008. As in religious giving, individuals contribute the majority, 61 percent, to secular causes.

Table 1
Per household measure of giving to the religious subsector
Includes contributions from all sources divided by number of households

Year	Per household	# of households
1988	$902	91.12 million
1998	$879	102.53 million
2008	$915	116.78 million

Data: Giving to religious organizations from *Giving USA* estimate divided by the number of households in that year from the U.S. Bureau of the Census' Current Population Survey.

since 1988. This year is the most recent year for which data are available based on IRS Forms 990, which are used as the basis of estimation of giving to charitable subsectors.

Philanthropic Giving Index "present situation" for giving to the religious subsector drops to 64.4 in 2008 from 88.1 in 2007

In December 2008, the Philanthropic Giving Index (PGI), which measures the fundraising confidence of nonprofit fundraisers and is conducted semi-annually by the Center on Philanthropy, reported a "present situation" index of 64.4 (on a scale of 100) for respondents working in religious organizations.[3] This was the lowest "present situation" PGI for the religious

subsector since December 2003 (57.2). The late 2008 PGI reported that:

- Most fundraisers (83.3 percent) from religious organizations realized success with planned giving.

- Fundraisers from religious organizations were significantly more likely, at 77.8 percent, to report success with direct mail campaigns than were fundraisers from other types of charities. Significantly fewer fundraisers from religious organizations reported success with special events (47.1 percent) when compared with fundraisers in other types of charities.

Table 2 shows the reported success by type of fundraising reported by religious organization respondents in 2007 and 2008.

An aunt comforts her nephew.
Organization represented: Children's Institute, Inc., Los Angeles (www.childrensinstitute.org)
Photographer: Jeffrey Catania, Los Angeles

Table 2
Percentage of religious organization respondents reporting success
with fundraising vehicle, 2007–2008

	Direct mail	Telephone	Special events	Planned giving	Major gifts	Corporate	Foundation	Email	Internet
2007	61.1	33.3	55.6	77.8	77.8	22.2	72.2	27.8	33.3
2008	77.8	22.2	47.1	83.3	61.1	23.5	44.4	33.3	38.9

GuideStar poll results, giving to religion in 2008

Each year since 2002, GuideStar.org has posted a late-year poll asking readers of its e-newsletter to report changes in giving to their organizations compared to the prior year.[4] We present a summary of these findings here. Note that these findings are not nationally representative, nor are they drawn from a random sample. In 2008's poll, there were 177 respondents from religious organizations. Compared with 2007, out of this sub-group:

- 38 percent reported growth in contributions received, in contrast with the 57 percent that reported growth from 2006 to 2007;

- 20 percent reported that contributions to their organizations stayed about the same, which is roughly the same as the prior year; and

- 41 percent of respondents said that giving fell. This is far higher than the 17 percent reporting a drop in contributions in 2007, compared with 2006.

Among the GuideStar poll participants, those from religious organizations reported the highest percentage (41 percent) of decreases in contributions received in 2008 compared to 2007. It was also the only type of organization where the percentage of participants reporting a decrease was higher than the percentage reporting an increase.

Multimillion-dollar gifts to religious organizations

Despite a sluggish economy and the poll results from GuideStar, religious organizations continued to receive gifts of $1 million or more. The following list is only a sampling of gifts, which were published in either print or electronic media during 2008. Note that many religious organizations and their donors do not publicize major gifts, thus the total number of seven-figure and higher gifts to this subsector is unknown:

- Wycliffe Bible Translators received an anonymous gift of $50 million.[5]

- The Roman Catholic Diocese of Syracuse received $30 million from the $250 million estate of Robert L. and Catherine H. McDevitt.[6] The couple also left $50 million to Le Moyne College, a Jesuit college in Syracuse.[7]

- St. Brigid's Roman Catholic Church, New York City, received a $20 million anonymous gift. The gift will be used to restore the historic church, which was forced to close in 2001, and to provide funding for local Catholic parochial schools.[8]

- Temple Emanu-El, Palm Beach, Florida, received $5 million from Mel and Claire Levine to build an endowment for the 45-year-old congregation.[9]

- John Ferguson, a farmer from western Pennsylvania, left his local church, Hopewell United Methodist Church, a $2 million gift upon his death in early 2007. The church was informed of the gift in late 2008 after probate ended.[10]

Death of John Templeton could lift foundation assets

The founder of the John Templeton Foundation, Sir John M. Templeton, died in July 2008. As of mid-2009, it was still uncertain how much additional money Templeton bequeathed to his foundation, which is based in Pennsylvania. Dr. John M. Templeton Jr., head of the foundation, stated that he believed the foundation's assets could increase by 50 percent by the end of 2009.[11] The John Templeton Foundation funds research grants in academic areas like theology, philosophy, and science and, in 2008, issued over $70 million in grants. It is one of only a handful of major founda-

tions that provides grant funding for religious research.

Reform movement in Judaism launches new organizational structure

The Union for Reform Judaism (URJ), which represents more than 900 synagogues, announced organizational changes in early 2009, which resulted, in part, from the economic crisis' impact on funding.[12] These changes could have implications for fundraising success in 2009. The URJ restructured to form four Congregational Support Centers, replacing 14 regional offices. In addition, the Union reduced staff positions by 20 percent, including positions in the New York City offices of the movement's central administration.

Faith-based giving among Jewish youth assessed

Susan Schwartzman, who provided staff support for a youth philanthropy initiative at the Peninsula Jewish Community Teen Foundation, reported that the project's success can be traced to program strategies that give participating teens ownership of ideas and the capacity to use philanthropy in order to affect community problems.[13]

GOOD TO KNOW

Engaging younger generations in faith communities and in giving to religious organizations is a concern for many religious organizations in the United States. At least one group, the Peninsula Jewish Teen Community Foundation, has "reversed" the usual progression. Rather than starting with a faith group and teaching about giving, the program first offers teens the means to improve their community according to their desires. Scriptural and cultural teachings are incorporated into their program to guide the teen participants as they raise and allocate funds. This successful model could be adopted by ecumenical councils, specific faith communities, or other programs.

The foundation's teen program, which is not based in a synagogue but in a community foundation, combined religious teachings about philanthropy with a formal process and structure through which participants could give. The organizational component included a teen-led board, incentive funds to match what the teens gave or raised, and training opportunities with access to community leaders. Annually, the participating teens identify a community issue to work on, review proposals from organizations seeking funds, and then allocate the dollars raised, donated, and matched to the chosen organization(s).

Studies of donors to religion

Research findings in 2008 about donors and donations to religion include a number of studies summarized below. Each was conducted by scholars affiliated with a university or research institute.

New book questions extent and nature of Christian generosity

Passing the Plate: Why American Christians Don't Give Away More Money, released in September 2008, provides a sociological investigation into why a vast majority of Christians do not give more than a small percentage of their financial resources to charity and religious institutions each year.[14] Sociologists Christian Smith (Notre Dame), Michael O. Emerson (Rice University), and Patricia Schnell (Notre Dame) contend that Christians are not as financially generous as they could be.

Various sources of data analyzed show that, in the United States on average,

Christians give from 1 percent to 3 percent of their annual income. Over 20 percent of Christians give nothing at all to charity or religious institutions. Drs. Emerson, Schnell, and Smith posit nine hypotheses about why Christians do not give more of their money to churches and charity. These hypotheses range from a lack of discretionary financial resources to sporadic giving practices that hinder attempts at disciplined giving. An appendix is included with summaries of the different Christian denominational positions on tithing.

High-net-worth donors give average of $17,044 to religion in 2007

According to the 2008 *Bank of America Study of High Net-Worth Philanthropy*, which was researched and written at the Center on Philanthropy at Indiana University, 67.7 percent of high-net-worth households (with an income of more than $200,000 or a net worth of more than $1 million) made a donation to religious organizations in 2007.[15] The most recent prior study about high-net-worth philanthropy, in 2005, showed that 71.6 percent of high-net-worth households gave to religion. Religious organizations received the third largest share (14.6%) of all high-net-worth giving in 2007. The average gift size in 2007 was $17,044, third largest after giving to foundations and the education sector. Compared to 2005, however, the average amount given decreased by 14.8 percent in 2007. The median gift was unchanged at $4,000 in 2005 and in 2007.

The study also differentiated between giving through personal assets and

GOOD TO KNOW

Researchers are looking beyond income and other demographic traits to try to identify correlates of giving to religion, including levels of social trust, length of time in the community, and the level of engagement in social networks. Some of these findings make their way into articles with recommendations about whom to engage in a fundraising or volunteer-raising effort.

Congregations and religious leaders, however, will benefit from understanding that research studies showing a connection between charitable activity and other factors does not mean that these factors cause an increase (or decrease) in charitable behavior.

giving through foundations, funds, and trusts. In that division:

- 66.6 percent of high-net-worth households gave to religious organizations through their personal assets in 2007. The average amount donated through personal assets was $12,085, and the median gift was $3,500.

- 14.5 percent gave to religious organizations via foundations, funds, or trusts. The average amount donated through these avenues was $36,541, and the median gift was $7,350.

In terms of reasons for making charitable gifts, 51 percent cited "religious beliefs" as a major motivation for making donations. This figure is somewhat lower than that reported in geographical studies on charitable giving. For example, in a Memphis study, 71 percent of respondents reported that religious beliefs were a major motivation for giving, and a Georgia study revealed that religious beliefs were a motivation for giving for 67 percent of respondents.[16]

Social ties linked with religious giving
Lili Wang (now at Arizona State University) and Elizabeth Graddy

(University of Southern California) analyzed giving to religious and secular charities using data from the Social Capital Community Benchmark Survey. This survey was fielded in 2000 under the leadership of Robert Putnam (author of *Bowling Alone* and other works). Drs. Wang and Graddy found that higher religious giving is associated with certain factors, such as:

- Length of time living in the community (10 years or more);

- High level of trust in others; and

- Greater number of opportunities for interaction with others, such as through social networks and forms of civic engagement.[17]

Additionally, the authors advanced the idea that a higher level of religious giving is associated with a higher level of personal happiness. The authors cautioned, however, that the direction of causality between religious giving and these factors could not be determined considering that data was collected only at one point in time. Thus, giving to religion may be a source of happiness, or happier people may give more to religion.

Study finds that 5 percent of Americans tithed in 2007

A January 2008 survey, conducted by the Barna Group, found that 5 percent of respondents reported they tithed 10 percent or more of their income in 2007.[18] This percentage is consistent with the last seven years of data from the Barna Group, which has regularly found that between 5 and 7 percent of the total United States population tithed at this rate. Of further note regarding religious organizations, the study also found:

- 64 percent of all respondents gave money to a place of worship;

- Evangelicals and religious conservatives were the most likely groups to tithe at least 10 percent of their income; and

- Those who identified themselves as Christians in the study gave an average of $1,426 to nonprofits in 2007; non-Christian individuals gave an average of $905; and those who identified themselves as either atheists or agnostics gave an average of $467 to nonprofits in 2007.

Note that the research sample of approximately 1,000 in the Barna Group study is nationally representative; however, some of the results differ from the larger 2004 Center on Philanthropy Panel Study (COPPS). The COPPS research, which is a nationally representative study of the giving behavior of more than 8,000 U.S. households, found that 46 percent of households (compared with 64 percent of individuals in the Barna study) reported contributions to religion. Moreover, the average

household contribution to religion in 2004 was $1,832, which was similar to the average household contribution of $2,088 in 2008, after adjusting for inflation. COPPS data revealed 3 percent of households tithed in 2004 (the most recent year for which data are available).[19]

Smaller estates more likely to give a larger share to religion

The Internal Revenue Service released a report based on estate tax returns filed for people who died in 2004.[20] That study found, among other things, that when looking at estates valued at $3.5 million or less, 18.5 percent of the amount deducted for charitable bequests benefited religious organizations.[21] Among estates valued at $5 million or more, 3.2 percent of dollars claimed in charitable bequest deductions were for religious organizations, while more than 70 percent went to foundations.

Studies of religious organizations and their interaction with communities

In addition to playing an important role in an individual's life, religious organizations serve many functions in the life of a community, either locally or broadly speaking. Because donors are often motivated to give in response to the mission of the religious organization in reaching beyond its own congregants, this section covers some of the studies that appeared in 2008 that examined how congregations and their members interact with the wider world.

The studies on religious organizations summarized below generally find that:

GOOD TO KNOW

Giving to religion is the most frequent, single type of donation in the United States, with at least 46 percent of households in 2004 reporting a donation to religion (2005 wave of the Center on Philanthropy Panel Study, with findings released in 2008) and as many as 64 percent of individuals donating to religion (Barna Group, 2008).

Despite the range of charitable giving to religious organizations by individuals and households reported in these studies, with a growing share of the U.S. population reporting that they are unaffiliated with a religion (especially adults under age 30)[22] and a low incidence of tithing, religious charities cannot be guaranteed the rates of growth in giving that they have historically realized (average annual rate of growth of 1.6 percent, adjusted for inflation, from 1991 to 2005, *Giving USA 2008*).

- Religious organizations are an important source of private funding to developing countries;

- Some churches generate high donations based on their "market orientation," but not necessarily higher membership;

- The number of congregations serving a community is not connected to the amount those congregations are able to raise; and

- Religious attendance and giving can be expected to fall when "blue laws" that prevent businesses from opening on Sundays are repealed.

U.S. religious organizations are a significant source of private funding to developing countries

A joint study between the Hudson Institute's Center for Global Prosperity and the University of Notre Dame's Center for the Study of Religion and Society found that religious organizations were responsible for $8.8 billion in aid to developing nations in 2006.[23] The amount is equivalent to 37 percent of the United States government's official aid to developing nations, which totaled $23.5 billion in 2006. Development aid from religious organizations constituted 25 percent of all private philanthropic development aid from the U.S. Around 57 percent of the surveyed congregations reported donating to U.S.-based foreign aid agencies, while 33 percent reported donating directly to programs within developing nations. The average transfer from the congregation to the aid agency was about $34,000.

High market-oriented churches receive more dollars from members but do not have a significant advantage in attracting new members

A study by Darin White and Clovis Smith (both from the McAfee School of Business Administration, Union University) found that churches that embraced a comparatively high level of market-oriented features (i.e., customer service, market mentality) were able to increase donation levels and recruit more volunteer help from members than churches that exhibited either low or medium market-orientation.[24] High

GOOD TO KNOW

There is evidence that the percentage of people of faith in the U.S. is declining. This, along with the fact that congregations compete with secular activities in the engagement of potential congregants, has caused a decline in worship service attendance, in general. To the extent that other types of charities, such as those working in international development or health care, seek support from religious congregations, these donations may diminish over time if recent trends continue.

market-oriented churches also saw stronger growth in attendance at Sunday services, Sunday school, and midweek services. However, despite statistically higher growth rates in attendance, fundraising, and volunteer recruitment, the study found that high market-oriented churches' membership growth rates did not differ from those at low and medium market-oriented churches.

No link found between religious choice and greater giving

A study conducted by Francesca Borgonovi of the London School of Economics found that areas in the United States where individuals had a greater choice of religious services (i.e., religious pluralism) saw no increase in regular worship service attendance and, therefore, no increase in giving when compared with regions with less religious pluralism.[25] The study hypothesized that, with a wider range of options, individuals would be more likely to find a worship home that fit their personal interests. However, worship attendance rates were similar in areas with and without religious pluralism. This suggests that creating a

new congregation does not attract new congregants but recruits them from existing houses of worship.

Repealing blue laws causes decrease in giving and attendance at houses of worship

Jonathan Gruber (Massachusetts Institute of Technology) and Daniel M. Hungerman (University of Notre Dame) conducted a study on the effect of blue laws on church attendance.[26] Blue laws are state laws that prohibit or limit specific types of commercial activity in order to enforce a time of religious observance. For example, certain types of alcohol sales are banned on Sundays across many states. This study found that when blue laws were repealed in various states, houses of worship saw a statistically significant decline in church attendance. This drop in attendance, consequently, affected the level of tithing to congregations. In some cases, there was a 13 percent drop in giving to religious organizations. The results of this study imply that worship service attendance, and therefore religious giving, face competition from secular alternatives.

1   The 2008 estimate is based on a three-year rolling average rate of change drawn from data provided by 29 Protestant denominations reporting contributions to the National Council of Churches' *Yearbook on American and Canadian Churches*. The estimate also includes financial information from additional large religious organizations, including Catholic parishes and some religious denominations whose contribution information is publicly available through the Evangelical Council for Financial Accountability.

2   Giving during recessions, *Giving USA Spotlight*, #3, 2008, available from www.givingusa.org.

3   Center on Philanthropy, *Philanthropic Giving Index*, December 2008, www.phlanthropy.iupui.edu.

4   No author, Fasten your seatbelts: It's going to be a bumpy giving season, GuideStar Newsletter, November 2008, www.guidestar.org.

5   No author, Wycliffe receives its single biggest donation ever, November 11, 2008, www.wycliffe.org.

6   Renee K. Gadoua, Syracuse Diocese receives $30 million gift from Binghamton couple's will, *The Post-Standard*, December 9, 2008, www.syracuse.com.

7   *The Chronicle on Philanthropy*, Slate 60: Donor Bios, *Slate*, January 23, 2009, www.slate.com.

8   Chan, S., Donor gives $20 million to revive historic church, *The New York Times*, May 22, 2008, www.nytimes.com.

9   M. Kaiser, Couple gives $5 million to Emanu-El, *Palm Beach Post*, March 11, 2008.

10 Frugal farmer leaves $2 million to church, *The Telegram*, December 18, 2008, www.pressdisplay.com.

11 B. Gose, Templeton Foundation's assets expected to grow by 50%, *The Chronicle on Philanthropy*, August 7, 2008, www.philanthropy.com.

12 Union for Reform Judaism plans reorganization to strengthen congregations and build the Reform Jewish future, Press release, Union for Reform Judaism, March 16, 2009, www.urj.org.

13 S. Schwartzman, Jewish youth philanthropy: Learning to give Jewishly, in E. Dorff and L. Newman (eds), *Jewish Choices, Jewish Voices, Money*, Philadelphia: Jewish Publication Society, 2008.

14 Michael Emerson et al., *Passing the Plate: Why American Christians Don't Give Away More Money*, 2008, www.oup.com/us/.

15 Center on Philanthropy at Indiana University, *Bank of America Study of High Net-Worth Philanthropy*, 2008, www.philanthropy.iupui.edu.

16 *Giving Memphis 2008; Giving Georgia 2008.* Both studies were conducted by the Center on Philanthropy at Indiana University.

17 L. Wang and E. Graddy, Social capital, volunteering, and charitable giving, *Voluntas*, volume 19, number 2, March, 2008.

18 The Barna Group, Press release, New study shows trends in tithing and donating, April 14, 2008, www.barna.org.

19 The Center on Philanthropy Panel Study (COPPS) has a 98 percent response rate, whereas a typical telephone or Internet survey has a response rate between 20 percent (telephone) and 75 percent (a very high rate for an online study). The analysis of COPPS data was performed by Ke Wu at the Center on Philanthropy at Indiana University.

20 B. Raub, *Federal Estate Tax Returns Filed for 2004 Decedents*, Statistics of Income Bulletin, Spring 2008, www.irs.gov.

21 Same as Note 20.

22 The Pew Forum on Religion & Public Life, *U.S. Religious Landscape Survey: Religious Affiliation: Diverse and Dynamic*, February 2008, www.pewforum.org.

23 Hudson Institute Center for Global Prosperity, *Index of Global Philanthropy 2008*, 2008, www.gpr.hudson.org.

24 D. White and C. Simas, An empirical investigation of the link between market orientation and church performance, *International Journal of Nonprofit and Voluntary Sector Marketing*, 2008.

25 F. Borgonovi, Divided we stand, united we fall: Religious pluralism, giving, and volunteering, *American Sociological Review*, 2008.

26 J. Gruber and D. Hungerman, The church versus the mall: What happens when religion faces increased secular competition, *The Quarterly Journal of Economics*, May 2008.

A project worker holds cups containing colored objects that children carefully examine.
Organization represented: Compassion International, Colorado Springs, CO (www.us.ci.org)
Photographer: Chuck Bigger, Colorado Springs, CO

8 Giving to education

- It is estimated that gifts to the educational sector totaled $40.94 billion in 2008.

- This estimate reflects a drop of 5.5 percent (-9 percent adjusted for inflation) since 2007.

- Giving to the education sector is 13 percent of total estimated giving.

- Education organizations include nonprofit or state-funded schools from preschool through grade 12; nonprofit or state-funded vocational or technical schools, colleges and universities; nonprofit and public libraries; tutoring programs; adult continuing education; and student services and organizations.

Giving USA findings for giving to education organizations, 2008

The estimate for the change in giving to organizations in the education subsector is based on the historical relationship between giving to education charities and other broader economic trends. Specifically, the estimate looks at changes in personal income; wealth, as measured by the Standard & Poor's 500 stock index; and giving in the recent past.

The Council for Aid to Education (CAE) reported growth in the 2007–2008 fiscal year of 6.2 percent in higher education giving (2.3 percent adjusted for inflation). Nearly one-half of that growth was attributed to just 20 very large institutions that each raised a total of $285 million or more. If those institutions were excluded from the analysis, CAE found a decline of 4.2 percent in giving to higher education from the 2006–2007 academic year to the 2007–2008 academic year.

The decline in giving to education institutions estimated by *Giving USA* reflects the economic changes in the

last half of 2008, including, in particular, stock market changes. In its March 2009 release, the Council for Aid to Education noted that giving to higher education closely follows changes in the stock market.

Trends in giving to education

Using *Giving USA* data, two different ways of measuring trends in giving to education are presented. The first looks at giving to education during recession years. The second shows the trend in giving to education over time, measured per household (including all education donations divided by all households).

In prior recession years from 1967 to 2006, giving to education organizations averaged an inflation-adjusted drop of 1.1 percent from the prior year. The range was from a decrease of nearly 14 percent (1975) to growth of 7 percent (2001). Giving to this subsector increased (adjusted for inflation) in five of eleven recession years from 1967 to 2006.[1]

Using a standardized measure of giving to education allows us to compare contributions to this subsector over

Table 1
Per household measure of giving to education
Includes contributions from all sources divided by number of households
(adjusted for inflation)

Year	Per household	# of households
1988	$202	91.12 million
1998	$307	102.53 million
2008	$351	116.78 million

Data: Giving to education from *Giving USA* estimate divided by the number of households in that year from the U.S. Bureau of the Census' Current Population Survey.

time. One standard measure is to estimate giving per household. To do this, the sum of contributions from all sources (not just households) is divided by the number of households in the country. Table 1 shows the results for giving to education organizations per household since 1988. IRS Forms 990 are the basis of estimation of giving to other subsectors.

Philanthropic Giving Index for giving to the education sector falls to 63.3 from 93.7 one year earlier

The Philanthropic Giving Index (PGI), which measures the fundraising confidence of nonprofit fundraisers and is conducted semi-annually by the Center on Philanthropy, reported a "present situation" index of 63.3 (on a scale of 100) for education organizations in December 2008.[2] This is the lowest level of fundraising confidence expressed by education fundraisers since the PGI began in 1998. Among concerns about fundraising tracked on the PGI:

- More than 40 percent of development officers working in educational organizations reported a decrease in the scheduled payment of pledges in 2008, which is significantly lower

than other types of organizations.

- One-third of education fundraisers reported a decrease in the payment of the full pledged amounts, the lowest of any type of organization.

- Educational fundraisers were more likely than fundraisers in other nonprofit subsectors to report that giving of assets (rather than cash) decreased in 2008 (70 percent reported a decrease).

In a bit of good news, fundraisers from educational organizations were more likely, at 63.3 percent, than those working in other types of nonprofits to report success in donors using the IRA charitable rollover provision in order to contribute to their institutions. Note that contributions through IRAs are not counted as charitable contributions eligible for itemized deductions under the Internal Revenue Code. They are, instead, a tax-free transfer from an individual's Individual Retirement Account (IRA) directly to a charitable organization.

Table 2 summarizes the percentage of PGI respondents working in educa

Table 2
Percentage of education respondents reporting success
with fundraising vehicle, 2007–2008

	Direct mail	Telephone	Special events	Planned giving	Major Gifts	Corporate	Foundation	Email	Internet
2007	64.5	58.1	53.4	77.4	93.8	46.9	71.9	36.7	46.2
2008	71.0	77.4	46.7	80.6	67.7	38.7	67.7	42.9	39.3

tional institutions who reported success with each of several fundraising vehicles or channels. The same people are surveyed in each wave. The table shows the year-end results for 2007 and 2008.

Fundraisers in education organizations reported higher levels of success in:

- 2008 for direct mail, telephone, planned giving, email, and

- 2007 for special events, major gifts, corporate support, foundation grants, and Internet fundraising.

GuideStar poll finds lower giving levels to the educational subsector in 2008

Each year since 2002, GuideStar.org has posted a late-year online poll asking users of its site to report changes in giving to their organizations compared to the prior year.[3] We present a summary of these findings here. Note that these findings are not nationally representative, nor are they drawn from a random sample. There were 897 respondents from education organizations in 2008, with results as follows:

- 38 percent reported an increase in contributions to their organizations, compared with 49 percent in 2007.

- 24 percent reported that contributions to their organizations stayed

about the same, compared with 25 percent in 2007.

- 36 percent reported a drop in charitable contributions received, compared with only 21 percent reporting decreased contributions in 2007.

Council for Aid to Education finds total giving to higher education rose 6.2 percent through June 2008

The Council for Aid to Education (CAE), using results from its online survey "Voluntary Support for Education" (VSE), reported that contributions to higher education institutions rose by 6.2 percent in the fiscal year that ended in June 2008.[4] CAE estimated a total $31.60 billion contributed to higher education in the United States from July 2007 through June 2008. The top 20 institutions, led by Stanford University, raised 26.6 percent of the total estimated giving to higher education in the United States. The increase in gifts received at these 20 institutions accounted for nearly one-half (46.9 percent) of the total estimated change in giving to higher education from 2006–2007 to 2007–2008.

Among the other 1,032 institutions responding to the VSE survey, about half reported an increase in contributions received and about half reported a decline to June 2008. In interviews, Ann E. Kaplan, director of the VSE, found that, "Even at institutions that reported healthy gains in fiscal 2008, advancement professionals told us they had 'hit a wall' in January 2009 and that the decline was substantial."[5]

The CAE study estimates the share of donations to all higher education organizations that originate with various types of donors. In 2007–2008, alumni giving remained below foundation giving. Many alumni make gifts through a family foundation, which are then tracked as foundation donations, not alumni gifts. Figure 1 illustrates the funding that, in billions of dollars, CAE estimates was given in 2007–2008 by each type of donor.

Foundation grants are a significant share of higher education giving. Education generally, and higher education in particular, receives a significant share

of foundation grantmaking. Education overall received 23 percent of grant dollars tracked by the Foundation Center in its report of grantmaking in 2007.[6]

Announced gifts to education in 2008

At least seven individuals (or estates) gave $100 million or more to higher education organizations in 2008 for purposes other than medical centers or medical research. The medical gifts are reported later in this chapter. These gifts, reported on the Million Dollar List maintained at the Center on Philanthropy at Indiana University, include:

■ David Booth, founder and chief executive of the investment firm Dimensional Fund Advisors, gave $300 million to the University of Chicago School of Business to hire and retain professors and to expand its publications.[7]

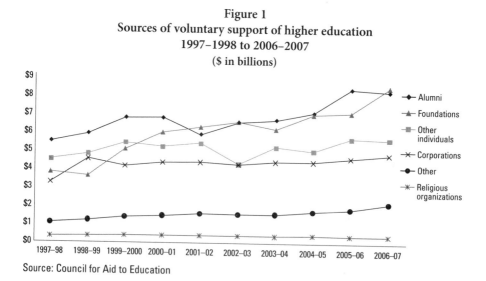

Figure 1
Sources of voluntary support of higher education
1997–1998 to 2006–2007
($ in billions)

Source: Council for Aid to Education

- Emily Rauh Pulitzer, widow of newspaper publisher Joseph Pulitzer, Jr., gave 31 works of art valued at $200 million and an additional $45 million to Harvard University's Art Museum.[8]
- A trust established by Frank Doble, an electrical engineer who founded his firm in 1920 and passed away in 1969, directed $136 million each to Lesley University and to Tufts University (1911 graduate), both in the Boston area.[9]
- Hansjörg Wyss, president of Synthes, a medical-implants and biomaterials company based in Pennsylvania, gave Harvard University $125 million to create the Hansjörg Wyss Institute for Biologically Inspired Engineering, the largest individual gift in the university's history.[10]
- Gerhard Andlinger donated $100 million to Princeton University to create the Gerhard R. Andlinger Center for Energy and the Environment within the School of Engineering and Applied Science in order to accelerate research on effective and sustainable solutions to problems of energy and the environment. In 1976, Mr. Andlinger established Andlinger & Company, Inc., a private investment and management firm.[11]
- David Rockefeller committed $100 million to Harvard University for programs focused on undergraduate education.[12]
- T. Boone Pickens, an oil and gas executive, announced a gift of $100 million for Oklahoma State University to endow faculty positions.[13]

Support for medical education and research

Gifts to universities are often directed to university hospitals or to medical research programs. At least five gifts of $100 million or more each were publicly announced for university-based medical centers in 2008. These are:

- The Eli and Edythe Broad Foundation gave $400 million to the Broad Institute of Harvard and MIT for biomedical research.[14]
- Kenneth Langone, a co-founder of Home Depot, and his wife Elaine, gave $100 million to New York Medical Center to start a campaign for a new medical center.[15] Their gift was followed by two more:
  - $150 million was given to New York University Langone Medical Center by Helen Kimmel, a trustee, to build a new patient pavilion.[16]
  - An anonymous gift of $110 million was given to New York University's Langone Medical Center to redesign Tisch Hospital.[17]
- Philip Knight, founder of Nike, and his wife Penny, gave $100 million to Oregon Health Sciences University Cancer Institute.[18]

Multimillion-dollar gifts announced for other education institutions

Gifts to higher education have long dominated the number and amount of gifts of $1 million or more, and these gifts vary by the type of educational institution.[19] In addition to gifts provided for medical education and research in 2008, gifts to other types of educational institutions also reached milestone levels. These include:

The William B. Hanrahan CCS Fellowship report for 2009 showed that among gifts of $1 million or more from 2000 through late 2007, 69 percent of the dollars (excluding gifts to foundations) went to higher education. This report also revealed that people who made their wealth through investments were among the most likely to support education, and people with inherited or family wealth were less likely than donors with wealth from other sources to give to education.[26]

- $100 million to New York Public Library from Steven Schwarzman, founder of the Blackstone Group, an investment firm, in a lead gift for the library's $1 billion capital campaign.[20]

- $70 million from Frank and Jane Batten, CEO of Landmark Communications in Norfolk, Virginia, to Culver Academies (Indiana) to fund an endowment and to provide a matching gift challenge.[21]

- $50 million from the Bernard Osher Foundation to fund an endowment to help low-income students attend community college in California.[22]

- $30 million from the Sunshine Lady Foundation, founded by Doris Buffett, to the Women's Independence Scholarship Program to continue to develop and enhance efforts to end domestic violence.[23]

- $25 million from Oscar Tang and his wife Argie Ligeros to Phillips Academy Andover to support several priorities, including need-blind admission for students across the economic spectrum and restoration and expansion of the Addison Gallery of American Art.[24]

Billion-dollar campaigns now common

The first billion-dollar fundraising campaign for higher education was announced in 1987 by Stanford University. In late 2006, Stanford announced a $4.3 billion campaign, again setting the fundraising pace for higher education.[25]

In the years since 1987, a number of campaigns of at least $1 billion have been undertaken. In 2008, at least nine were announced, which is particularly striking given the fact that the United States entered a recession in December 2007. Using information from the *Chronicle of Higher Education*, Table 3 shows the announced campaigns, and Table 4 shows the campaigns that were announced as closed in 2008 or early 2009.[27]

Donor reactions to economy leads to anticipated decline in growth to educational giving

Upon the release of the *Giving USA 2008* report showing that giving to education grew 3.4 percent in 2007, John Lippincott, president of the Council of Advancement and Support of Education, suggested that this increase in giving was likely due to the many colleges and universities running capital campaigns.[28] Lippincott anticipated slower growth for 2008 educational giving because, as of June 2008, development officers were reporting that the economic climate was causing

Table 3
Billion-dollar higher education campaigns announced in 2008

Institution	Announced	Planned to close	Goal ($)	Raised ($)	As of
Boston College	2008	2015	$1.5 B	$546.3M	12/31/2008
Carnegie Mellon University	2008	2013	$1B	$565.5M	12/31/2008
Emory University	2008	2012	$1.6B	$898.2M	1/31/2009
Rice University	2008	2012	$1B	$513.5M	12/31/2008
University of California at Berkeley	2008	2013	$3B	$1.42M	12/31/2008
University of Cincinnati	2008	2013	$1B	$474.5M	12/31/2008
University of Tennessee at Knoxville	2008	2011	$1B	$812.1M	12/31/2008
University of Texas at Austin	2008	2014	$3B	$753M	12/31/2008
University of Utah	2008	2013	$1.2B	$600.2M	12/31/2008

M = million; B = billion
Data: *The Chronicle of Higher Education*

Table 4
Billion-dollar higher education campaigns announced as closed in 2008 or early 2009

Institution	Announced	Planned to close	Goal ($)	Raised ($)	As of
Johns Hopkins University	2002	2008	$3.2B	$3.741B	12/31/2008
New York University	2004	2008	$2.5B	$3.075B	8/31/2008
North Carolina State University	2005	2008	$1B	$1.307B	5/31/2008
University of Chicago	2002	2008	$2B	$2.38B	6/30/2008
University of Michigan system	2004	2008	$2.5B	$3.2B	12/31/2008
University of Missouri at Columbia	2005	2008	$1B	$1.039B	1/31/2009
University of Washington	2004	2008	$2.5B	$2.684B	6/30/2008

M = million; B = billion
Data: *The Chronicle of Higher Education*

donors to be more cautious with their gifts. Higher educational institutions saw three principal types of donor reactions to the economic climate:

- Extending pledge payments;
- Delaying commitment until seeing how their financial situation has changed; and
- Scaling back gifts to comfortable amounts.

The 2008 Philanthropic Giving Index (PGI) found that over 40 percent of development officers working in educational organizations reported that scheduled pledge payments in 2008 were missed or renegotiated by donors. The finding is significantly different from other types of organizations, where lower percentages of development officers reported slowed pledge payments.[29]

CASE index finds giving flat in 2008 and predicts a decline in 2009

The Council for Advancement and Support of Education's biannual fundraising index found that giving to colleges and universities would likely be flat in 2008 with 0.3 percent growth for 2008. The January 2009 index forecasts that giving to education may decline by 1.7 percent in 2009.[30] Flat growth in 2008 shows the impact of the difficult economic situation, as well as the resiliency of philanthropy to higher education.

Gates Foundation redirects educational funding

The Bill & Melinda Gates Foundation announced a change in direction regarding its educational mission from concentrating on school structure to focusing on: quality instruction; teacher tenure and performance; curriculum relevance; and national standards for measuring progress.[31] In particular, two new areas of concentration will be improving teacher quality and community colleges. The foundation is increasing its educational investment to $3 billion over the next five years, with the goal of increasing the number of low-income students who complete a post-secondary degree program after high school.

Reports released about giving to education

Many organizations and scholars study giving to higher education. This section summarizes some of the reports and articles appearing in 2008.

GOOD TO KNOW

Continuing expansion of philanthropic opportunities, growing competition for philanthropic resources, and variable factors, such as the economic situation, mean that educational fundraisers must become more sophisticated in understanding the complex interests of their potential supporters.

Fundraisers for educational organizations need to communicate with donors and educate them about the importance of support for education in the face of rising tuition and other factors that might tend to undermine such support.

*Educational attainment is a predictor
of giving to educational organizations*
Russell N. James III, University of
Georgia, examined various donor
characteristics and found, overall,
educational donors "had significantly
greater income, wealth, and education
than other donors."[32] Although individuals with higher levels of educational
attainment support a broad range of
charities, James found that educational
attainment is a strong predictor of
giving to educational organizations.
The tendency to give to educational
institutions greatly increased at each
successive educational level. Individuals
holding graduate degrees were found
to be the most likely to support educational institutions, at 22 percent, and
individuals with a high school diploma
among the least likely (at less than 1
percent). James' work illustrates that
educational donors are most likely
individuals who have benefited from
higher education and that development professionals, particularly at educational institutions, can use education
as a distinctive characteristic when
evaluating prospective donors.[33]

*Predicting alumni giving in higher
education*
Justin Weerts, University of Minnesota-
Twin Cities, and Justin Ronca, University of Wisconsin-Madison, employed
classification and regression tree
methodology to study alumni giving
at a public research university.[34] The
authors found that alumni giving
levels are related to: household
income; religious preference; level of
education and type of degree; nature
of continued engagement with the

institution; and beliefs regarding what
the institution needs, as well as the
competition of other institutions in
acquiring donations from an alumni.

*Nontraditional alumni are less likely
to support on-campus initiatives and
annual funds*
Few differences were found between
traditional and nontraditional alumni
giving preferences in Frederick Hurst's
dissertation, in which he studied
Northern Arizona University alumni
giving.[35] Nontraditional alumni were
significantly less likely to support gifts
that benefit the campus, such as scholarships for traditional students, new
faculty, on-campus research, campus
building renovations, and unrestricted
annual giving. However, the study
found nontraditional alumni[36] were
equally as likely as traditional alumni
to support academic programs of
interest, collegiate athletics, and the
alumni association. Hurst found nontraditional alumni prefer giving to:

- Scholarships for nontraditional
  students and students in their
  geographical region;
- Construction to make education
  more accessible in their town; and
- Faculty support and research in
  their town.

*Private donations positively affect
alumni giving*
University of Pennsylvania doctoral student Michael A. Gottfried employed an
economic approach to study crowding-
in theories in higher education philanthropy.[37] Crowding-in is the term used
to describe what non-economists might

call the "bandwagon" effect: People who might not otherwise give to an institution are motivated to make a gift when they see that others are giving.

Gottfried's economic model found that private donations from secondary constituencies, such as parents, corporations, and foundations, create a statistically significant crowd-in effect for alumni charitable behavior when using samples of private colleges, public universities, and all higher educational institutions in aggregate. Gottfried suggested:

- Alumni of public institutions may be more heavily influenced by private gifts because increased donations from non-alumni may be a signal of the quality of the institution.

- Private institution alumni may not be as easily influenced by private gifts because they tend to be more affluent and have a stronger tradition of giving.

HBCUs urged to cultivate a philanthropic culture among alumni

Rodney Cohen of the Presbyterian College in South Carolina examined the role that alumni of Historically Black Colleges and Universities (HBCUs) have played in donating to their alma mater.[38] HBCUs, institutions that are often financially challenged, have traditionally relied upon alumni for funding support. Despite this reliance on alumni, Cohen identified 30-year giving trends of HBCU alumni that negatively affect HBCU fundraising efforts. One trend includes a decline in both alumni giving and in membership in HBCU alumni associations. The results of this study point to the importance for HBCUs to engage their alumni in the philanthropic process. Cohen suggested that HBCU fundraisers should place more emphasis on fostering an understanding in alumni donors of the personal and practical benefits of giving.

Educational giving ranks low among charitable preferences for Hispanics

University of New Hampshire professors, Jerry Marx and Vernon Brooks Carter conducted a study on Hispanic charitable giving, which included giving to the education subsector. These researchers advise that development professionals should be aware of the increasing gift opportunities among the growing Hispanic population, and they stress that fundraisers should cultivate an understanding of the unique giving preferences of Hispanic donors.[39] According to their research, which used data from the "Giving and Volunteering in the U.S. 2001"

GOOD TO KNOW

Publicizing the giving of non-alumni donors, such as parents, community members, corporations, or foundations, can be a signal that encourages more giving among alumni of public institutions of higher education, in particular. This crowding-in effect of giving to private institutions of higher education may be lower than that for public institutions.

As the general population, along with the population of students and alumni, continues to become more diverse, fundraisers must become much more sensitive to the myriad cultural values and philanthropic traditions/ways of giving of potential donors. By understanding these factors, educational fundraisers may begin to provide appropriate ways for people to become more fully and intimately involved with and supportive of those educational institutions and programs that are important to them.

survey conducted by Westat for the INDEPENDENT SECTOR:

- Giving to educational institutions ranked fifth among all respondents' charitable preferences;

- Hispanics reported higher giving amounts to educational organizations than to other organizations;[40]

- Hispanics are twice as likely to make a gift to educational organizations if solicited by phone than those not solicited by phone; and

- Volunteerism is a predictor of Hispanic charitable giving.

Colleges challenged to adjust fundraising strategies to counter new trends affecting alumni giving

The rising costs of tuition; globalization of the student population; the fact that women are outpacing men in bachelor degree completion; more students are attending community colleges; more competition for student loyalty from graduate schools; and rising student debt are all reasons that college alumni offices need to adjust fundraising strategies to remain relevant.[41] Consulting firm Changing Our World identified these trends and issued a report calling for college development offices to get to know students before they graduate and to increase partnership with student

affairs. Additionally, successful alumni fundraising requires that development offices recognize the growing diversity among alumni populations. Along these lines, the study encourages development offices to:

- Be aware of cultural characteristics in the U.S. student and alumni populations;

- Use appropriate language;

- Increase presence abroad to expand alumni networks; and

- Understand how charitable giving and philanthropy are viewed and approached in different world cultures.

Donors called to solve the human capital challenges in K-12 educational institutions

In "Achieving Teacher and Principal Excellence: A Guidebook for Donors," Education Sector co-founder Andrew Rotherham found that the majority of philanthropic gifts to K-12 educational institutions supported "low-leverage activities" in the current educational system.[42] Low-leverage activities, according to education analyst Jay P. Greene, are those that support and maintain existing teacher recognition programs, policies, and educational programs.[43] In contrast, the author identified human capital challenges, particularly with a focus on performance, as the leading concern in K-12 school reform. In his guidebook for donors, Rotherham claims that effective philanthropy is performance focused and invests in new initiatives. Hence, he recommends five priorities that philanthropists should use in improving the level of quality of educators. Additionally, he summarizes the advice of educational donors to assist novice philanthropists in effectively investing in educational organizations. These suggestions are:

- Be clear about the objectives that the gift is desired to accomplish;

- Think strategically to leverage the gift;

- Understand the people involved in the project, as well as their capabilities;

- Consider requiring matching contributions from the organization, as well as federal matching opportunities;

- Plan ahead for future funding of new initiatives;

- Pair-up with other donors to learn from their experiences and to leverage resources, and encourage collaboration among researchers and educational institutions;

- Communicate with the grantee organization to follow up on the progress and impact of the gift; and

- Do not feel pressure to fund every initiative. Rather, stay committed to effective grantmaking and decline requests that do not fit with the original vision.

Multiple-phases and attention to goals significantly influence campaign giving behaviors

Wesley Lindahl, North Park University, examined donor giving behavior in a traditional two-phase, higher-education campaign and found a positive relationship between capital campaign progression and a typical donor's willingness to make a pledge to the campaign.[44] Lindahl's findings challenge the traditional notion of when a campaign should be publicly announced—when 40-60 percent of the goal has been reached. Lindahl found that 1) donors are much more likely to give when a higher percentage of the goal has been reached, and 2) donors are significantly less likely to make a gift once the campaign goal is achieved. This study suggests:

- It may be of strategic benefit for an education organization to manage capital campaigns in three phases: quiet, growth, goal line;

- A final public initiative should be implemented during the goal line phase to increase the number of donors; and

- Development offices should manage goals carefully by knowing when donors are more or less likely to give to a specific campaign contingent on the percentage of donations received.

With increasing pressure by nonprofit boards and institutional leadership on development offices to announce campaigns prior to reaching 40 percent of the goal and with the expectation such publicity will create a wave of gifts, this study suggests it is wise to delay the announcement until a greater percentage of leadership giving is secured.

Bank of America Study of High Net-Worth Philanthropy findings about giving to education

According to the 2008 *Bank of America Study of High Net-Worth Philanthropy*, which was researched and written at the Center on Philanthropy at Indiana University, 77.8 percent of high-net-worth households (with an income of more than $200,000 or a net-worth of more than $1 million) made a donation to education organizations in 2007.[45] The figure for 2005 was slightly higher at 79.4 percent. The median gift size to educational organizations in 2007 was $2,000, and the average gift size was $27,379, which is a 2.5 percent decrease compared to the prior Bank of America study about giving in 2005 (adjusted for inflation). Compared to other types of organizations, education received the second-highest average gift in 2007, after foundations. Moreover, education organizations received, compared to the other nonprofit sectors, the largest share of giving (27.1 percent) by high-net-worth households.

The study also asked about giving through personal assets and foundations, funds, and trusts. Comparing the two sources of funds:

■ 27.3 percent of high-net-worth households gave an average gift of $20,022 (median = $1,600) to education organizations through their personal assets in 2007.

■ 21.5 percent gave by utilizing foundations, funds, or trusts, and the average gift amount was $45,057 (median = $7,000).

Key findings from annual studies about giving to education

Several organizations issue annual reports about giving to education. Three years of data from various regular reports are summarized in Table 5.

Table 5
Key findings from other studies about giving to educational organizations

$10 Million Dollar List, gifts from individuals to education Center on Philanthropy at Indiana University, www.philanthropy.iupui.edu (percentages exclude gifts to foundations)			
	2006	2007	2008
Number, higher education	202	238	333
Largest gift, higher education	$105 million to Stanford University from Phillip H. Knight, for the business school	$400 million commitment from John Kluge from his eventual estate, to Columbia University for scholarships	$300 million to University of Chicago from David Booth
Dollars to higher education as percentage of all gifts on list	56.2 percent	21.1 percent	31.8 percent
Number, K–12 education	16	20	2
Largest gift, K–12 education	$25 million to the Peddie School from the estate of Randall Terry	$128.5 million to George School in Pennsylvania to support financial aid, staff compensation and environmental sustainability over 20 years	$70 million to Culver Academies from Frank Batten, Sr. and his wife Jane: $20 million to endowment; $50 million in matching funds for campaign
Education gifts as a percentage of all individual gifts of $10 million or more.	3.9 percent	2.0 percent	0.8 percent

Foundation Giving Trends: Update on Funding Priorities Grants to education Foundation Center, www.foundationcenter.org			
	2005	2006	2007
Average grant amount	$150,748	$150,979	$164,271
Median grant amount	$30,000	$30,000	$30,000
Education funding as a percentage of grant dollars	24.0 percent	22.5 percent	22.8 percent

CASE Report of Educational Fundraising Campaigns
Council for Advancement and Support of Education, www.case.org
(percentages are as of the reporting date for that year)

From all reporting institutions	2005–2006 (reported as mean)	2006–2007 (reported as median)	2007–2008 (percent of goal raised to date)
Percentage of goal received from top 10 percent of donors	80	91	92
Percentage of goal received from top 1 percent of donors	59	73	76
Mean percentage of alumni who gave to campaign	25	19.5 (25% mean)	18 (23% mean)

National Independent School Facts at a Glance
National Association of Independent Schools
Taken from reports dated 2005–2006; 2006–2007; and 2007–2008, www.nais.org

	2005–2006	2006–2007	2006–2007
Average annual giving per student	$1,572	$1,806	$1,698
Average endowment per student	$33,639	$35,494	$42,161
Giving by alumni Average gift Participation	$357 16.3%	$472 17.7%	$381 15.6%
Giving by current parents Average gift Participation	$1,039 63.1%	$1,118 63.3%	$1,199 61.8%
Giving by trustees Average gift Participation	$5,147 93.1%	$5,425 93.8%	$6,875 93.7%

IRS tax-exempt organizations in education
Charities and Other Tax-exempt Organizations, 2003, 2004, and 2005
Statistics of Income Bulletin, www.irs.gov

	2003	2004	2005
Number of organizations	47,117	48,920	52,530
Charitable revenue*	$59.86 billion	$64.47 billion	$69.93 billion

*Includes direct public support (from individuals, foundations, and corporations, as in *Giving USA*) and indirect public support (transfers from other nonprofits, such as the United Way, a membership association, or other collective funding source).

Voluntary Support of Education Council for Aid to Education** www.cae.org			
	2005–2006	2006–2007	2007–2008
Giving by alumni Average gift Participation	$1,195 11.9%	$1,166 11.7%	$1,259 11%

**CAE does not measure trustee giving or parent giving in ways that are comparable to the NAIS research.

Giving by individuals, estimated total for all institutions ($ billion)	$12.00	$12.14	$14.82
Charitable bequests, reporting institutions, ($ billion)	$2.10	$2.47	$2.65
Deferred gifts, reporting institutions, present value, ($ billion)	$0.58	$0.61	$0.75

1   Giving during recessions, *Giving USA Spotlight*, #3, 2008, available from www.givingusa.org.

2   Center on Philanthropy at Indiana University, Philanthropic Giving Index, December 2008, www.philanthropy.iupui.edu.

3   Seventh Annual GuideStar Nonprofit Survey: Charitable Organizations and the Economy, Oct. 6-20, 2008, Released in the fall, 2008, www.guidestar.org.

4   Council for Aid to Education, Press release, February 25, 2008, www.cae.org.

5   Council for Aid to Education, Press release, February 25, 2008, p. 4.

6   S. Lawrence et al., *Foundation Giving Trends: Update on Funding Priorities*, released February 2008, www.foundationcenter.org.

7   R. Guth, Chicago Business School Gets Huge Gift, *The Wall Street Journal*, November 7, 2008, www.wsj.com.

8   C. Vogel, Harvard Art Museum Receives Pulitzer Prize, *The New York Times*, Oct. 17, 2008, www.nyt.com.

9   Lesley University, Press release, April 8, 2008, www.lesley.edu, and Tufts University, Feature story, April 9, 2008, www.tufts.edu.

10 Hansjorg Wyss gives $125 million to create institute for biologically inspired engineering, Harvard University Science Department,

Oct. 6, 2008, www.harvard.edu.

11 S. Schultz, International business leader Gerhard R. Andlinger makes $100 million gift to transform energy and environment research at Princeton, Princeton University, July 1, 2008, www.princeton.edu.

12 David Rockefeller gives $100 million to Harvard undergraduate programs, *Harvard University Gazette Online*, April 25, 2008, www.harvard.edu.

13 Largest academic donation in Oklahoma history: Gift will more than double OSU endowed faculty chairs, Oklahoma State University, May 21, 2008, www.osu.okstate.edu.

14 H. Bridger, Eli and Edythe L. Broad announce $400 million endowment for the Broad Institute of Harvard and MIT, Broad Institute, Sept. 4, 2008, www.broad.mit.edu.

15 NYU Medical Center Changes Name to Honor Chairman of Board and Wife, New York University, Press release, April 16, 2008, www.nyu.edu.

16 NYU Langone Medical Center Announces Two Gifts Totaling $260 Million to Support Major Expansion of Campus in Multi-Year Transformation, New York University, Press release, Nov. 12, 2008, www.nyu.edu.

17 Same as note 16.

18 Knights to give $100 million to OHSU Cancer Institute, Oregon Health & Science University, Press release, Oct. 29, 2008, www.ohsu.edu.

19 Center on Philanthropy, *An analysis of Million Dollar Gifts: January 2000 – September 2007*, a report funded through the William B. Hanrahan CCS Fellowship, www.ccsfundraising.com.

20 New York Public Library Unveils $1 Billion Transformation Plan, New York Public Library, Press release, March 11, 2008, www.nypl.org.

21 Culver Academies Receives Commitment up to $70 million for Endowments, *Philanthropy News Digest,* The Foundation Center, Dec. 11, 2008, www.foundationcenter.org.

22 $70 million gift to help California students, *Community College Times,* May 19, 2008, www.communitycollegetimes.com.

23 A. Umble, Doris Buffett awards $30 million for scholarships for Domestic Abuse Survivors, *Philanthropy News Digest,* Sept. 30, 2008, www.foundationcenter.org.

24 Phillips Academy Receives Record $25 Million Gift, Phillips Academy, Press release, Feb. 6, 2008, www.andover.edu.

25 H. Hall, Raising Big Sums, *the Chronicle of Philanthropy,* March 22, 2007, www.philanthropy.com.

26 Same as note 19.

27 Data derived from various articles in the *Chronicle of Higher Education,* available online at www.chronicle.com.

28 H. Hall and C. Moore, How Different Types of Charities Fared Last Year, *The Chronicle of Philanthropy,* June 26, 2008, www.philanthropy.com.

29 Center on Philanthropy at Indiana University, Philanthropic Giving Index, December 2008, www.philanthropy.iupui.edu.

30 P. Russell, Fundraisers Forecast Slight Decline in Giving to Education in 2009, Council for Advancement and Support of Education, January 16, 2009, www.case.org.

31 C. Wallis, Bill & Melinda Gates Go Back to School, *Fortune,* December 8, 2008.

32 R. James III, Distinctive Characteristics of Educational Donors, *International Journal of Educational Advancement,* March 2008.

33 R. James III used data from the Consumer Expenditure Survey that is produced by

the U.S. Bureau of Labor Statistics to investigate donor characteristics of 56,663 U.S. households.

34 D. Weerts and J. Ronca, Using classification trees to predict alumni giving for higher education, *Education Economics,* Volume 16, Issue 1, March 22, 2009.

35 F.M. Hurst, Philanthropic giving preference differences: Nontraditional and traditional alumni at Northern Arizona University, Union Institute and University, 2008.

36 In higher education terminology, a "nontraditional student" is one who is not proceeding to a two-year or four-year college degree program directly from high school. It can include students who attend right after high school, but who are taking courses on a part-time basis while they work or undertake other responsibilities.

37 M. Gottfried, College Crowd-in: How Private Donations Positively Affect Alumni Giving, *International Journal of Educational Advancement,* June 2008.

38 R. Cohen, Alumni to the Rescue: Black College Alumni and Their Historical Impact on Alma Mater, *International Journal of Educational Advancement,* March 2008.

39 J. Marx and V. Brooks Carter, Hispanic Charitable Giving: An Opportunity for Nonprofit Development, *Nonprofit Management and Leadership,* Winter 2008.

40 Authors excluded data regarding amounts given to religious organizations; likewise, they did not include average gifts due to outliers that influenced the data.

41 K. Moser, Report Calls on Colleges to Update Strategies for a New Era of Fundraising, *The Chronicle of Higher Education,* May 23, 2008, www.chronicle.com.

42 A. Rotherham, *Achieving Teacher and Principal Excellence: A Guidebook for Donors,* Philanthropy Roundtable, 2008, www.philanthropyroundtable.org.

43 Same as note 40, p. 27.

44 W. Lindahl, Three-Phased Capital Campaigns, *Nonprofit Management and Leadership,* Spring 2008.

45 Center on Philanthropy at Indiana University, *Bank of America Study of High Net-Worth Philanthropy,* 2008, www.philanthropy.iupui.edu.

Chores are done! Time for splashing summer fun until the supper bell is rung! The motto at Rodeheaver Boys Ranch: "It's better to build boys than to mend men." Daily chores, good food and healthy fun are important boy-building blocks.

Organization represented: Rodeheaver Boys Ranch, Palatka, FL (www.rbr.org)

Photographer: Greg Lepera, St. Augustine, FL, for www.giftcounsel.com, Ponte Vedra Beach, FL

Giving to foundations

- The Foundation Center and *Giving USA* estimate that giving to foundations in 2008 was $32.65 billion.

- This is a decline of 19.2 percent (-22.2 percent adjusted for inflation) from the revised value of $40.43 billion for 2007. The figure for 2007 is based on IRS Forms 990 and 990-PF as analyzed by the Foundation Center.

- Gifts to foundations are an estimated 11 percent of total giving.

Giving USA findings

Foundations included in this estimate are independent, community or operating foundations that are not established by corporations. Independent foundations are also sometimes called private foundations; independent foundations include family foundations.[1] The estimate for giving to foundations is based on the historical record of foundation gifts as a percentage of combined individual and bequest giving.

The estimate of gifts to foundations in 2008 does not include payments by Warren Buffett on his pledge to the Gates Foundation. Mr. Buffett's gifts to the Gates Foundation are intended to be distributed within a few years of their receipt. They will be tracked in *Giving USA* as part of foundation grantmaking.

Estimated donations to foundations are 13 percent of combined individual and charitable bequest giving for 2008. That percentage is consistent with gifts to foundations as a share of combined individual giving and charitable bequests from 1997 through 2006.

Using FoundationSearch.com to search for foundations newly registered in

2008, *Giving USA* finds more than 3,000 new foundations of all types (including corporate) reported on IRS records (as of March 2009).[2] This includes trusts and scholarship funds. Gifts to new foundations will be tabulated when those entities file their first IRS Forms 990-PF. Not all newly registered foundations were grantmaking by 2007, therefore not all were tracked by FoundationSearch.

Trends in giving to foundations

Using *Giving USA* data, two different ways of measuring trends in giving to foundations are presented. The first looks at giving to foundations during recession years. The second shows the trend in giving to foundations over time, measured per household (including all foundation donations divided by all households).

In prior recession years from 1978 to 2006, giving to foundations averaged an inflation-adjusted increase of 6.85 percent from the prior year. The range was from a decrease of nearly 21.9 percent (1980) to growth of 57.6 percent (1982). Giving to this subsector increased (adjusted for inflation) in four of the six recession years from 1978 to 2006.[3]

Table 1
Per household measure of giving to foundations
Includes contributions from all sources divided by number of households
(adjusted for inflation)

Year	Per household	# of households
1988	$78	91.12 million
1998	$257	102.53 million
2008	$280	116.78 million

Data: Giving to foundations from *Giving USA* estimate divided by the number of households in that year from the U.S. Bureau of the Census' Current Population Survey.

Using a standardized measure of giving to foundations allows us to compare contributions to this subsector over time. One standard measure is to estimate giving per household. To do this, the sum of contributions from all sources (not just households) is divided by the number of households in the country. Table 1 shows the results for giving to foundations per household since 1988. IRS Forms 990 are used as the basis of estimation of giving to all subsectors.

Multimillion-dollar gifts and pledges to foundations

The estimate of gifts to foundations in 2008 includes major donations that were announced in 2008 but were not likely to have been paid in full to foundations that year. These gifts are shown in Table 2.

Table 2
Announced contributions of more than $100 million to foundations, 2008

Amount to foundation	Donor	Recipient	Mission or purpose
$4.5 billion	James LeVoy Sorenson (Estate)	Sorenson Legacy Foundation, Salt Lake City	Promote charitable, artistic, religious, educational, literary, and scientific endeavors.
$1 billion	Peter G. Peterson	Peter G. Peterson Foundation, New York	Increase public awareness of the nature and urgency of key fiscal challenges threatening America's future and to accelerate action on them.
$360 million	Harold Alfond (Estate)	Harold Alfond Foundation, Portland, Maine	Support higher education, healthcare, and the arts in Maine.
$350 million	William P. Carey	W.P. Carey Foundation New York, Dallas and London	Support educational institutions with the larger goal of improving America's competitiveness in the world.
$225 million	Dorothy Patterson (Estate)	Patterson Foundation, Sarasota	In development as of mid-2009.

Amounts reported by *The Chronicle of Philanthropy*, January 29, 2009 and on the Million Dollar List maintained by the Center on Philanthropy at Indiana University.

Financial crisis undermines earlier gifts to foundations

The full extent of the impact of the financial crisis on foundation assets and numbers will not be known until the Foundation Center has access to data to be filed on IRS Forms 990-PF for 2008. However, some highly publicized cases dramatize the impact of the economic crisis and imprudent investment decisions on foundation assets.

At least two dozen foundations lost nearly all of their assets due to a Ponzi scheme allegedly run by Bernard Madoff. Nicholas Kristof of *The New York Times* web-published a list showing 147 foundations that lost at least some assets with Madoff. Of those foundations, 27 had 90 percent or more of their 2007 assets invested in funds linked to Madoff.[4] One especially high-profile case is that of the Picower Foundation, which lost its entire endowment due to this Ponzi scheme.[5] That foundation reported total assets of $958 million in 2007.[6]

While not forced to close in 2008, the Starr Foundation lost a significant share of its endowment when invest-ments it owned in insurance giant AIG declined dramatically in value, reportedly losing at least $1 billion of its previous $3 billion endowment.[7] The chairman of the Starr Foundation at the time was Maurice Greenberg, former chief executive officer of AIG.

The bankruptcy and failure of financial firms Bear Stearns and Lehman Brothers also affected independent foundations created by executives of those two firms.[8] However, specifics on how these and numerous other foundations were affected and by how much were not available publicly in mid-2009 as *Giving USA* went to press.

Bank of America Study about giving to foundations

According to the 2008 *Bank of America Study of High Net-Worth Philanthropy*, foundations (including family foundations) received 16.5 percent of the total amount donated by high-net-worth households (those with an annual income of more than $200,000 or a net worth of more than $1 million) in 2007.[9] This was the second largest share among all types of recipients. This study was written and researched

According to the *Bank of America Study of High Net-Worth Philanthropy*, giving to foundations by high-net-worth households ranks second, after giving to religious organizations, in the amount donated.

Most family foundations have less than $1 million in assets and grant less than $50,000 per year, according to the Foundation Center's *Key Facts about Family Foundations* for 2009.[10] Additionally, most make grants in the areas where family members live. While many foundations give less in times of economic downturn, they are not ceasing to grant funds to nonprofits. Therefore, nonprofits can still benefit from introducing their work to family foundations that are located, in particular, in close proximity.

for Bank of America by the Center on Philanthropy at Indiana University.

The median gift amount to foundations by high-net-worth households in the 2008 study was $9,000. The average gift size to foundations in the 2008 study (about giving in 2007) was $60,578. This was the highest average gift amount to all the types of organizations included in the study. However, the average gift in 2007 of $60,578 was 7.5 percent lower (adjusted for inflation) than the average gift to foundations reported in a 2006 giving study analyzing 2005 data.

Foundation donations in 2007 hit new high

The Foundation Center released data in March 2009 showing that gifts to foundations in 2007 reached $40.43 billion.[11] The Foundation Center reported that in 2007 there were a total of 72,679 independent, community, and operating foundations with assets totaling $660.30 billion. The Foundation Center tracks foundations that file IRS Forms 990-PF (or IRS Forms 990 for community foundations) and foundation closures or mergers.

IRS finds giving to foundations especially prevalent among the highest-net-worth estates

Bequests from high-net-worth estates are a major source of contributions to foundations. In 2006, when total gifts to foundations were $30.60 billion, an estimated $9.56 billion was bequeathed to foundations through estates.[13] This is 31 percent of the total for 2006.

In 2007, with total foundation donations reaching $40.43 billion, the Foundation Center identified a gift of $2.70 billion from the estate of Susan Thompson Buffett to the Buffett Foundation as among the top ten foundation gifts made that year. The IRS categorizes types of recipient organizations using a coding system that places foundations in the category of "philanthropy and voluntarism," which can also include United Way, Jewish federations, and other charities. For 2007, the "philanthropy and voluntarism" segment of charitable bequests claimed on estate tax returns was $10.08 billion. This is equivalent to 25 percent of the total gifts to foundations for 2007. Figure 1 illustrates the estimated amount of giving to foundations from 2002 through 2007 that came from estates claiming deductions for a gift to a foundation.

Gifts from other sources include contributions from living individuals; donations from estates below the estate tax filing threshold; and corporate donations of products, such as medicines, to operating foundations created to provide low-cost or free drugs to patients in need.

The Foundation Center anticipates that some private family foundations will transfer assets to community foundations when the cost of operating a private foundation outweighs the benefits.[12]

GOOD TO KNOW When tracking foundations, be sure to verify whether the one of interest is operating independently or whether it has merged or transferred its assets.

While estate gifts are important to foundations, gifts from other sources total a larger amount each year than do transfers from estates that file estate tax returns (the estates most likely to leave significant amounts to charity).

Social trust within community promotes more giving to community foundations

Elizabeth Graddy (University of Southern California) and Lili Wang (now at Arizona State University) used data collected by Robert Putnam (of *Bowling Alone*) to examine factors within a community and among households that shape giving to a community foundation.[14] They found that on a per capita basis, giving to community foundations is higher when there is a higher level of "social trust" among the people living in that area. Social trust was indicated by survey participants who said they did (or did not) usually trust other people. In contrast, other forms of civic engagement, such as formal or informal networks of people, and organized group activism were not associated with differences in the per capita amount contributed. Drs. Graddy and Wang point out that for fundraisers, it is important to develop trust in the organization receiving the funds. Their work shows that overall trust in others in the community is also important. While not a short-term strategy for success, a long-term goal for some community foundations might be to develop and extend programs that help area residents gain more trust in one another.

Figure 1
Contributions to foundations from estates filing estate tax returns and from other donors, 2002–2007

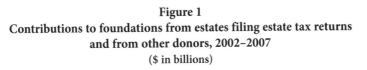

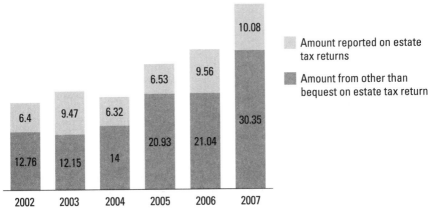

Data: Total foundation gifts received according to the Foundation Center (independent, community and operating foundations), based on year gift received. Amount from estates: U.S. Department of the Treasury, based on year estate tax return filed.

Key findings from other studies summarized

Table 3 presents three years of data from studies released annually about contributions to foundations. Web site addresses are provided so readers can access the full reports.

Table 3
Key findings from other studies about giving to foundations

Gifts to foundations *Foundation Yearbook*, 2007, 2008 and 2009 editions www.foundationcenter.org			
	2005*	2006	2007
Independent foundations, new gifts received	$17.37 billion	$21.59 billion	$31,28 billion
Community foundations	$5.59 billion	$6.03 billion	$6.23 billion
Operating foundations	$4.51 billion	$4.57 billion	$4.92 billion
Total for these three types of foundation	$27.46 billion	$32.20 billion**	$40.43 billion**

* The *Foundation Yearbook* publishes actual foundation giving totals from two years prior.
** Includes amounts transferred to the Bill & Melinda Gates Foundation by Warren Buffett and, at his request, to be granted within three years. These amounts are excluded by *Giving USA* in its estimate of giving to foundations.

1   Gifts to corporate foundations and operating foundations created by corporations, about a dozen of which are patient assistance foundations that distribute pharmaceuticals to qualified individuals, are covered in the chapter about corporate giving.
2   FoundationSearch.com using "foundations first filing since 2008" as one of the search terms, March 1, 2009.
3   Giving during recessions, *Giving USA Spotlight*, #3, 2008, available from www.givingusa.org.
4   N. Kristof, Madoff and America's (poorer) foundations, *The New York Times*, January 29, 2009, www.nytimes.com.
5   G. Fabrikant, Foundation that relied on Madoff fund closes, *The New York Times*, December 19, 2008, www.nytimes.com.
6   Same as note 5.
7   G. Fabrikant, Economy expected to take toll on charitable giving, *The New York Times*, September 29, 2008, and Foundation that relied on Madoff closes, *The New York Times*, December 19, 2008, both at www.nytimes.com.

8   Same as note 7.
9   Center on Philanthropy at Indiana University, *Bank of America Study of High Net-Worth Philanthropy*, 2008, www.philanthropy.iupui.edu.
10 S. Lawrence and R. Mukai, *Key Facts on Family Foundations*, January 2009, the Foundation Center, www.foundationcenter.org.
11 S. Lawrence and R. Mukai, *Foundation Growth and Giving Estimates*, released March 31, 2009, includes final numbers for 2007, www.foundationcenter.org.
12 Same as note 11, p.7.
13 U.S. Treasury, *Key Facts about Charitable Giving*, 2008, appearing in *Giving USA 2008*.
14 E. Graddy and L. Wang, Community foundation development and social capital, *Nonprofit and Voluntary Sector Quarterly*, June 2009; published online on June 1, 2008, http://nvsq.sagepub.com.

10 Giving to human services

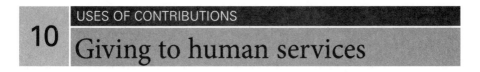

- Giving to human services organizations reached an estimated $25.88 billion in 2008. This is a decline of 12.7 percent (-15.9 percent adjusted for inflation).

- Donations to human services organizations are an estimated 9 percent of total giving for 2008.

- Human services organizations include charities focused on courts and legal services; employment and vocational training; food and nutrition; long-term housing and temporary shelter; public safety and community disaster relief; recreation and sports; youth development; family and children's services; emergency assistance for families; and independent living and self-sufficiency for women, seniors, veterans, and individuals with disabilities.

Giving USA findings for giving to human services organizations, 2008

Giving USA estimates for giving to human services organizations for 2007 and 2008 are based on the historical relationship between giving to human services organizations and broader economic trends. Specifically, the estimate looks at changes in personal income, changes in wealth as measured by the Standard & Poor's 500 stock index, and changes in giving in the recent past.[1] The giving data are from IRS Forms 990 analyzed by the National Center for Charitable Statistics. The 2008 data from IRS Forms 990 will be available in about 2010. *Giving USA* will revise its estimates then.

Trends in giving to human services
In prior recession years, giving to human services organizations averaged an inflation-adjusted change of 0.7 percent from the prior year, although the range was from a drop of 9 percent (1980) to an increase of 14.4 percent (1974). Giving to this subsector

increased (adjusted for inflation) in five of the eleven recession years between 1968 and 2006.[2]

Using a standardized measure of giving to human services organizations allows us to compare contributions to this subsector over time. One standard measure is to estimate giving per household. To do this, the sum of contributions from all sources (not just households) is divided by the number of households in the country. Table 1 shows the results for giving to the human services subsector since 1988. IRS Forms 990 are used as the basis of estimation of giving to charitable subsectors.

Philanthropic Giving Index "present situation" indicator drops 22 percent for human services organizations from one year earlier

In December 2008, the Philanthropic Giving Index (PGI), which measures the fundraising confidence of nonprofit fundraisers and is conducted by the Center on Philanthropy, reported a "present situation" index of 61.9 (on

Table 1
Per household measure of giving to the human services subsector
Includes contributions from all sources divided by number of households
(adjusted for inflation)

Year	Per household	# of households
1988	$112	91.12 million
1998	$200	102.53 million
2008	$222	116.78 million

Data: Giving to human services subsector from *Giving USA* estimate divided by the number of households in that year from the U.S. Bureau of the Census' Current Population Survey.

a scale of 100) for human services organizations in December 2008.[3] The index of 61.9 is the lowest level of fundraising confidence expressed by human services fundraisers since the summer of 2003 (60.3). The late 2008 PGI reported that:

- Significantly fewer human services fundraisers reported success with telephone solicitations, planned giving, email, and Internet, when compared with fundraisers from other types of charities.

- While success with major gifts dropped in 2008, it remained one of the most successful fundraising techniques.

- More human services fundraisers had success with special events than any other type of fundraising technique.

Table 2 shows success by type of fundraising tactic reported by human services organization respondents in 2007 and 2008.

Compared with 2007, human services organization respondents reported particularly pronounced declines in corporate gifts (from an index of 63.6 in 2007 to 29.4 in 2008) and in foundation grants (from 81.8 in 2007 to 64.7 in 2008). While success with telephone fundraising was lower for human services charities in 2008 than it was for other types of organizations, it rose compared to the end of 2007.

GuideStar poll results, 2008

Each year since 2002, GuideStar.org has posted a late-year online poll asking readers of its e-newsletter to report changes in giving to their organizations compared to the prior year.[4] We present a summary of these findings here. Note that these findings are not nationally representative, nor are they drawn from a random sample.

Table 2
Percentage of human services organization respondents reporting success
with fundraising vehicle, 2007–2008

	Direct mail	Telephone	Special events	Planned giving	Major gifts	Corporate	Foundation	Email	Internet
2007	54.5	27.3	72.7	72.7	77.3	63.6	81.8	27.3	36.4
2008	41.2	29.4	76.5	29.4	64.7	29.4	64.7	11.8	11.8

There were 2,040 respondents from human services organizations. In 2008:

- 38 percent of responding human services charities said their contributions increased. In 2007, among human services respondents, 52 percent reported an increase in contributions.

- 24 percent of human services charity respondents reported that contributions to their organizations stayed about the same compared to the previous year.

- 36 percent of participants representing human services organizations reported a decrease in contributions compared to the previous year.

Giving USA topical survey of human services organizations

For *Giving USA 2009*, the Center on Philanthropy invited a nationally representative, random sample of human services organizations to answer questions about how they fundraise. This section of *Giving USA* summarizes key findings from the survey, revealing trends in which types of donors changed their giving in the year and how human services charities seek public support. There were 228 responses, which is 7 percent of those contacted.

Changes in giving by type of donor

In the *Giving USA* survey, across all donor types, nearly 60 percent of respondents said their giving fell or stayed the same. Individual giving was the most likely type of donation to increase (40 percent said individual giving rose). Figure 1 shows the percentage reporting an increase, no change, or decrease in funds received by donor type.

Total sources of revenue for human services charities

Among surveyed charities, philanthropic gifts provided an average of 28 percent of total revenue in 2008. On average, organizations received revenue from three sources in addition to philanthropic fundraising. By frequency of their use, other sources of funding were:

- 62 percent charged fees for services (excluding memberships, such as at YMCA).

- Just under half (49 percent) had some investment earnings.

- Nearly half (46 percent) reported receiving government grants.

- Nearly one-third received donated in-kind services, such as accounting help or legal counsel.

- Less than a quarter (23 percent) had revenue from memberships.

Human services organizations serve many purposes that range from providing for households' basic needs to supporting youth development. Each type of organization has a unique funding pattern and combination of charitable giving. Figure 2 illustrates the charitable giving sources by type of human services organizations. Basic needs organizations receive nearly half (49 percent) of their charitable donations from corporations and one quarter from individuals. Basic needs charities include food banks, which often receive considerable in-kind corporate

Figure 1
Change in charitable revenue received, 2008, by type of donor

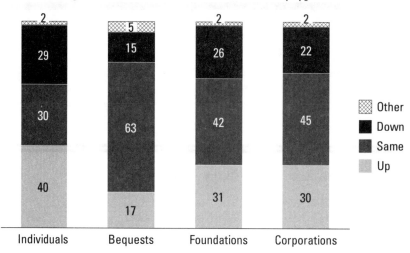

Data: *Giving USA* survey of human services organizations, n = 228

Figure 2
Funding received by each type of human services organization

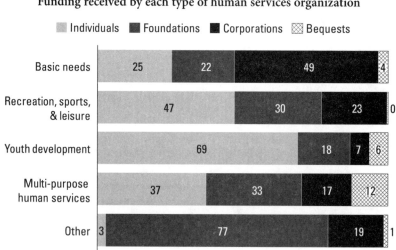

Data: *Giving USA* survey of human services organizations, n = 228

support. In contrast, recreation, sports, and leisure groups received just under half (47 percent) of their charitable dollars from individuals and nearly one-quarter from corporations.

How human services charities raise funds

This survey asked participating organizations what vehicles they use for their fundraising and which ones resulted in more than 30 percent or less than 5 percent of total funds raised (see Figure 3). Among all the organizations responding to the survey:

- 78 percent used proposals as a fundraising technique, with 47 percent reporting proposals accounting for more than 30 percent of fundraising receipts;

- 74 percent held special events to raise charitable dollars, with 29 percent of these organizations reporting that more than 30 percent of their charitable revenue derived from special events;

- Half of all organizations reported that their donors are able to make a gift through an online Web site to their agency, with 39 percent of these organizations reporting that these online donations account for less than 5 percent of the total amount raised; and

Figure 3
Fundraising vehicles: percentage using each, and percentage of respondents raising less than 5 percent, 5-30 percent and more than 30 percent through vehicle

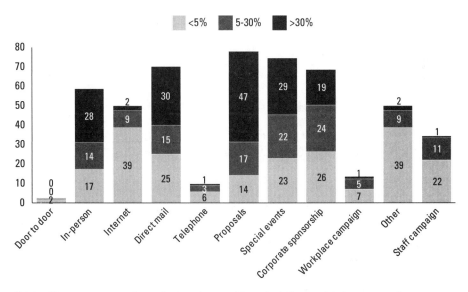

Height of bar = percentage of organizations that use this method. The data labels represent the percentage of ALL respondents who reported that charitable dollars from the listed giving vehicles are either above 30 percent, 5 to 30 percent, or below 5 percent of their total fundraising receipts.

Data: *Giving USA* survey of human services organizations, n=228

- 13 percent reported fundraising revenue from workplace campaigns, and 10 percent reported charitable donations from telephone solicitations.

Human services organizations saw increase in demand for services, decrease in funding

The survey also asked participating charities for their perspective on the changing demands on their organizations in 2008 and whether they would be adequately funded for 2009. Charities in this subsector are among the first to report increasing needs for their services and slower growth in contributions when the national economy slows.

The survey results showed that:

- Compared with 2007, 54 percent of human services charities saw an increase in need for their services in 2008; 30 percent saw little change in need; and 16 percent saw a decline; and

- For 2009, 60 percent of the surveyed human services organizations were cutting expenses, including limiting services or downsizing staff, due to funding shortages.

Figure 4 shows the change in demand for services by type of human services organizations.

Figure 4
Percentage of organizations reporting change in demand for their services in 2008, by each type of human services organizations

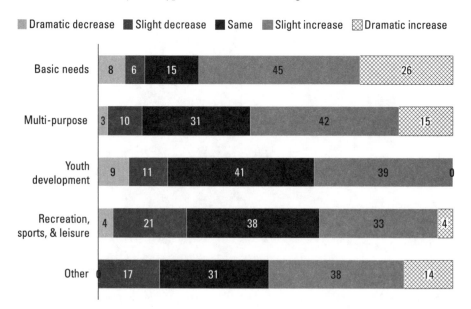

Data: *Giving USA* survey of human services organizations, n = 228

Organizations providing households' basic needs such as food and shelter were the most likely to report an increase in demand for their services (45 percent reported a slight increase, 26 percent a dramatic increase). Youth development organizations were the most likely to report that demand stayed the same (41 percent) while recreation, sports, and leisure groups were the most likely to report a decrease in demand for their services (25 percent).

Half (50 percent) of the organizations considered themselves underfunded for 2009 and were planning ways to trim costs. Another 10 percent said

they were severely underfunded and were closing or drastically reducing programming. A combined total of 40 percent reported that they had: adequate funding (18 percent), cash reserves (20 percent), or enough savings to consider implementing additional services (2 percent).

Figure 5 presents the change in revenue available to meet the demand for services in 2008. The type of human services agency most likely to be underfunded was youth development. Seventy-four percent of youth organizations reported that they are underfunded or severely underfunded, meaning that current available funding was insufficient to

Figure 5
Percentage of organizations reporting change in revenue to meet the demand for services in 2008, by type of human services organization

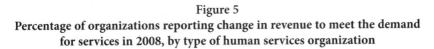

Severe underfunding cutting services or staff | Underfunded, thinking of ways to cut expenses | Just enough | Adequate, some cash reserves | Funds now available for new programs/services

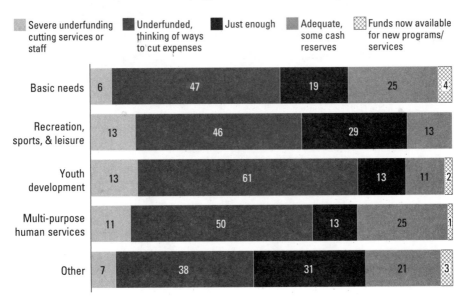

	Severe underfunding	Underfunded	Just enough	Adequate	Funds now available
Basic needs	6	47	19	25	4
Recreation, sports, & leisure	13	46	29	13	
Youth development	13	61	13	11	2
Multi-purpose human services	11	50	13	25	1
Other	7	38	31	21	3

Data: *Giving USA* survey of human services organizations, n = 228

Ladies try on chapeaus during "Hat Day" at a United Way-affiliated organization that provides senior services.
Organization represented: United Way of Greater Houston (www.unitedwayhouston.org)
Photographer: Justin Calhoun, Houston

meet current demand. Among organizations working to meet people's basic needs (i.e. food, shelter, and clothing), more than half (53 percent) said they are underfunded or severely underfunded for 2009.

Interestingly, there was no correlation between changes in demand for services and current perception of resources available to meet demand (being adequately funded or underfunded).[5] There may be a few reasons why this is true. Nonprofits may not be changing their fundraising effort in response to needs; donors may not be responding to changes in demand for human services organizations; or the response is too varied among organizations for a clear pattern to emerge.

Largest gifts to human services organizations

There were three publicly announced gifts of $25 million or more made to human services organizations in 2008. One was from an individual and the other two were from a foundation and a corporation.

- The Doris Buffett Foundation gave $30 million to the Women's Independence Scholarship Fund for scholarships that help women go back to school after leaving abusive partners.[6]

- The Home Depot Foundation gave $30 million in financial and in-kind support of technical resources and training to Habitat for Humanity International to establish a new national green building initiative called Partners in Sustainable Building.[7]

- David Rockefeller pledged $25 million from his eventual estate to the Stone Barns Center for Food and Agriculture. (Agriculture and farmland preservation are coded in the human services subsector by the National Taxonomy of Exempt Entities.)[8]

Overview of events of the year

By the end of 2008, nearly every sector of the American—and global—economy was affected by the current recession, which began at the end of 2007.[9] Layoffs in the U.S. mounted and official levels of unemployment rose from 4.9 percent at the beginning of the year to 7.2 percent by December.[10] Human services charities, especially those providing "safety net" services including employment counseling, food, and shelter, reported growing demands. Many also reported declining revenues from multiple sources, including government funds and donations. However, some funders, particularly foundations and some companies, responded with major commitments to agencies serving those most in need. Additionally, households and individual donors provided enough funds to surpass 2007 fundraising totals at some of the largest non-profit entities, including Catholic Charities USA and the Salvation Army. This section presents news stories from the year.

Some charities set new records

As of December 11, 2008, Catholic Charities USA had raised $7.2-million, a 15 percent increase over the same period in 2007. Perhaps, in response to the declining economic situation, donors stepped up their online giving. In the last week of November, the average gift was $148.50; in the first week of December, it rose to $201.[11]

The U.S. Salvation Army topped all records with its Red Kettle campaign in 2008, raising $130 million for use in local communities served by the charity.[12] This total surpassed the previous record of $118 million set in 2007. The Salvation Army attributed the 10 percent increase to corporate partnerships, increased donations from individuals, and innovative uses of technology.

Among the new approaches were "cashless" kettles pilot-tested in two regions, which allowed people to contribute with debit or credit cards. Donations made online rose 28 percent in 2008, perhaps in part due to increased social networking through sites such as Facebook and Twitter. The Salvation Army also provided donors a way to give using mobile phones.

Foundations commit special funds to recession-hit charities
The Council on Foundations surveyed funders early in 2008 and found that 86 percent said their grantmaking "directly or indirectly aids families,

provides human services, assists lower income populations, or supports economic development (p. 3)."[14] Among the 320 survey responses, 31 percent reported increasing their grantmaking to help those most impacted by the economic downturn, and 5 percent said they began providing human service assistance for the first time in 2008.

As of May 2008, 37 percent of foundations in the survey projected increasing their funding for such assistance in 2009.[15] This study was conducted before the stock market declines and investment firm failures that undermined foundation asset levels in the last quarter of 2008. Thus, as of this writing, it is unclear how many foundations will be able to fully meet future commitments.

In late 2008, using mapping features, the Foundation Center began tracking grants made as foundations responded to the needs arising from the economic crisis. For fiscal year 2008, the site listed 735 grants totaling $127.6 million, including donations from corporate foundations and corporate giving programs. As of late March 2009, another $24 million had been announced in grants to 504 recipients.[16]

GOOD TO KNOW

The Salvation Army and other charities are having success with new technologies, including mobile giving (text messages from cellular phones) and social networking. During the 2008 Christmas season, Internet giving at the Salvation Army rose 28 percent from 2007 for a total of $10 million.[13] While an impressive gain, Internet giving remains a very small percentage of total contributions to the Salvation Army.

While foundations want to make grants to assist during tough economic times, their own assets fell along with the decline in the stock market throughout 2008. This decline in asset values will make it more difficult for many funders to issue grants. Charities with strong existing relationships with a funder may be able to continue to receive grants, however, others should not expect major funding until foundation assets have improved and remained high for two to three years.

Food banks face food and funding shortages

Several trends converged to create severe shortages in the nation's food banks by year-end 2008. These were 1) the growing economic crisis, which increased the need for access to low-cost or free food; 2) a shift in American eating habits toward perishable foods and away from the types that food banks can easily stock; 3) greater efficiencies in food production and distribution, reducing the overages that formerly stocked food banks; and 4) grocers and food packagers' preferences to sell near-expiration-date products through discount grocers rather than donate items to charity.[17] News outlets in many major cities ran stories about the urgent need for food and monetary donations.[18] As a result, many companies increased their commitments, including Walmart, Kroger Stores, and others.[19]

An additional note: America's Second Harvest, a network serving food banks, adopted a new name, Feeding America, effective September 2008.[20]

American Red Cross copes with multiple disasters

The year 2008 began with an announcement that the American Red Cross faced a $200 million operating deficit and nearly exhausted disaster relief funds. The organization trimmed its staff at national headquarters, even as it conducted a search for a new CEO.[21] Gail McGovern began as president of the American Red Cross in April, 2008, becoming the sixth CEO of the organization since 2001.[22]

In late spring 2008, there were significant, natural disasters in the United States and in countries abroad. In the country of Myanmar, a cyclone caused cataclysmic destruction, killing up to 100,000 people and displacing up to one million people.[23] Days later, China's Sichuan Province was struck by a 7.9 earthquake, killing over 70,000 people.[24] Also beginning in May, tornados and floods hit areas in the U.S. from Minnesota to Oklahoma to West Virginia. Americans responded by contributing donations to many different charities, including the American Red Cross, which reported that it responded in ten weeks to 40 large-scale disasters—about half the total it typically faces in a full year.[25] While major contributions for relief went to the American Red Cross (and other agencies),[26] the intensity of these disasters drew down the organization's already depleted disaster relief fund.

Natural disasters continued throughout the year, with Hurricanes Gustav and Ike destroying parts of Louisiana and Texas. These disasters were particularly devastating as both regions were still rebuilding from the 2005 tragedies of Katrina, Rita, and Wilma. Many charities, including the Red Cross, also responded to these disasters and may have even overresponded. Hurricane Gustav was predicted to be as strong as Katrina (but wasn't) and advance preparations pushed some first-response charities, including the American Red Cross, into debt.[27] While it mounted a fundraising campaign to replenish the disaster relief fund, the Red Cross also sought $150 million in emergency funding from the U.S. Congress, and eventually received $100 million.[28]

Studies of giving to human services organizations

Several annual studies of giving to human services organizations are presented in Table 3. In addition, findings from a study of high-net-worth household giving, including the share that went to help meet people's basic needs and the share that went to help agencies working on issues related to youth and family services are summarized.

Bank of America Study of High Net-Worth Philanthropy, 2008

In a survey of high-net-worth households sponsored by the Bank of America, and written at the Center on Philanthropy at Indiana University, participants answered questions about how much they gave to different types of charitable organizations, including two that form part of the human services

subsector: organizations that help people meet their basic needs and organizations that serve youth and families. More than 600 respondents, all from high-net-worth households (those with an annual income of more than $200,000 or a net worth of more than $1 million, provided giving information about contributions they made in 2007. This updates a similar survey conducted in 2005. The Bank of America and the Center on Philanthropy have posted free copies of the report.[29]

Giving to help people meet their basic needs

Among Bank of America study participants, 81.4 percent made a donation to basic needs organizations in 2007. This is higher than for any other type of organization listed in the study. Moreover, basic needs organizations are the only type (excluding "other") for which the percentage of high-net-worth households who gave increased compared to 2005. The rate for 2005 was 74.6 percent. Basic needs organizations provide people with food, shelter, clothing, heating assistance, and other essentials.

However, the average 2007 gift for basic needs was one of the lowest ($3,578) when compared with other types of organizations. In addition, the average gift decreased by 14.4 percent compared with 2005 (adjusted for inflation), and the median gift in 2007 was $700 (down 34 percent). Despite the high incidence of giving for basic needs among high-net-worth households, the low average gift meant that these organizations received only 3.7 percent of the estimated total giving. This is the third lowest share, with only environmental (2 percent), and international (1.5 percent) organizations receiving less. The highest shares went to education, religion, and to private or community foundations, donor-advised funds, and charitable trusts.

The study also differentiated between giving through personal assets and through foundations, funds, and trusts. In this case:

- 79.3 percent of high-net-worth households gave to basic needs organizations through their personal assets in 2007. The average amount

donated through personal assets was $2,215, with a median gift of $500.

- 16.9 percent gave through foundations, funds, or trusts. In this case, the average amount was $10,565, with a median gift of $2,000.

Gifts to youth and family services were also examined in the Bank of America Study of High Net-Worth Philanthropy.

Key findings from annual studies

Table 3 presents three years of data from studies released annually about contributions to human services organizations. Web site addresses are provided so readers can access the full reports.

Table 3
Key findings from other studies about giving to human services organizations

Million Dollar List, gifts from individuals $10 million and above (2006–2008) to human services organizations (does not include gifts to foundations) Center on Philanthropy at Indiana University, www.philanthropy.iupui.edu			
	2006	2007	2008
Number of gifts to human services organizations	4	2	2
Largest gift to human services organizations	$64 million to the Salvation Army in Phoenix from the estate of Ray and Joan Kroc to help expand and renovate the South Mountain Youth Center (asset transfer from previously announced gift)	$50 million challenge gift from the estate of Joan Kroc to the Salvation Army Eastern Michigan Division to build and endow a new community center	$25 million pledge from David Rockefeller to Stone Barns Center for Food and Agriculture
Human services gifts as a percentage of all individual gifts of $10 million and above	0.9 percent	0.4 percent	0.3 percent

Foundation Giving Trends: Update on Funding Priorities
Grants to human services organizations
Foundation Center, www.foundationcenter.org

	2005	2006	2007
Average grant amount	$71,159	$73,401	$82,778
Median grant amount	$25,000	$25,000	$25,000
Human services funding as a percentage of grant dollars (surveyed foundations, including corporate foundations)	14.8 percent	13.8 percent	14.9 percent

IRS tax-exempt organizations in human services
Charities and other tax-exempt organizations.
Statistics of Income Bulletin, www.irs.gov

	2003	2004	2005
Number	100,835	104,837	108,283
Charitable revenue*	$58.76 billion	$62.85 billion	$70.07 billion

*Charitable revenue includes gifts and foundation grants (which is comparable to what Giving USA tracks), as well as government grants and allocations from other nonprofit agencies, such as the United Way and United Jewish Communities (which are not included in Giving USA estimates for contributions).

1   The model used to estimate giving was tested in late fall 2007 and early 2008 by Partha Deb (Hunter College, NY) and was found to be the most accurate method of predicting giving to human services organizations. More information about the estimating procedure appears in the chapter about methodology.

2   Giving during recessions, Giving USA Spotlight, #3, 2008, www.givingusa.org.

3   Center on Philanthropy at Indiana University, Philanthropic Giving Index, December 2008, www.philanthropy.iupui.edu.

4   Seventh Annual GuideStar Nonprofit Survey: Charitable Organizations and the Economy, Oct. 6-20, 2008, Released in the fall, 2008, www.guidestar.org.

5   Correlation coefficient was 0.013 and was not significant. Categorical responses 0 to 4 for each question.

6   A. Umble, Doris Buffett Foundation endows scholarships, Free Lance Star, September 16, 2008, www.fredericksburg.com.

7   Habitat for Humanity International and the Home Depot Foundation Announce National Green Building Effort, Habitat for Humanity International, Press release, March 20, 2008, www.habitat.org.

8   David Rockefeller Announces $25 Million Bequest to Stone Barns Center for Food and Agriculture, Stone Barns Center for Food and Agriculture, Press release, Oct. 3, 2008, www.stonebarnscenter.org.

9   Current news about the recession and the effects of the recession on the national and global economies can be found at www.recession.org, accessed June, 2009.

10 U.S. Bureau of Labor Statistics, using data from the monthly Current Population Survey, which uses a sample of U.S. households'

employment status. This sample includes persons who are without jobs and are currently seeking employment and are available to work, as well as people who are on layoff. According to an alternative measure of unemployment (U-6 in Table A-12 of the Employment Situation Report) released by the BLS in December 2008, 13.5 percent of the over-16 population was either unemployed, working part-time for economic reasons, or "marginally attached to the labor force" (looked for work unsuccessfully in the past year but not in the past month). In December 2007, the corresponding alternative unemployment measure was 8.7 percent. The difference is a faster rate of growth than in the official unemployment rate, which doesn't include the part-time employed or the marginally attached.

11 H. Hall and P. Wasley, Holiday-Giving Update: Social-Services Groups See a Surge, But Most Groups Face Big Slowdown in Donations, *The Chronicle of Philanthropy*, December 15, 2008, www.philanthropy.com.

12 $130 Million Raised During 2008 National Fundraising Campaign, Salvation Army, Press release, March 17, 2009, www.salvationarmyusa.org.

13 Same as note 12.

14 Council on Foundations, *Foundations Support Families Hit by Economic Downturn*, May 2008, www.cof.org.

15 Same as note 14.

16 The Foundation Center, MapShots, 2008 fiscal year and 2009 fiscal year, all foundation types, all recipient types, and all states, www.foundationcenter.org, viewed March 29, 2009.

17 R. Guth and R. Thurow, A different banking crisis in need of fresh capital, *The Wall Street Journal*, November 20, 2008, www.wsj.com.

18 Google news search conducted March 25, 2009 found articles from 2008 in *The New York Times, Atlanta Journal Constitution, Denver Post, Omaha World-Herald, Baltimore Sun, Seattle Post-Intelligencer, San Francisco Chronicle, Pittsburgh Post-Gazette, Sacramento Bee,* and *USA Today.*

19 Same as note 17.

20 Feeding America, Sept. 2008, www.feedingamerica.org.

21 S. Strom, Short on fundraising, Red Cross will cut jobs, *The New York Times*, January 16, 2008, www.nytimes.com.

22 P. Rucker, New Red Cross CEO will inherit a large deficit, *Washington Post*, April 9, 2008.

23 M. Casey, Why the Cyclone in Myanmar Was So Deadly, *National Geographic News*, May 8, 2008, www.nationalgeographic.com.

24 No author, Sichuan Earthquake, *The New York Times*, May 6, 2009, www.nytimes.com.

25 American Red Cross, *Standing Ready with a Helping Hand: The American Red Cross Response to the Central U.S. Floods and Tornados*, December 2008, www.redcross.org.

26 Lilly Endowment Awards $50 Million for Indiana Recovery Efforts, Lilly Endowment, Press release, June 23, 2008; also summarized at *Philanthropy News Digest*, June 25, 2008, www.foundationcenter.org.

27 P. Rucker, Gustav relief sends Red Cross into debt, *Washington Post*, Sept. 6, 2008, www.washpost.com; also summary at *Philanthropy News Digest*, www.foundationcenter.org.

28 P. Rucker, Red Cross asks Congress for millions in storm aid, *Washington Post*, September 16, 2008, www.washpost.com; also summary at *Philanthropy News Digest*, www.foundationcenter.org.

29 Center on Philanthropy at Indiana University, *Bank of America Study of High Net-Worth Philanthropy*, 2008, www.philanthropy.iupui.edu.

Founded in Evanston, Illinois in 1923, The Cradle is a not-for-profit, nonsectarian adoption and child welfare agency that has placed more than 14,500 children with loving families. The Cradle's onsite newborn nursery provides a safe, temporary, nurturing home for around 100 infants each year whose birthparents are considering an adoption plan. Half of the babies admitted to the nursery each year have some degree of special medical need. Here, Infant Aide Ellen Warsaw gently cradles baby Sarah Horist.

Organization represented: The Cradle, Evanston, IL (www.cradle.org)

Photographer: Brian MacDonald, copyright macdonaldphotography.com

11 Giving to health

- Estimated contributions to healthcare organizations reached $21.64 billion in 2008. This is a drop of 6.5 percent (-10.0 percent adjusted for inflation) compared with the estimate for 2007.

- Contributions to the health subsector are 7 percent of total estimated giving in 2008.

- Contributions to healthcare organizations include, but are not limited to:
  - Gifts to hospitals, clinics, and other healthcare facilities;
  - Organizations providing support for and conducting research on a vast scope of diseases and disorders;
  - Institutions providing services, research or advocacy about mental health issues; and
  - Medical research centers independent of other types of charities, such as a university.

Giving USA findings for giving to health organizations, 2008

The *Giving USA* estimate is based on a tested model incorporating economic variables and the historical record of giving to healthcare organizations. The economic variables are changes in stock market prices, personal income, and other economic trends.[1] *Giving USA* will revise the estimates of giving to health and all other subsectors as more data become available. The final figures will be based on data compiled from IRS Forms 990 by the National Center for Charitable Statistics, which are expected to be available in about two years.

Trends in giving to organizations in the health subsector

In prior recession years from 1967 to 2006, giving to health organizations averaged an inflation-adjusted increase of 0.6 percent from the prior year.[2] The range was from a growth of 8 percent (2001) to a decrease of 7.7 percent

(1980). Giving to this subsector increased (adjusted for inflation) in six of eleven recession years from 1967 to 2006.

Using a standardized measure of giving to health allows us to compare contributions to this subsector over time. One standard measure is to estimate giving per household. To do this, the sum of contributions from all sources (not just households) is divided by the number of households in the country. Table 1 shows the results for giving to health organizations per household since 1988. IRS Forms 990 are used as the basis of estimation of giving to charitable subsectors.

Philanthropic Giving Index "present situation" for giving to the health subsector drops to 62.2 in 2008 from 95.1 in 2007

In December 2008, the Philanthropic Giving Index (PGI), which measures the fundraising confidence of nonprofit fundraisers and is conducted semi-

Table 1
Per household measure of giving to health
Includes contributions from all sources divided by number of households
(adjusted for inflation)

Year	Per household	# of households
1988	$125	91.12 million
1998	$171	102.53 million
2008	$185	116.78 million

Data: Giving to health from *Giving USA* estimate divided by the number of households in that year from the U.S. Bureau of the Census' Current Population Survey.

annually by the Center on Philanthropy, reported a "present situation" index of 62.2 (on a scale of 100) for health organizations in December 2008.[3] This is the lowest PGI "present-situation" level for the health subsector since the summer of 2003 (60.7). The late 2008 PGI reported that:

- More health organization fundraising professionals reported success with major gifts and special events (85.7 percent each).

- Significantly more health fundraisers (61.9 percent) reported success with corporate giving than their peers working in other types of organizations.

- Significantly fewer development officers in health reported success with email solicitations compared to the other subsectors (10.0 percent).

Table 2 shows the reported success by type of fundraising reported by

health organization respondents in 2007 and 2008.

Compared with 2007, health organization respondents in 2008 reported:

- Greater success with telephone appeals;

- About the same level of success in direct mail, special events, major gifts, corporate support, foundation grants, and Internet fundraising; and

- Lower levels of success in planned giving and email.

Fifty-two percent of Association for Healthcare Philanthropy members made no change to giving forecast in response to recession

Among members of the Association for Healthcare Philanthropy (AHP) surveyed in December 2008, slightly more than half (52 percent) reported that their organization made no change to the amount forecasted for gifts in fiscal year 2008–2009 (or calendar 08).[4] However, nearly as many, 46 percent,

Table 2
Percentage of health organization respondents reporting success
with fundraising vehicle, 2007–2008

	Direct mail	Telephone	Special events	Planned giving	Major gifts	Corporate	Foundation	Email	Internet
2007	68.0	18.2	88.0	84.0	88.0	62.5	80.0	36.4	29.2
2008	66.7	35.0	85.7	71.4	85.7	61.9	66.7	10.0	28.6

said their organizations reduced the amount of the philanthropic revenue forecast. In this latter group, the average reduction was 17 percent. The respondents who projected a lower total for the year attributed it to the financial crisis that prevailed in late 2008. Thirty-six percent of these respondents elaborated that their organizations would delay or terminate plans to expand or renovate facilities, and 8 percent said that community services (e.g., free clinics) would be cut.

GuideStar poll finds lower giving levels in 2008

Each year since 2002, GuideStar.org has posted a late-year online poll asking readers of its e-newsletter to report changes in giving to their organizations compared to the prior year.[5] We present a summary of these findings here. Note that these findings are not nationally representative, nor are they drawn from a random sample.

There were 925 respondents from health organizations in 2008. In 2008:

- 38 percent of participants representing health organizations reported an increase in contributions;

- 21 percent of participants reported that contributions to their organiza-

tions stayed about the same compared to the previous year. This was a slight decrease compared to 25 percent in 2007; and

- 38 percent of participants representing health organizations reported a decrease in contributions.

The change from 53 percent reporting an increase in contributions in 2007 to 38 percent reporting an increase in contributions in 2008 marks the difficulties in fundraising in 2008. The corresponding shift is that only 19 percent reported a decline in 2007, and in 2008, that share was 38 percent.

All subsectors in the GuideStar poll show the same pattern: A larger percentage of charities reported a decline in 2008 compared with 2007, and a smaller share reported growth.

Medical research conducted in university settings is in the Education chapter

Among the largest gifts in the United States are gifts and grants for medical research undertaken at universities. Following the National Taxonomy of Exempt Entities, contributions to higher education institutions are recorded in education, even when their purpose

Studies by GuideStar, the Center on Philanthropy at Indiana University, and the Association for Healthcare Philanthropy about health philanthropy in 2008 showed a sizeable portion (38 percent to 46 percent) of charities reporting a lower amount of giving in 2008 compared with 2007.

Healthcare fundraisers reported more success than their peers in other subsectors with major gifts and planned gifts. The PGI and the AHP member survey both found that these two vehicles were areas in which healthcare fundraisers plan to focus in 2009.

is healthcare or medical research.[6] Among the gifts announced in 2008 that are in this group is the $400 million to Harvard University and Massachusetts Institute of Technology from the Eli and Edythe Broad Foundation for biomedical research.[7]

Largest gifts to health organizations announced in the media in 2008

At least seven gifts of $40 million or more each were given to health organizations in 2008 and publicly announced in the media:

- The Robert W. Woodruff Foundation gave $200 million to Grady Memorial Hospital in Georgia for its capital needs over the next four years.[8]

- $168.7 million was donated by the Bill & Melinda Gates Foundation to PATH for its Malaria Vaccine Initiative.[9]

- The Harold and Annette Simmons Family gave $50 million to the Parkland Foundation in Texas for its five-year capital campaign for a new hospital to replace Parkland's aging main facility.[10]

- Steven and Alexandra Cohen gave $50 million to NewYork-Presbyterian to significantly expand and enhance emergency pediatric care at Morgan Stanley Children's Hospital.[11]

- $43 million was donated by the Hall Family Foundation to Children's Mercy Hospitals and Clinics in Kansas City to support the first phase of expansion.[12]

- Andy Grove, co-founder of Intel, pledged to bequeath a portion of his estate, up to $40 million, to the Michael J. Fox Foundation for Parkinson's Research to help it continue to push for a cure.[13]

- The Bill & Melinda Gates Foundation gave $40 million to the Carter Center and World Health Organization to help eliminate the relatively few remaining cases of Guinea worm disease. While the Carter Center is classified in the international affairs subsector and the World Health Organization is based in Switzerland, this gift is of importance to the health subsector and, therefore, is included here.[14]

2008 sees nearly $100 million in major gifts to support nursing

In analyzing progress toward reducing the nursing shortage, researchers Denise Davis and Michelle Napier (both at the Robert Wood Johnson Foundation) studied foundation grant-making for nursing education, nursing research, and for scholarship or loan support for nursing students. From 2000 to 2004, the examined foundations gave $375 million, predominately (69 percent) through grants of less than $500,000 each and, often, to support local projects.[15]

For 2008, the number of donors and foundations who gave for nursing education or to encourage nursing rose dramatically compared to 2007, as well as in comparison to the 2000–2004 period studied by researchers Davis and Napier. The Million Dollar List maintained by the Center on Philanthropy at Indiana University for 2008 shows 26 gifts and grants from other funders that were publicly announced in 2008 to fund university or hospital programs focused on nursing education or promoting nursing as a career. [16] Each was at least $1 million and they totaled just under $100 million. In comparison, in 2007, only six such gifts were listed, totaling $12.35 million.

State revenue shortfalls threaten healthcare programs

When states face budget shortfalls, they need to cut funding to programs. Healthcare, as a major state expenditure, is among the programs that faced cuts in 2008 in many states. At least 29 states and the District of Columbia faced budget shortfalls for fiscal year 2009 (which began July 1, 2008 in many states).[17] As of March 2009, the national economic crisis was significantly worse, and 43 states reported budget shortfalls for fiscal year 2009. Another four predicted shortfalls in fiscal year 2010 (beginning July 1, 2009).[18] Of the 43 with budget shortages for fiscal year 2009, at least 18 states had already implemented cuts that reduced access to care.[19] The three states not reporting budget deficits were Montana, North Dakota, and Wyoming.

IRS study finds 8 percent of patients in nonprofit hospitals were uninsured

In its first-ever review of the finances and compensation practices at 544 hospitals, the Internal Revenue Service found that the share of uninsured patients ranged from 7 to 8 percent across the types of hospitals studied.[20]

The surveyed hospitals spent 7 percent of their total revenue on uncompensated (charity) care. The data were collected beginning in 2006 on hospital operations in the most recently completed tax period. In a separate study, the American Hospital Association found an increase in 2008 in the costs of uncompensated care among the 557 hospitals it surveyed late in the year.[21]

Public health issues receive private and foundation funding

Global health concerns include vaccination and disease prevention, both priorities of the Bill & Melinda Gates Foundation; safe drinking water, which is a growing priority for a number of funders; and maternal and child health. Several of these have been covered in earlier editions of *Giving USA*. In 2008, U.S.-based donors have demonstrated through their giving that health concerns are both an important part of American society and are of increasing concern globally. Many areas that are being funded by philanthropists are related to prevention and wellness, including obesity, tobacco use, potable drinking water, childhood vaccinations, and healthy babies. The following news items report gifts toward these and other public health issues.

Ideas for more roles that foundations can play in protecting women's health
Speaking at a conference about world health, Dr. William H. Foege, Presidential Distinguished Professor of International Health at Emory University and Senior Medical Advisor for the Bill & Melinda Gates Foundation,

offered his perspective about four roles that foundations are situated to play to improve the health of women in poor countries.[22] Dr. Foege's remarks were included in a report from the meeting and are incorporated here as information that can benefit charities seeking to work on health-related issues, generally, and on topics of interest to the Bill & Melinda Gates Foundation in particular.

- Find what works and analyze why so that it can be publicized and replicated.

- Examine and confront the role(s) that women are allowed or forbidden to play in various developing and poor countries as health programs and education programs are being introduced. Addressing questions of access to the decision-making power process in implementation of these programs is important in making lasting change.

- Fund multiple programs to do parallel research, even when it is known that most of the funded projects won't show the expected results.

- Work as a field to encourage more spending on women's health by governments of both poor and rich countries.

Continued research and program funding to reduce obesity

Obesity, in particular, has been an increasing healthcare issue of concern for many grantmakers and donors. For example, in 2007, the Robert Wood Johnson Foundation launched a national initiative directed at reducing childhood obesity.[23] Additionally, in 2008, four major gifts and grants further contributed to the nonprofit sector's efforts to improve health through better diets, more exercise, and better knowledge of the physiology of obesity. These gifts include:

- $25 million from Stephen and Diana Goldberg to the Children's National Medical Center in Washington, D.C.[24]

- $16 million from the medical provider Kaiser Permanente to LiveWell Colorado to help develop community-based initiatives statewide to fight obesity.[25]

- $16 million from the Robert Wood Johnson Foundation to the University of Illinois at Chicago to study policy and environmental factors that influence youth behaviors related to nutrition, physical activity, obesity, and tobacco use.[26]

- Two grants totaling $2.57 million from the New Balance Foundation to hospitals in the Boston area for nutrition counseling and other services aimed at combating childhood obesity.[27]

In addition to these grants that emphasize treatment of childhood obesity, Eli

Lilly & Company awarded $3 million to the Joslin Diabetes Center to investigate the underlying causes of obesity and insulin resistance.[28]

Michael Bloomberg contributes another $250 million to reduce global tobacco use

Michael Bloomberg, founder of the financial news network Bloomberg and mayor of New York City, contributed $250 million through Bloomberg Philanthropies to the Bloomberg Initiative to Reduce Tobacco Use.[29] This initiative was launched in 2006 and emphasizes grants to projects that "develop and deliver high-impact tobacco control interventions" in "low- and middle-income countries."[30] Grants have gone to programs in countries such as Argentina, Bangladesh, Burkina Faso, China, Niger, Russia, and Vietnam. American-based charities that work in countries of interest to the Initiative have also been funded, including the Adventist Development and Relief Agency, which had a project in Laos.

Nurse-Family Partnership funded for expansion

Nurse-Family Partnership is a clinically proven program that improves health outcomes for newborns and their families by sending visiting nurses to provide counseling and care for low-income, first-time parents. [31] This initiative received at least seven grants in 2008 totaling $43.6 million, with a portion of that intended to expand its model to new service areas. In 2008, the Nurse-Family Partnership actively sought new partner agencies, including state-wide initiatives.

Highest grossing "a-thons" raise nearly 8 percent more in 2008

The Run-Walk-Ride Fundraising Council (RWRFC) announced that total receipts at the nation's top 30 sports-related fundraising events reached $1.76 billion in 2008, a growth of 7.6 percent compared with 2007.[32] The highest receipts were for the American Cancer Society's "Relay for Life" at $430 million, followed by $125.5 million generated by the Leukemia & Lymphoma Society's "Team in Training" events.

Twenty-six of the top 30 "a-thon" events asked participants to collect funds for health-related causes. The specific health issues supported were: AIDS, Alzheimer's disease, arthritis, autism, birth defect prevention, cancer (including blood cancers), cystic fibrosis, diabetes, Down Syndrome, heart disease prevention and treatment, mental illness, and multiple sclerosis. The report covers total revenue, not net proceeds,

GOOD TO KNOW

Numerous funders are tackling health concerns affecting the U.S. and other nations. This helps spread the financial risk and enables the funded agencies to have a wider reach by linking with a broader network of stakeholders. It also creates opportunities for nonprofit agencies working on the same issue, as they might be in a better position to leverage funding towards working on a joint mission.

Sports-related event fundraising continued to grow in 2008, although more slowly compared to 2007. The nation's largest events benefit health causes.

after expenses. While 8 percent growth exceeds growth in total giving for 2008, it is a slow-down compared to 2007 when the top 30 events grossed 12 percent more than in 2006.[33]

The Run-Walk-Ride Fundraising Council, formed in 2007, provides resources and research for for-profit and nonprofit organization staff who manage athletic event fund-raising programs.

Studies

Studies that advance the understanding of contributions for health organizations were released in 2008. Summaries of two appear below.

Bank of America Study of High Net-Worth Philanthropy finds average health donation of $12,013

According to the *2008 Bank of America Study of High Net-Worth Philanthropy*, which was researched and written at the Center on Philanthropy at Indiana University, 68.2 percent of high-net-worth households (with an annual income of more than $200,000 or a net worth of more than $1 million) made a donation to health organizations in 2007.[34] This is a slight drop from Bank of America's earlier study on high-net-worth philanthropy in 2005, when 70.3 percent of respondents surveyed reported gifts to health.

The average gift size for health organizations in 2007 was $12,013, an increase of 51.2 percent compared to 2005 (adjusted for inflation). The median gift in 2007 was $800. Health received 10.4 percent of all the giving by high-net-worth households in 2007.

The study also differentiated between giving through personal assets and through foundations, funds, and trusts. When looking at the source of funds:

- 66 percent of high-net-worth households gave to health organizations through their personal assets in 2007, while 14.3 percent gave by utilizing foundations, funds, or trusts.

- The average donation amount through personal assets was $8,970, and the median was $500.

- The average gift from foundations, funds, and trusts was $24,206, and the median was $5,000.

Association of Healthcare Philanthropy, 2007

The Association for Healthcare Philanthropy (AHP) estimated in their *FY2007 Report on Giving* for the United States, published in late 2008, that $8.3 billion was contributed to healthcare institutions. This amount included $6.1 billion that was paid during the year and an additional $2.2 billion that was pledged. The 460 institutions that responded to the study reported that most of the donations, 61 percent, came from individuals.[35]

In response to questions about the type of donation made, organizations reported that more than two-thirds of contributions came in cash; about one-quarter of the amount reported was in planned or pledged gifts and not yet paid; and the balance was from securities or non-monetary assets that were sold for cash. Figure 1 shows the percentage of funds raised by AHP respondents by type of donation.

The AHP report also includes information about how donations are expended. Among the funds raised, the largest share supported construction and renovation (29 percent). The second largest expense category was equipment (17 percent). Charitable care expenditures accounted for 6 percent of the funds raised.[36]

Figure 1
Philanthropic revenue by type, 2007

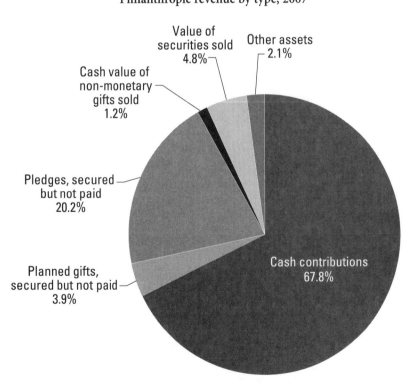

Data: FY07 Report on Giving, Association for Healthcare Philanthropy
Adapted from page 4. Used with permission

Key findings from annual studies

Table 3 presents three years of data from studies released annually about giving for healthcare and health-related causes. Web site addresses are provided so readers may access complete reports.

Table 3
Key findings from other studies of giving to health

Million Dollar List, gifts from individuals $10 million and above (2006–2008) to health organizations (does not include gifts to foundations) Center on Philanthropy at Indiana University, www.philanthropy.iupui.edu			
	2006	2007	2008
Number of health gifts	18	15	23
Largest gift to health	$125 million from Michael Bloomberg to various organizations to support programs to help smokers quit and educate children to prevent them from starting	$600 million from Jon and Karen Huntsman to the Huntsman Cancer Foundation in Utah to support cancer research	$50 million from the Harold and Annette Simmons family to the Parkland Foundation in Texas for a new hospital. $50 million to New York-Presbyterian Hospital from Steven and Alexandra Cohen for emergency pediatric care at Morgan Stanley Children's Hospital
Health sector gifts as a percentage of all individual gifts of $10 million or above	3.7 percent	11.5 percent	4.2 percent

Foundation Giving Trends: Update on Funding Priorities Grants to health Foundation Center, www.foundationcenter.org			
	2005	2006	2007
Average grant amount	$199,410	$240,660	$249,401
Median grant amount	39,720	35,000	35,000
Health funding as a percentage of grant dollars (surveyed foundations, including corporate foundations)	20.8 percent	23.0 percent	22.7 percent

Report on Giving FY 2005, 2006, and 2007 Association for Healthcare Philanthropy, www.ahp.org			
	2005	2006	2007
Estimated total giving to member organizations; includes pledges	$7.1 billion	$7.9 billion	$8.3 billion
Estimated cash contributions (includes value of non-monetary and security gifts sold)	$5.1 billion	$5.9 billion	$6.1 billion
Median return on $1 spent for fundraising, all institutions	$3.58	$4.17	$3.49

IRS tax-exempt organizations in health category Charities and other tax-exempt organizations, 2003, 2004, 2005 Statistics of Income Bulletin, www.irs.gov			
	2003	2004	2005
Number	35,144	36,737	35,669
Charitable revenue*	$44.31 billion	$46.56 billion	$52.15 billion

*Charitable revenue includes gifts and foundation grants (which is comparable to what *Giving USA* tracks), as well as government grants and allocations from other nonprofit agencies, such as the United Way and United Jewish Communities (which are not included in *Giving USA* estimates for contributions).

1   The model used to estimate giving was tested in late fall 2007 and early 2008 by Partha Deb (Hunter College, NY) and found to be the most accurate method over time of predicting giving to human services. Professor Deb looked at other potential variables, such as the percentage of the population in different age categories or the percentage that is uninsured, and found that they did not improve the estimating procedure.

2   Giving during recessions, *Giving USA Spotlight*, #3, 2008, available from www.givingusa.org.

3   Center on Philanthropy at Indiana University, Philanthropic Giving Index, December 2008, www.philanthropy.iupui.edu.

4   Association for Healthcare Philanthropy, *The Effect of the Economic Recession on Health Care Philanthropy*, December 2008, www.ahp.org/ric-online/recession-toolkit/pdfs/AHP_Recession_Survey_December2008.pdf.

5   Seventh Annual GuideStar Nonprofit Survey: Charitable Organizations and the Economy, Oct. 6-20, 2008, Released in the fall, 2008, www.guidestar.org.

6   Information about NTEE codes provided by the National Center for Charitable Statistics, The Urban Institute, www.nccs.urban.org.

7   Eli and Edythe L. Broad endow the Broad Institute of Harvard and MIT with additional $400 million, Harvard Science, Press release, Sept. 4, 2008, www.harvardscience.harvard.edu.

8   M. Kempner, Woodruff's $200M gift critical to Grady's survival, *Atlanta Journal-Constitution*, April 7, 2008, www.ajc.com.

9   Bill Gates Announces $168 Million to Develop Next-Generation Malaria Vaccine, Bill & Melinda Gates Foundation, Press release, Sept. 25, 2008, www.gatesfoundation.org.

10 S. Jacobson, Parkland hospital kicks off its capital campaign with big donor support, *Dallas Morning News*, September 10, 2008, www.dallasnews.com.

11 $50 Million Gift to Expand and Enhance Emergency Care at Morgan Stanley Children's Hospital, NewYork-Presbyterian Hospital, Press release, Jan. 16, 2008. www.nyp.org.

12 J. Karash, $43 million gift by Hall founda-
    tion boosts Children's Mercy expansion,
    Kansas City Star, February 22, 2008,
    www.kansascity.com.

13 K. Dolan, Andy Grove Puts Millions into
    Parkinson's Fight, *Forbes*, January 10, 2008,
    www.forbes.com.

14 Guinea Worm Cases Hit All-Time Low:
    Carter Center, WHO, Gates Foundation,
    and U.K. Government Commit $55 Million
    toward Ultimate Eradication Goal, The
    Carter Center, Press Release, December 5,
    2008, www.cartercenter.org.

15 D. Davis and M. Napier, Grantwatch
    Report: Strategically addressing the nursing
    shortage: A closer look at the Nurse
    Funders Collaborative, *Health Affairs*,
    May/June 2008.

16 Million Dollar List for 2008, analysis for
    Giving USA by the Center on Philanthropy,
    www.philanthropy.iupui.edu.

17 I. Lav and E. McNichol, 29 States Faced
    Total Budget Shortfall of at Least
    $48 Billion in 2009, January 15, 2008,
    http://www.cbpp.org.

18 E. McNichol and I. Lav, *State Budget
    Troubles Worsen*, http://www.cbpp.org/files/
    9-8-08sfp.pdf. Updated March 13, 2009.

19 Legislation passed in February 2009
    re-funded the Children's Health Insurance
    Program and portions of the "economic
    stimulus package" (the American Recovery
    and Reinvestment Act of 2009), also approved
    in February 2009, extended access to care
    among low-income residents in states.

20 IRS Exempt Organizations (TE/GE)
    Hospital Compliance Project, Final Report,
    Feb., 2009, www.irs.gov/pub/irs-tege/
    frepthospproj.pdf

21 American Hospital Association, *Report
    on the Economic Crisis: Initial Impact on
    Hospitals*, www.aha.org.

22 W. Foege, The Role of Charitable Foundations
    in the Protection of Women's Health in
    Least Developed and Developing Countries,
    Emory International Law Review, 2008.

23 Robert Wood Johnson Foundation, May 28,
    2009, http://www.rwjf.org/childhoodobesity/
    index.jsp.

24 P. Rucker, Couple Gives $25M to Children's
    Hospital, *Washington Post*, April 17, 2008,
    www.washingtonpost.com.

25 Kaiser Permanente Approves $29 Million
    in Community Benefit Grants, Kaiser
    Permanente, Press release, February 12,
    2008, www.kaiserpermanente.org.

26 UIC Receives $16M to Study Impact of
    Environment on Kids' Health, University of
    Illinois at Chicago, Press Release, December
    15, 2008, www.uic.edu.

27 BMC Receives $1.57M from New Balance
    Foundation to Expand Nutrition and
    Fitness for Life Efforts to Reduce Obesity,
    New Balance, Press release, October 29,
    2008, www.newbalance.com; Children's
    Hospital Boston Receives $1 Million
    from New Balance Foundation to
    Expand Childhood Obesity Program
    and Research, Children's Hospital Boston,
    Press release, September 10, 2008,
    www.childrenshospital.org.

28 Joslin Diabetes Center Receives $3 million
    from Eli Lilly and Company Foundation
    for Obesity Studies, Joslin Diabetes
    Center, Press Release, October 14, 2008,
    www.joslin.org.

29 Michael Bloomberg and Bill Gates Join to
    Combat Global Tobacco Epidemic, Bill &
    Melinda Gates Foundation, Press Release,
    July 23, 2008, www.gatesfoundation.org.

30 Bloomberg Initiative to Reduce Tobacco
    Use, viewed March 20, 2009, http://www.
    tobaccocontrolgrants.org/, para.1.

31 Nurse-Family Partnership at www.
    nursefamilypartnership.org, assessed May
    15, 2009, announced that the organization
    is seeking partner sites.

32 2008 Run Walk Ride 30 overview, March 5,
    2009, assessed March 20, 2009 from
    www.runwalkride.com.

33 H. Hall, Gifts to walkathons and other events
    rise 12%, *The Chronicle of Philanthropy*,
    March 6, 2008, www.philanthropy.com.

34 Center on Philanthropy at Indiana
    University, *Bank of America Study of
    High-Net Worth Philanthropy*, 2008,
    www.philanthropy.iupui.edu.

35 Association Research, Inc. (ARI), FY 2007
    Report on Giving USA, Association for
    Healthcare Philanthropy, 2008.

36 Association Research, Inc. (ARI), FY 2007
    Report on Giving USA, Association for
    Healthcare Philanthropy, 2008, p. 6.

12 Giving to public-society benefit

- Gifts to public-society benefit organizations reached an estimated $23.88 billion in 2008.

- This reflects an increase of 5.4 percent since 2007 (1.5 percent adjusted for inflation).

- Public-society benefit giving is 8 percent of total giving.

- The public-society benefit sector includes organizations that raise funds to redistribute to a wide range of charities (United Way, Jewish federations, Combined Federal Campaign, and others) that promote philanthropy and volunteerism, or that conduct research in the biological, physical, and social sciences, including public policy research. Other causes or purposes included in this subsector include: community and economic development, civil liberties and civil rights, voter education, and consumer protection.

Giving USA findings for giving to public-society benefit organizations, 2008

The estimate for the change in giving to organizations in the public-society benefit subsector is based on the historical relationship between giving to public-society benefit charities and other broader economic trends. Specifically, the estimate looks at changes in personal income, changes in wealth as measured by the Standard & Poor's 500 stock index, and changes in giving in the recent past.

Giving USA will revise the estimates of giving to public-society benefit and all other subsectors as more data become available. The final figures will be based on data compiled from IRS Forms 990 by the National Center for Charitable Statistics.

Trends in public-society benefit giving, 1968–2006

In prior recession years, giving to public-society benefit organizations averaged an inflation-adjusted change of 3.9 percent from the prior year, although the range was from a drop of 29 percent (1973) to an increase of 29 percent (1974). Giving to this subsector increased (adjusted for inflation) in eight of the eleven recession years between 1968 and 2006.[1]

Using a standardized measure of giving to public-society benefit organizations allows us to compare contributions to this subsector over time. One standard measure is to estimate giving per household. To do this, the sum of contributions from all sources (not just households) is divided by the number of households in the country. Table 1 shows the results for giving to the public-society benefit sector since 1988. IRS Forms 990 are used as the basis of estimation of giving to charitable subsectors.

Table 1
Per household measure of giving to public-society benefit subsector
Includes contributions from all sources divided by number of households
(adjusted for inflation)

Year	Per household	# of households
1988	$102	91.12 million
1998	$180	102.53 million
2008	$204	116.78 million

Data: Giving to public-society benefit subsector from *Giving USA* estimate divided by the number of households in that year from the U.S. Bureau of the Census' Current Population Survey.

Philanthropic Giving Index "present situation" for giving to the PEAI (public-society benefit, environment/animals, and international affairs) subsector drops to 54.9 in 2008 from 79.1 in late 2007

In December 2008, the Philanthropic Giving Index (PGI), which measures the fundraising confidence of nonprofit fundraisers and is conducted semi-annually by the Center on Philanthropy, reported a "present situation" index of 54.9 (on a scale of 100) for a combination of organizations that includes those in three subsectors: public-society benefit; environment/animals; and international affairs (PEAI).[2] This is the lowest level of fundraising confidence expressed for the PEAI cluster since the PGI began in 1998. The late 2008 PGI reported that:

■ PEAI fundraisers, along with those in human services, had the lowest PGI in December 2008, indicating that charities in these areas had the least amount of success in raising gifts and were the least optimistic about fundraising in the coming six-month period (the expectations index) compared to other subsector organizations.

■ Fundraisers in this group were among the least likely to report success with email fundraising, at just 12.5 percent. This compares with one-third of religious fundraisers and 43 percent of education fundraisers reporting success.

■ However, more fundraisers in the PEAI cluster reported success with special events (93.8 percent) than did fundraisers in other subsectors. In most other types of charities, special events were less likely to be reported as successful when compared to major gifts. In comparison, 62.5 percent of the PEAI cluster reported success with major gifts.

Table 2 shows the fundraising success according to type reported by public-society benefit, environment/animals, and international affairs organization respondents (PEAI) in 2007 and 2008.

Compared with 2007, PEAI organization respondents reported particularly pronounced declines in corporate gifts (from 52.9 percent reporting success in 2007 to 37.5 reporting success in 2008) and in planned giving and major gifts (both dropping from 76.5 percent success rates in 2007 to 62.5 percent in 2008).

Table 2
Percentage of public-society benefit, environment/animals, and international affairs
(PEAI) respondents reporting success with fundraising vehicle, 2007–2008

	Direct mail	Telephone	Special events	Planned giving	Major gifts	Corporate	Foundation	Email	Internet
2007	58.8	25.0	70.6	76.5	76.5	52.9	76.5	12.5	29.4
2008	43.8	43.8	93.8	62.5	62.5	37.5	68.8	12.5	37.5

GuideStar poll results, giving to the public-society benefit subsector in 2008

Each year since 2002, GuideStar.org has posted a late-year online poll asking users of its site to report changes in giving to their organizations compared to the prior year.[3] We present a summary of these findings here. Note that these findings are not nationally representative, nor are they drawn from a random sample. In 2008's poll, there were 177 respondents from religious organizations. Compared with 2007, out of this sub-group:

- 36 percent reported more charitable revenue, which is a drop from 51 percent of organizations that saw an increase in 2007 when compared to 2006.

- Twenty-five percent reported that contributions stayed about the same compared to 2007.

- Thirty-six percent reported that charitable revenue decreased in 2008, which is equal to the percentage that realized growth in charitable revenue. In 2007, only 19 percent of organizations reported a decline in revenue.

Million-dollar gifts awarded to public-society benefit organizations

The largest publicly announced gifts to public-society benefit organizations in 2008 came from corporations, foundations, and the estate of an early Microsoft staff member.

- Intel Corporation gave $105 million to the Society for Science & the Public (SSP), a nonprofit 501(c)(3) organization dedicated to public engagement in scientific research and education. The gift will support SSP's science competitions and will create an educational outreach program and an alumni and membership program. The society also organizes the Intel Science Competition, which recognizes original scientific work by high school students.[4]

- The estate of Ric Weiland, one of the first five employees of Microsoft Corporation, directed $65 million to Washington state's Pride Foundation. The funding will support anti-discrimination campaigns and programs to help youths, develop future leaders and provide scholarships. A portion of the funds will be distributed to 10 other organizations over eight years.[5]

- Lilly Endowment granted $45 million for flood and tornado relief to the Indiana Association of United Ways. The foundation also awarded $2.5 million each to the American Red Cross and the Salvation Army to support their relief work efforts.[6]

Two men working on the construction of a building pass a large stone up a ladder at Najile Girl's School in Kenya.

Organization represented: Compassion International, Colorado Springs, CO (www.us.ci.org)

Photographer: Chuck Bigger, Colorado Springs, CO

- Comcast Corporation pledged $27 million worth of public outreach and financial support to City Year in Boston for its community outreach programs.[7]

- The Stardust Foundation gave $25 million to the Valley of the Sun United Way Foundation in Phoenix to provide matching funds for a five-year endowment campaign.[8]

Of the 20 gifts of $10 million or more to public-society benefit organizations, only two were from individual donors or families. The other 18 were from corporations or foundations.

United Way sets priorities, focuses on 10-year goals to achieve impact

In May 2008, the United Way of America announced a new focus on education, income, and health issues.[9] This new, 10-year strategic plan, titled "Goals for the Common Good," aims to heighten the impact of the organizations that it supports. Instead of allocating funds to organizations with wide-ranging goals, United Ways that adopt these priorities will shift their funding to support only those programs which offer well-defined approaches to achieve specific goals within these three areas.[10] These goals include:

- Reduce by half the number of young people who drop out of high school;

- Reduce by half the number of working families lacking financial stability; and

- Increase by one-third the percentage of healthy young people and adults.

The national focus on three core areas is an extension of an earlier strategy by many United Way affiliates that had sought funding for "community impact" or support for specific, locally identified needs. Among 172 United Ways that adopted the community impact strategy, donations averaged 20 percent more than giving to United Ways that did not.[11]

The United Way system recognizes that this new strategic plan poses challenges for charitable organizations that have received United Way funding in the past; these organizations may not be eligible under the new funding guidelines.[12] Charities in several cities, including those in Philadelphia,[13] Washington D.C.,[14] and Austin,[15] reported frustration with the switch in priorities.

GOOD TO KNOW

In an article in *The Chronicle of Philanthropy*, officials from different United Ways offered this advice to charities:[16]

"Make sure you've got outcomes related to the work you're doing, and think about how the work can affect conditions in the community if you can get it to a greater scale."

Leslie Ann Howard, United Way of Dane County, Madison, Wis.

"Think about who's doing something similar to you, so you can unite forces. Collaboration and coordination is going to be the key."

Debra Usher, United Way for Southeastern Michigan, Detroit, Mich.

Numerous newspapers and media outlets, including the *Boston Globe*, *Miami Herald*, *Denver Post* and *Los Angeles Times*, reported stories in 2008 about scams involving solicitation of funds for veterans. Charitable organizations seeking to raise funds for veterans' services may be well advised to take extra steps in sharing with donors evidence of the charity's legal status, successful programs, and financial standing.

"Live United" launched

United Way has long been characterized by its workplace fundraising campaigns. However, in implementing its new 10-year strategy, United Way has launched a new branding effort under the slogan "Live United." The campaign features television advertising, radio advertising, YouTube videos, and a new United Way Web site.[17] The aim is to reach individuals and encourage them to support the United Way in their local communities through giving, volunteering, and advocacy in reaching the "Goals for the Common Good," as listed above.

Foundations partner to expand services for veterans

Organizations focused on veterans, such as the American Legion, Disabled American Veterans, Iraq War Veterans, and others, are categorized in the public-society benefit subsector. Organizations that receive funding for services to veterans may be in public-society benefit or in any other subsector. Several major foundation initiatives in 2008 supported health-related or education-related services for veterans.

- The McCormick Foundation and Major League Baseball teamed up to raise more than $6 million in a program called "Welcome Back Veterans."[18] The initial round of

funding was granted in November 2008 to programs providing mental health services, job training and placement, and family care.

- The Wal-Mart Foundation granted $3.6 million to 12 charities working to provide educational assistance to veterans. The largest portion of the funds went to the American Council on Education to support educational assistance programs for veterans at 20 colleges and universities.[19]

- A $1 million grant from the Lilly Foundation to the American Psychiatric Foundation (APF) and Give an Hour (GAH) will be used to recruit and train volunteer mental health professionals to treat U.S. veterans returning from Iraq and Afghanistan.[20] This grant is particularly important considering a RAND study found that at least 31 percent of soldiers deployed in combat in these areas report post-war psychological problems.[21]

Announcing the "National Fund for Workforce Solutions"

In September 2008, leaders from foundations, businesses, government, and nonprofit organizations announced the result of a strategic collaboration: the creation of the National Fund for Workforce Solutions. This initiative will use grants and investments to strengthen and expand local workforce development partnerships across the nation. Major national contributors include the Annie E. Casey, Ford, Mott, and Rockefeller foundations, as well as the U.S. Department of Labor.[22] Additional support is being offered by the Harry and Jeanette Weinberg Foundation, the Hitachi Foundation, the John S. and James L. Knight Foundation, Microsoft, the Prudential Foundation, and the Wal-Mart Foundation.[23]

Growth of independent donor-advised funds

Financial institutions began sponsoring donor-advised funds in the 1990s, when Fidelity Investments created a public charity that took the advice of donors when redistributing donated funds to nonprofit beneficiary groups. Independent donor-advised funds, which are not affiliated with a sponsoring community foundation or other nonprofit, now include the rapidly growing National Christian Charitable

Foundation, National Philanthropic Trust and the U.S. Charitable Gift Trust. However, three of the four largest commercially sponsored donor-advised funds are those sponsored by investment companies, as indicated in Table 3.[24]

More options for those considering donor-advised funds

The recent popularity of donor-advised funds has led to variations on traditional planned giving programs. A donor-advised fund enables a donor or advisor to designate a percentage of the fund's assets for dispersal to a charitable organization.

- A donor-advised fund may be paired with an Irrevocable Life Insurance Trust (or a "Wealth Replacement Trust") to replace assets donated to charity. This ensures an inheritance for any trust beneficiaries.[25]

- Calvert Foundation's "Calvert Giving Fund" invests donated money placed in donor-advised funds in nonprofit organizations, microfinance institutions, and social enterprises. By

Table 3
Four of the largest commercially sponsored donor-advised funds
Assets, distributions, and new gifts received, circa 2008

	Assets at end of fiscal year	Charitable distributions during year	Percentage of assets distributed	New gifts received
Fidelity	$4.717 billion	$1.164 billion	25%	$1.594 billion
Schwab	>$2 billion	$0.37 billion	18%	$0.89 billion
Vanguard Charitable Fund	$1.85 billion	$0.43 billion	23%	$0.67 billion
National Christian Charitable Foundation (2007)	$873 million	$331.5 million	38%	$452 million

Data: IRS Form 990 to June 30, 2008: Fidelity and Vanguard ; Audited financial report for FY ending June 30, 2008: Schwab; and GuideStar: National Christian Charitable Foundation providing investment strategies that align with philanthropic goals, the Calvert program heightens the impact of donor contributions.[26]

- The Schwab Charitable Microfinance Guarantee Program operates in a similar fashion by investing a percentage of donor-advised Charitable Gift Accounts into microfinance loan programs to assist "the world's poorest entrepreneurs to start, maintain or expand small businesses."[27] Funds that are put into an account in order to guarantee microloans are invested, therein heightening the impact of the original donation.

Bank of America findings, combined funds

According to the *2008 Bank of America Study of High Net-Worth Philanthropy*, which was researched and written at the Center on Philanthropy at Indiana University, 59.1 percent of high-net-worth households (those with an annual income of more than $200,000 or a net worth of more than $1 million) made a donation to combination organizations (e.g., United Way) in 2007.[28] This is essentially the same as the 60.1 percent who donated to organizations serving a combination of purposes in 2005, as reported in the *2006 Bank of America Study of High Net-Worth Philanthropy*.

The average gift size in 2007 was $9,038 and the median was $1,000. Average giving for 2007 was a 29.9 percent increase as compared to 2005 (adjusted for inflation). The only other type of organization with a higher average gift amount in 2007, compared to 2005, was health, which realized a 51.2 percent increase. In terms of total dollar amount, combination organizations received 6.8 percent of all giving by high-net-worth households in 2007.

The study also distinguished between giving through personal assets and through foundations, funds, and trusts. The results include the following: 56.4 percent of high-net-worth households gave to combination organizations through their personal assets in 2007, while 13.8 percent gave via foundations, funds, or trusts. The average amount donated through personal assets to combination charities was $3,491 and the median was $1,000. For those who gave through foundations, funds, and trusts, the average amount was $36,937 and the median amount was $5,000.

Key findings from annual studies

Table 4 presents three years of data from several studies appearing annually about giving to organizations in the public-society benefit subsector. Web site addresses are provided so readers can access the full reports.

Table 4
Key findings from other studies about giving to public-society benefit organizations

$10 Million Dollar List, gifts from individuals to public-society benefit (does not include gifts to foundations) Center on Philanthropy at Indiana University, www.philanthropy.iupui.edu			
	2006	2007	2008
Number of public-society benefit gifts	6	7	5
Largest gift to public-society benefit	$33 million from the estate of Hector and Doris Di Stefano to the Disabled American Veterans Charitable Service Trust	$47 million from George Soros to the Open Society Institute	$65 million from the estate of Ric Weiland to the Pride Foundation, a civil rights organization in the state of Washington
Public-society benefit dollars given as percentage of all individual gifts on list of $10 million and above	1.8 percent	0.7 percent	0.7 percent

Foundation Giving Trends: Update on Funding Priorities Grants to public-society benefit organizations Foundation Center, www.foundationcenter.org			
	2005	2006	2007
Average grant amount	$116,166	$121,526	$137,438
Median grant amount	$45,000	$30,000	$30,000
Public-society benefit funding as a percentage of grant dollars (surveyed foundations, including corporate foundations)	11.2 percent	10.7 percent	10.9 percent

Results of United Way campaigns and other fundraising United Way of America, www.liveunited.org			
	2005–2006	2006–2007	2007–2008
Total raised in campaigns	$3.69 billion	$4.07 billion	$4.19 billion
Gifts to specific initiatives	$107 million	$107.5 million	$150.1 million
Realized bequests, endowment gifts, and other realized planned gifts	$67 million	$83.6 million	$72.4 million
Resources under management (amount donated less designated gifts)	$3.3 billion	$3.12 billion	$3.2 billion

United Jewish Communities Annual report, www.ujc.org			
	2006	2007	2008
Total raised, annual campaign	Nearly $900 million	$900 million	> $1 billion
Special initiatives	More than $350 million, Israel Emergency campaign More than $28 million, Katrina relief	$450 million, Israel Emergency Campaign $90M cash $360M pledges	Not in annual report separately
Planned giving	More than $1.1 billion	$1.3 billion	$2.6 billion (includes all contributions to endowment funds)

Combined Federal Campaign Office of Personnel Management, www.opm.gov/cfc			
	2005	2006	2007
Total amount raised	$268.5 million	$271.6 million	$273.1 million

IRS tax-exempt organizations in public-society benefit subsector Charities and Other Tax-Exempt Organizations, 2003, 2004, and 2005 *Statistics of Income Bulletin*, www.irs.gov			
	2003	2004	2005
Number	23,339	24,148	18,182
Charitable revenue*	$28.67 billion	$32.35 billion	$6.19 billion

*Charitable revenue includes gifts and foundation grants (which is comparable to what *Giving USA* tracks), as well as government grants and allocations from other nonprofit agencies, such as the United Way and United Jewish Communities (which are not included in *Giving USA* estimates for contributions).

1   Giving During Recessions, *Giving USA Spotlight*, #3, 2008, www.givingusa.org.

2   Center on Philanthropy at Indiana University, Philanthropic Giving Index, 2008, www.philanthropy.iupui.edu.

3   Fasten your seatbelts: It's going to be a bumpy giving season, Guidestar Newsletter, November 2008, www.guidestar.org.

4   Intel Encourages More Youth to Participate in Math and Science, Intel, Press release, Oct. 20, 2008, www.intel.com.

5   K. Heim, Seattle man who helped launch Microsoft left $65M for gay rights, *Seattle Times*, February 24, 2008, http://seattletimes.nwsource.com.

6   Lilly Endowment announces $50 million for 2008 Indiana storm relief and recovery efforts, Lilly Endowment, Press release, June 23, 2008, www.lillyendowment.org.

7   Comcast Pledges $27 Million in support to City Year, Cityyear.org, Press release, June 6, 2008, www.cityyear.org.

8   E. Scott, Developer makes $25 million pledge to United Way, May 2, 2008, www.azcentral.com.

9   United Way Outlines Ambitious 10 Year Goals Around High School Graduation Rates, Financial Stability and Health, United Way of America, Press release, May 15, 2008, www.liveunited.org.

10   E. Schwinn, Charity's Cutting Edge, *The Chronicle of Philanthropy*, August 21, 2008, www.philanthropy.com.

11   E. Schwinn, United Way hopes to attract new donors as it alters the fundraising landscape, *The Chronicle of Philanthropy*, August 21, 2008, www.philanthropy.com.

12   E. Schwinn, Charity's cutting edge, *The Chronicle of Philanthropy*, August 21, 2008, www.philanthropy.com.

13   A. Lubrano, United Way funding sparks social-service scramble, *Philadelphia Inquirer*, October 16, 2008.

14   P. Rucker, D.C. area nonprofits fear loss of funding as United Way retools, *Washington Post*, May 16, 2008, www.washingtonpost.com.

15   E. Schwinn, Charity's cutting edge, *The Chronicle of Philanthropy*, August 21, 2008, www.philanthropy.com.

16   Same as Note 11, quotations from entire article.

17   www.liveunited.org, viewed May 19, 2009.

18   Major League Baseball, McCormick Foundation Raise Nearly $6 Million For Veterans Through "Welcome Back Veterans," McCormick Foundation, Press release, November 18, 2008, www.mccormicktribune.org.

19   Walmart Foundation Gives $3.6 Million to Veteran's Educational Programs, November 10, 2008, www.walmartstores.com.

20   Anonymous, American Psychiatric Foundation, Lilly Foundation and Give an Hour Join Forces to Provide Mental Health Care to Iraq and Afghanistan Veterans; Expanded Network of Volunteer Mental Health Professionals Will Respond to a Growing Public Health Crisis for Thousands of Veterans and Their Families, *PR Newswire*, May 19, 2008, www.prnewswire.com.

21   T. Tanielian and L.H. Jaycox, (ed.s), *Invisible Wounds: Mental Health and Cognitive Care Needs of America's Returning Veterans*, RAND Center for Military Health Policy Research, 2008, www.rand.org.

22   The National Fund for Workforce Solutions: A History of Collaboration, *Annie E. Casey Foundation*, 2008, www.nfwsolutions.org.

23   www.nfwsolutions.org, viewed May 19, 2009.

24   Information regarding these foundations' revenues, assets, and grants assessed at www.guidestar.org; Information regarding Schwab's charitable distributions on Table 3 can be found at www.schwabcharitable.com.

25   W. Hersch, Taking The Pulse of Charitable Planning, *National Underwriter, Life & Health*, December 1, 2008, www.lifeandhealthinsurancenews.com.

26   Anonymous, What's in Your Philanthropy? New Platform Puts 'Idle' Donor Advised Fund Assets to Work for More Social Impact through Investment, *PR Newswire*, November 18, 2008.

27   Schwab Charitable Pioneers Innovative Microfinance Guarantee Program, Schwab, Press release, Sept. 24, 2008, www.schwabcharitable.org.

28   Center on Philanthropy at Indiana University, *Bank of America Study of High Net-Worth Philanthropy*, 2008, www.philanthropy.iupui.edu.

In Houston, a United Way-affiliated organization offers after-school and summer cultural enrichment programs for youth, such as music lessons.

Organization represented: United Way of Greater Houston (www.unitedwayhouston.org)

Photographer: Justin Calhoun, Houston

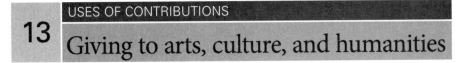
- The arts, culture, and humanities subsector received an estimated $12.79 billion in contributions in 2008.

- This is a drop of 6.4 percent from the estimated total for 2007 (-9.9 percent adjusted for inflation).

- Arts, culture, and humanities giving is 4 percent of total estimated giving.

- The subsector for arts, culture, and humanities includes performing arts; museums of all kinds; historical societies; humanities organizations; and media and communication charities, including public broadcasting. Religious radio, television, and publishers are in the religion subsector.

Giving USA findings for giving to arts, culture, and humanities organizations, 2008

The *Giving USA* estimate is based on a tested model incorporating economic variables and on the historical record of giving to arts, culture, and humanities organizations. The economic variables include changes in stock market prices, personal income, and other economic trends.[1] *Giving USA* will revise the estimates of giving to arts, culture, and humanities and all other subsectors as more data become available. The final figures will be based on data compiled from IRS Forms 990 by the National Center for Charitable Statistics, which are expected to be available in about two years.

Trends in giving to arts, culture, and humanities

Using *Giving USA* data, two different ways of measuring trends in giving to arts, culture, and humanities organizations are presented. The first looks at giving to these organizations during recession years. The second shows the trend in giving to this subsector over time, measured per household (including all arts, culture, and humanities donations divided by all households).

In prior recession years from 1968 to 2006, giving to arts, culture, and humanities organizations averaged an inflation-adjusted increase of 1.8 percent from the prior year. The range was from a decrease of over 13 percent in 1970 to a growth of nearly 14 percent just one year earlier, in 1969. Certainly, at least part of the decline in 1970 can be attributed to the substantial rise in giving in 1969. Giving to this subsector increased (adjusted for inflation) in seven of 11 recession years from 1968 to 2006.[2]

Using a standardized measure of giving to arts, culture, and humanities organizations allows us to compare contributions to this subsector over time. One standard measure is to estimate giving per household. To do this, the sum of contributions from all sources (not just households) is divided by the number of households in the country. Table 1 shows the results for giving to arts,

Table 1
Per household measure of giving to arts, culture, and humanities;
Includes contributions from all sources divided by number of households
(adjusted for inflation)

Year	Per household	# of households
1988	$66	91.12 million
1998	$127	102.53 million
2008	$110	116.78 million

Data: Giving to arts, culture, and humanities from *Giving USA* estimate divided by the number of households in that year from the U.S. Bureau of the Census' Current Population Survey.

culture, and humanities organizations per household since 1988. IRS Forms 990 are used as the basis of estimation of giving to charitable subsectors.

Philanthropic Giving Index for arts drops to 64.3 in 2008, from 90.5 in 2007

In December 2008, the Philanthropic Giving Index (PGI), which measures the fundraising confidence of nonprofit fundraisers and is conducted semi-annually by the Center on Philanthropy, reported a "present situation" index of 64.3 (on a scale of 100) for arts, culture, and humanities organizations.[3] While the overall index was down from 2007, which measured at 90.5, there were several bright spots in arts fundraising that distinguished it from other types of charitable sectors.

- Fundraisers from arts, culture, and humanities organizations were the most likely (47.1 percent) to report an increase in donations received from donors who give a total of less than $1,000.

- Arts and cultural organizations (47.1 percent) were more likely to be in the midst of a capital campaign compared with education and health organizations, but much

less likely compared with religious organizations.

- More development professionals from arts, culture, and humanities organizations reported success with raising funds through planned giving (88.2 percent) than any other fundraising technique or any other type of organization.

Table 2 summarizes the percentage of PGI respondents working in arts, culture, and humanities organizations who reported success with each of several fundraising vehicles or channels. The same people are surveyed in each wave. The table shows the year-end results for 2007 and 2008.

The least successful fundraising techniques reported by these organizations continue to be the Internet, with only 18.8 percent reporting success. The percentages reporting success in the two years were about the same for direct mail, telephone, and Internet.

GuideStar poll finds lower giving levels in 2008

Each year since 2002, GuideStar.org has posted an online poll in the fall asking users of its site to report changes in

Table 2

Percentage of arts, culture and humanities organization respondents
reporting success with fundraising vehicle, 2007–2008

	Direct mail	Telephone	Special events	Planned giving	Major gifts	Corporate	Foundation	Email	Internet
2007	75.0	50.0	58.3	66.7	100.0	58.3	66.7	16.7	16.7
2008	76.5	57.1	70.6	88.2	70.6	47.1	52.9	25.0	18.8

giving to their organizations compared to the prior year.[4] Note that GuideStar asks for responses from any users on their Web site, so the findings are not nationally representative nor are they drawn from a random sample. There were 401 respondents from arts, culture, and humanities organizations in 2008.

In 2008, among poll respondents from arts, culture, and humanities organizations:

- 39 percent reported an increase in contributions received, compared with 2007 when more than half (54 percent) reported an increase;

- 20 percent of participants reported that contributions to their organizations stayed about the same compared to the previous year. This figure did not change markedly compared with the 2007 figure of 21 percent; and

- 37 percent reported a decline in contributions. This figure is markedly higher than that of 2007, when only 21 percent reported a decrease in contributions compared with 2006.

Multimillion-dollar gifts awarded to arts, culture, and humanities organizations

At least six gifts of $25 million or more each were given by individuals to arts, culture, and humanities organizations

and publicly announced in the media in 2008:

- David Koch, whose family founded Koch Industries (the largest private company in the U.S.), gave $100 million to the New York State Theater at Lincoln Center as the lead gift in a capital campaign to enhance and update the auditorium and audience amenities.[5]

- $45 million was given by Stewart and Lynda Resnick, owners of the Franklin Mint, to the Los Angeles County Museum of Art to finance a new 45,000-square-foot exhibition pavilion. The Resnicks also contributed artwork valued at $10 million.[6]

- Siblings Ross Perot, Jr., Katherine Perot, Carolyn Rathjen, Suzanne McGee, and Nancy Mulford gave $50 million to the Museum of Nature and Science in Texas to support construction of a new museum at Dallas' Victory Park, which will be named after their parents.[7]

- John Gunn, CEO of Dodge and Cox Investment Managers, and his wife Cynthia Fry gave $40 million to the San Francisco Opera to fund several opera productions, outreach efforts, and the general director's chair.[8]

- Banker Adrienne Arsht gave $30 million to the Adrienne Arsht

Center for the Performing Arts of Miami-Dade County to help build an endowment and stabilize the Center.[9]

■ Sidney Kimmel, founder of Jones Apparel Group, gave $25 million to the endowment of the Kimmel Center, a performing arts venue in Philadelphia, as part of a larger transfer of funds from numerous philanthropists, foundations, and the City of Philadelphia to secure the Kimmel Center for a "financially healthy and artistically vibrant future."[10]

In 2007, there were five gifts of $90 million or more each. Of those, three included a significant portion in-kind (donated artworks). For 2008, only one announced gift was $100 million. The top gifts were donations to fund activities or capital improvements, and just $10 million was reported in-kind.

Arts organizations think strategically about funding

This section provides information about some of the types of opportunities and challenges faced by arts organizations in 2008 and how they were planning for 2009.

Surviving the economy

Several foundations with a history of arts funding continued to support cultural institutions, some with innovative approaches. Major arts foundation funding includes:

■ The Doris Duke Foundation, which created a new multimillion-dollar program to assist arts organizations across the nation in addressing financial problems innovatively.[11]

■ The John S. and James L. Knight Foundation, which created a $40 million grant program to support endowment growth for Miami-area arts organizations. Recipients included the Miami Art Museum, the Museum of Contemporary Art, and the New World Symphony.[12]

■ The Wallace Foundation, which continued its Excellence Awards program and gave grants to support the arts in Seattle and Minneapolis. Several arts organizations in each community received grants, with at least one award supporting a regional collaboration that will focus on audience development.[13]

Among new and creative ways to raise funds, organizations sought corporate sponsorships and partnerships, as well as partnerships with other nonprofit organizations. Examples of creative sponsorships and partnerships include:

■ The Metropolitan Opera Company, soprano Renee Fleming, and Coty Inc. (a fragrance company) have partnered to create a high-end fragrance inspired by Ms. Fleming, with all of the proceeds to be given to the Met;[14]

■ Bank of America expanded its Museums on Us™ Program, which provides free admission for Bank of America account holders to the partnered museums on the first weekend of each month;[15]

■ The Metropolitan Opera and one of its donors partnered to offer reduced-price admission tickets for the third season in a row. In this program, the donor purchases the tickets at full price and the Met resells them at a lower rate in a strategy to draw in spectators who would otherwise not be able to attend the opera;[16]

- Arts organizations in Indianapolis founded MusicCrossroads, a new entity dedicated to supporting local music and arts organizations in the city and assisting with inter-organizational partnerships;[17] and

- The Chicago History Museum and the Motorola Foundation partnered to create a dedicated grant program designed to celebrate the bicentennial of Abraham Lincoln, which will fund, among other things, arts and cultural organization programs.[18]

"A charitable divide" between large and small organizations affects the arts
The Chronicle of Philanthropy reported that there is a significant "charitable divide" between large and small orga-

nizations.[19] Smaller, more local organizations struggle to raise funds to stay in operation, compared with larger organizations that work with more high-end donors. Evidence of this difference between organization size in the arts subsector was confirmed in studies released in 2008, such as:

- The Greater Philadelphia Cultural Alliance found that small and medium-sized arts organizations in that region depend more on foundation support than do the larger organizations;[20]

- The 2007 Annual Field Report from Opera America found that smaller opera companies depended upon individual giving to a greater extent than did the larger companies;[21] and

- Theatre Communications Group found that 15 percent of organizations with budgets of $10 million and up experienced cash flow problems in 2008, compared with 55 percent of organizations with annual expenses under $500,000. In the middle ranges (budgets from $500,000

GOOD TO KNOW

Arts organizations have many opportunities to build loyalty among donors. Here are some suggestions from members of the Giving Institute:

- Consider cultivating funding opportunities that take advantage of the programming that is already underway. This can include inviting donors to a technical rehearsal or offering members an increased number of exclusive hours to view a special exhibit.

- Offer incentives for subscribers or donors to renew membership early, using a less-costly channel, such as online or by telephone, and by using volunteers rather than sending renewals through the mail.

- Follow the formula that public broadcasting stations use. Offer donors an "installment plan" for gifts and include the option to make a monthly contribution of a certain amount to receive premium benefits.

to $9.9 million), 40 to 48 percent had cash flow problems.[22]

Budgetary emergencies force reductions, closures

2008 found arts organizations, especially smaller entities, across the country contemplating closing their doors due to a widening gap between funds raised and expenditures. For instance:

- The Lincoln Museum in Fort Wayne, IN, closed on June 30, 2008 due to fewer visitors;[23]

- The Baltimore Opera Company in Baltimore, MD, filed for Chapter 11 Bankruptcy and cancelled the remaining productions for the 2008/2009 season;[24]

- The Columbus Symphony Orchestra, which had been threatened with closing earlier in the year, reduced its season and musician salaries in order to remain open;[25] and

- Shakespeare Santa Cruz was able to raise more than $400,000 only after making an emergency plea to its community in order to remain open in 2009.[26]

As the economy worsened toward the end of 2008, even organizations that had a good year began planning for a longer economic downturn. These budgetary and programming decisions included: Cutting budgets, reducing the number of productions, substituting plays with a smaller cast for larger shows, and increasing fees for special exhibits planned for 2009.

Americans for the Arts and Business Committee for the Arts plan merger

With the approval of each organization's board, two advocacy organizations for the arts—Americans for the Arts and the Business Committee for the Arts—announced plans to merge.[27] In a statement announcing the merger, Robert Lynch, president of Americans for the Arts, said, "Despite recent modest gains in overall giving, the market-share of private funding for the arts is nearly one-third less than it was in the early 1990s. By combining our interests and strengths, we will be able to effectively address the challenges ahead." The transaction requires approval of the New York Attorney General and the New York Supreme Court and is expected to be completed in 2009.

GOOD TO KNOW

According to the National Endowment for the Arts, donations by individuals account for 72 percent of private, contributed income at arts organizations; foundations account for 21 percent; and corporations represent 7 percent.[28]

Unlike individual donors, corporations and foundations often know their giving budgets months in advance. Contact a representative for institutions that have funded your organization in the past and ask about their plans for the coming year. If they're not able to give now, keep them in the cultivation loop so they may be reengaged later. Additionally, try to learn when budget decisions for the next year are made so that you can provide timely information.

Reports about arts philanthropy

A number of studies released in 2008 showcased the changing nature of arts funding in the United States. Some of this research is summarized here.

68 percent of high-net-worth households surveyed gave to the arts, 2007

According to the *2008 Bank of America Study of High Net-Worth Philanthropy*, researched and written at the Center on Philanthropy, 68.4 percent of high-net-worth households (with an annual income of more than $200,000 or a net worth of more than $1 million) made a donation to arts, culture, and humanities organizations in 2007.[29] The figure for 2005 in a similar study was 70.1 percent. The average gift size in 2007 was $4,792, which is 71 percent lower than the average gift size in the prior study of giving by high-net-worth households (adjusted for inflation). The median gift for 2007 was $700. The arts, culture, and humanities organizations received 4.2 percent of all the donations made by high-net-worth households in 2007.

This study also distinguished between giving through personal assets and via foundations, funds, and trusts. In 2007,

- 65.4 percent of high-net-worth households gave to arts, culture, and humanities organizations through their personal assets. The average amount donated through personal assets was $3,147, and the median amount donated was $500.

- 17.1 percent gave utilizing foundations, funds, or trusts. The average donation was $11,013, and the median amount donated was $3,500.

Symphony orchestra funding associated with population and area income, but competes with opera funding

Robert Flanagan, a professor at the Stanford Graduate School of Business, studied financial data from 62 orchestras for the years between 1987 and 2003 in order to analyze a number of issues related to orchestra funding. In examining the drivers of charitable giving to symphony orchestras, Dr. Flanagan found two factors that were associated with giving: population of the community in which the orchestra is located and per capita income in the community. Larger communities with larger per capita incomes generated high levels of giving. Unemployment rates and stock market indices were not significant factors in giving to orchestras.

However, the presence of at least one opera company in the same market area is associated with a decline of about 7 percent in the total philanthropic gifts to the symphony. Interestingly, Dr. Flanagan found that an increase in development expenditures by opera companies in one year were associated with declines in orchestra philanthropic gifts received in the following year, after controlling for population size, per capita income, and other variables.

Dr. Flanagan also found that higher fundraising expenses were associated, as expected, with receiving more in donations. However, among large symphonies (budget over $9 million in the late 1990s), even with 14 years of data, an additional dollar in fundraising expense resulted in 51 cents in donations. In contrast, smaller orchestras (< $9 million budget) raised $1.96 per dollar in fundraising costs over the years of the study. There are many possible explanations for this difference, but one important point that Dr. Flanagan makes is that orchestras in larger cities with higher per capita income might be expending on fundraising when orchestra patrons in that area would give anyway. Further, he recognizes that deferred gifts and

major gifts take many years of engagement with a donor, which impacts upon these differences.

Key data from annual studies summarized

Table 3 presents three years of data from several studies appearing annually about giving to the arts, culture, and humanities organizations. Web site addresses are provided so readers can access the full reports.

Table 3
Key findings from other studies about giving to arts organizations

Million Dollar List, gifts from individuals $10 million and above (2006–2008) to arts organizations Center on Philanthropy at Indiana University, www.philanthropy.iupui.edu			
	2006	2007	2008
Number of gifts to arts, culture, and humanities	25	15	13
Largest gift to arts, culture, and humanities: Cash	$35 million to the San Francisco Opera from Jeannik Mequet Littlefield	$90 million to the New World Symphony from an anonymous donor	$100 million to New York State Theater in Lincoln Center from David Koch
In-kind		$1 billion (estimated) combined value of eight collections donated to the Seattle Art Museum	
Arts, culture, and humanities gifts as a percentage of all individual gifts on list of $10 million or above	2.6 percent, not including Warren Buffet's pledge to the Gates Foundation	3.6 percent	3.5 percent

Foundation Giving Trends, 2007, 2008, and 2009 editions Grants for the arts Foundation Center, www.foundationcenter.org			
	2005	2006	2007
Average grant amount	$109,885	$115,934	$106,552
Median grant amount	$25,000	$25,000	$25,000
Arts funding as percentage of grant dollars (surveyed foundations)	12.5 percent	12.2 percent	10.6 percent

State of North America's Art Museums Survey Association of Art Museum Directors, www.aamd.org			
Survey conducted about significant change in:	2005 n=129	2006 n=167	2007 n=125
Overall revenue			
Decline	16%	6%	17%
Increase	47%	58%	55%
No change	37%	36%	28%
Individual gifts			
Decline	7%	4%	10%
Increase	70%	73%	67%
No change	23%	23%	23%
Foundations			
Decline	12%	8%	13%
Increase	50%	33%	45%
No change	38%	46%	42%
Corporations			
Decline	20%	18%	31%
Increase	34%	33%	31%
No change	46%	49%	38%
Earned income			
Decline	16%	1%	25%
Increase	44%	65%	51%
No change	40%	34%	24%

Theatre Facts Theatre Communications Group, www.tcg.org			
	2004	2005	2006
Number of theatres that responded to the TCG Fiscal Survey each year over 5 years ("Trend" Theatres)	n=100	n=105	n=117
Average contributions to "Trend" Theatres	$2,879,549	$3,202,216	$2,798,173
Average percentage of contributions, as a portion of total revenue, to "Trend" Theatres from: Individuals Foundations Corporations Government Other (in-kind, events, arts funds)	36.6 18.8 11.3 14.9 18.5	37.2 19.7 10.8 12.8 19.5	38.4 20.5 10.8 8.6 21.7
Contributions as a percentage of net income in "Trend" Theatres	44.2	42.3	39.1

IRS tax-exempt organizations in arts, culture, and humanities Charities and Other Tax-exempt Organizations, 2003, 2004, and 2005 Statistics of Income Bulletin, www.irs.gov			
	2003	2004	2005
Number of organizations	27,285	28,615	28,972
Charitable revenue*	$14.01 billion	$14.15 billion	$15.86 billion

*Charitable revenue includes gifts and foundation grants (which is comparable to what *Giving USA* tracks), as well as government grants and allocations from other nonprofit agencies, such as the United Way and United Jewish Communities (which are not included in *Giving USA* estimates for contributions).

1 The model used to estimate giving was tested in late fall 2007 and early 2008 by Partha Deb (Hunter College, NY) and found to be the most accurate method of predicting giving to arts, culture, and humanities over time.

2 Giving during recessions, *Giving USA Spotlight*, #3, 2008, available from www.givingusa.org.

3 The Center on Philanthropy at Indiana University, Philanthropic Giving Index, December 2008, www.philanthropy.iupui.edu.

4 Seventh Annual GuideStar Nonprofit Survey: Charitable Organizations and the Economy, Oct. 6-20, 2008, Released in the fall, 2008, www.guidestar.org.

5 P. Cole, David Koch to give $100 million to N.Y. opera, ballet, *Bloomberg*, July 10, 2008, www.bloomberg.com.

6 J. Adelman, LA County Museum of Art gets $45 million cash gift, ABC News, September 29, 2008, www.abcnews.com.

7   J. Farmer, Perot family donates $50 million for science museum, Texas Cable News, May 30, 2008, www.txcn.com.

8   M. Boehm, Quick Takes: S.F. Opera gets $40-million gift, *Los Angeles Times*, September 16, 2008, www.latimes.com.

9   P. Boroff, Miami arts center renamed for Arsht after $30 million donation, Bloomberg, January 10, 2008, www.bloomberg.com.

10 No author, Kimmel Center in PA receives multi-million dollar grants, Broadway World, April 23, 2008, www.broadwayworld.com.

11 Doris Duke Charitable Foundation and Nonprofit Finance Fund Kick Off Bold $15.125 Million Arts Initiative to Address Sector-Wide Challenges; 10 Arts Organizations Receive Grants to Explore Promising New Business Practices and Programs, *PR Newswire*, October 14, 2008.

12 D. Chang, $40M cash bonanza for arts groups, *The Miami Herald*, February 7, 2008, www.herald.com.

13 Wallace Foundation, press release, The Wallace Foundation awards $6.9 million to Minneapolis St. Paul arts community, November 13, 2008; Wallace Foundation, press release, The Wallace Foundation awards $7.7 million to support Seattle arts community, November 19, 2008, both at www.wallacefoundation.org.

14 Coty Inc. to Launch La Voce by Renee Fleming; Beauty Company to Donate Proceeds from Sales of Limited Edition Prestige Fragrance to the Metropolitan Opera, *PR Newswire*, July 14, 2008.

15 Bank of America Announces Significant Expansion to Museums on Us™ Program; Free access now available first weekend of every month; 28 geographic markets now participating in program, *PR Newswire*, April 28, 2008.

16 M. McKinney, The Spirit of Giving, *Opera News*, December 2008.

17 J. Whitson, City becoming music magnet, *Indianapolis Business Journal*, May 19, 2008.

18 Motorola Celebrates Lessons from Abraham Lincoln's Life with Dedicated Grant Program, *Business Wire*, February 11, 2008.

19 H. Hall, A Charitable Divide, *The Chronicle of Philanthropy*, January 10, 2008, www.philanthropy.com.

20 Greater Philadelphia Cultural Alliance, *Key Findings 2008 Portfolio*, 2008.

21 L. Bomback and A. Cekay, Opera America, *Highlights from the 2007 Annual Field Report*, Winter 2008.

22 Theatre Communications Group, *Snapshot Survey: Taking Your Fiscal Pulse*, www.tcg.org.

23 J. Boen, Lincoln Museum to close June 30: Foundation plans to move key artifacts to other museums, *The News-Sentinel*, March 4, 2008, www.FortWayne.com.

24 D. Itzkoff, Baltimore Opera files for bankruptcy, *The New York Times*, December 9, 2008, www.nytimes.com.

25 J. Sheban, Music director leaving Columbus Symphony, *Columbus Dispatch*, November 14, 2008, www.dispatch.com.

26 As We See It: Hits and Misses, *Santa Cruz Sentinel*, December 23, 2008, www.santacruzsentinel.com.

27 Americans for the Arts, press release, Americans for the Arts and Business Committee for the Arts Merge Operations, October 30, 2008, www.artsusa.org.

28 National Endowment for the Arts Office of Research and Analysis, *How the United States Funds the Arts*, Second edition, January 2007, www.nea.gov.

29 The Center on Philanthropy, *The 2008 Bank of America Study of High Net-Worth Philanthropy*, March 2009, www.philanthropy.iupui.edu.

Pictured are two young circus performers, Donald and Menar, from the Peace through Pyramids project—
a collaboration between the St. Louis Arches, an American youth circus troupe, and the Galilee Circus,
a Jewish/Arab youth troupe from Israel.

Organization represented: Circus Harmony, St. Louis, MO (www.circusharmony.org)

Photographer: Chris Mrozewski, St. Louis, MO

14 — USES OF CONTRIBUTIONS
Giving to international affairs

- Giving to organizations in the international affairs subsector is estimated to be $13.3 billion in 2008.

- This is an increase of 0.6 percent (-3.1 percent adjusted for inflation) compared with the value for 2007.

- Giving for international affairs is 4 percent of total estimated giving in 2008.

- The international affairs subsector includes charities formed for international aid, development, or relief; those that promote international understanding (including exchange programs); and organizations working on international peace and security issues. It also includes research institutes devoted to foreign policy and analysis, and organizations working in the domain of international human rights.

Giving USA findings for giving to international affairs, 2008

The amount estimated in giving to organizations in the international subsector[1] includes gifts of cash, cash equivalents (securities), and gifts in kind (food, medicine, equipment, and other items of value). The *Giving USA* estimate is based on a tested model that uses the historical relationship between giving to international affairs organizations and changes in stock market prices, personal income, and other economic trends.

Support for international activities that is not included in the *Giving USA* estimate for international affairs includes:

- Gifts that support health or education endeavors working internationally, which are placed in the health and education subsectors; and

- Gifts made directly to organizations located abroad. For corporations and individuals, gifts made abroad are not included in *Giving USA* because the amount is not known—

the gifts are not eligible for a tax deduction as a charitable contribution under U.S. tax law. No national data about such gifts is available. For foundation grantmaking, the amount of the donation is known and included in *Giving USA* in the "unallocated" portion of total giving.

Trends in international affairs giving

Using *Giving USA* data, two different ways of measuring trends in giving to international affairs organizations are presented. The first looks at giving to these organizations during recession years. The second shows the trend in giving to the international affairs subsector over time, measured per household (including all international affairs donations divided by all households).

In prior recession years from 1987 to 2006, giving to international affairs organizations averaged an inflation-adjusted increase of 9.1 percent from the prior year. The range was from a decrease of over 9 percent in 1991 to a growth of over 24 percent a year earlier,

Table 1
Per household measure of giving to international affairs subsector
Includes contributions from all sources divided by number of households
(adjusted for inflation)

Year	Per household	# of households
1988	$18	91.12 million
1998	$65	102.53 million
2008	$114	116.78 million

Data: Giving to international affairs organizations from *Giving USA* estimate divided by the number of households in that year from the U.S. Bureau of the Census' Current Population Survey.

in 1990. Certainly, part of the decline in 1991 can be attributed to the substantial rise in giving in 1990. Note, as well, that data collection on international giving only began in 1987; therefore only three recession years are included in this analysis. Two of these three recession years saw an increase in charitable giving to this subsector.[2]

Using a standardized measure of giving to international organizations allows us to compare contributions to this subsector over time. One standard measure is to estimate giving per household. To do this, the sum of contributions from all sources (not just households) is divided by the number of households in the country. Table 1 shows the results for giving to international affairs organizations per household since 1988. This year is the most recent year for which data are available based on IRS Forms 990, which are used as the basis of estimation of giving to charitable subsectors.

Philanthropic Giving Index "present situation" drops to 54.9 for public-society benefit, environment, animals, and international affairs (PEAI)

In December 2008, the Philanthropic Giving Index, which is conducted semi-annually by the Center on Philanthropy to assess senior fundraisers' perceptions of the climate for fundraising, reported a "present situation" index of 54.9 (on a scale of 100) for a combination of organizations that includes those in three subsectors: public-society benefit; environment and animals; and international affairs (PEAI).[3] This is a decrease from the "present situation" index of 79.1 reported in December 2007[4] and is the lowest level of fundraising confidence expressed for the PEAI cluster since the PGI began in 1998. The December 2008 PGI reported that:

- PEAI fundraisers, along with those in human services, had the lowest PGI in December 2008, indicating that charities in these areas had less success overall in raising gifts and were less optimistic about fundraising in six months (the expectations index).

- Fundraisers in this group were among those least likely to report success with email fundraising, at just 12.5 percent. This compares with one-third of religious fundraisers and 43 percent of education fundraisers.

Table 2
Percentage of public-society benefit, environment and animals,
and international affairs (PEAI) respondents reporting success
with fundraising vehicle, 2007–2008

	Direct mail	Telephone	Special events	Planned giving	Major gifts	Corporate	Foundation	Email	Internet
2007	58.8	25.0	70.6	76.5	76.5	52.9	76.5	12.5	29.4
2008	43.8	43.8	93.8	62.5	62.5	37.5	68.8	12.5	37.5

- More fundraisers in the PEAI cluster reported success with special events (93.8 percent) than did fundraisers in other subsectors. In most other types of charities, special events were less likely to be reported as successful compared with major gifts. In comparison, PEAI subsector respondents reported 62.5 percent success with major gifts.

Table 2 shows the success by type of fundraising reported by public-society benefit, environment and animals, and international affairs organization respondents in 2007 and 2008.

Compared with 2007, PEAI organization respondents reported particularly pronounced declines in corporate gifts (from 52.9 percent reporting success in 2007 to 37.5 reporting success in 2008) and in planned giving and major gifts (both dropping from 76.5 percent success rates in 2007 to 62.5 percent in 2008).

Million-dollar-and-up gifts to international affairs announced in 2008

Not including gifts from the Bill & Melinda Gates Foundation, at least two gifts of $25 million or more were given to international aid/relations/affairs organizations in 2008 and publicly announced in the media. These include:

- $30 million from Lorry I. Lokey to the American Committee for the Weizmann Institute of Science to further international scientific education and research. The Weizmann Institute is located in Israel, so the U.S.-based fundraising arm is coded in the international subsector by GuideStar.org. A science research institute based in the United States would be in the public-society benefit subsector.[5]

- $30 million from the Adelson Family Foundation to the Birthright Israel Foundation to support a program that funds trips to Israel for Jewish youths.[6]

GOOD TO KNOW

The Foundation Center and the Conference Board both reported growth in gifts and grants by institutional donors directly to charitable entities located in other countries.[7]

Trends emerging in international aid giving

International aid giving is being directed toward ending global poverty in a variety of new ways. International aid organizations focus on women's health and education, as well as increasing the aid given to support agriculture. Microfinance and support for innovation continue to be priorities for many other organizations. As mentioned in the section on giving to the environment, safe water has also gained in importance for many donors.

Programs for international aid focus on women

The Microcredit Summit Campaign, which provides small loans to impoverished people, seeks women borrowers for micro-loans because experience shows that women are a better credit risk and are more likely to invest money in providing for their families. In addition, women themselves benefit from the empowerment and independence of owning their own businesses.[8] Other microcredit lending organizations have also begun to follow this policy, including CARE, Women's World Banking, and Oxfam.

Increased giving to agricultural programs

The surge in global food prices during 2008 increased the risk for starvation and social unrest in poor countries, prompting an increase in charitable giving to international agriculture. In January 2008, the Bill & Melinda Gates Foundation announced a $306 million package of agricultural development grants designed to boost the yields and incomes of millions of small farmers in Africa and throughout the developing world. The largest Gates grant of $164.5 million went to the Alliance for a Green Revolution in Africa (AGRA), an Africa-based partnership focused on helping small farmers increase their productivity and incomes. Five other agricultural grants totaling $141.5 million went to CARE, Heifer International, International Development Enterprises, International Rice Research Institute, and TechnoServe.[9] This expanded the Gates' support for agricultural programs by approximately 50 percent, increasing from $160 million in 2007 to $240 million in 2008.[10] The Rockefeller Foundation also supported the International Rice Research Institute with a $4 million grant and gave $3 million to the UN World Food Programme.[11]

Funders support the UN World Food Programme and P4P initiative

The World Food Programme (WFP) announced the Purchase for Progress (P4P), a new partnership initiative designed to expand market access for small farmers, primarily in Sub-Saharan Africa and Central America. The Bill & Melinda Gates Foundation committed $66 million and the Howard G. Buffett Foundation committed $9.1 million to support pilot projects in several countries.[12]

Additionally, YUM! Brands announced a $50 million cash pledge to WFP over the next five years to provide meals to children at school.[13] Actress Drew Barrymore also made a personal donation of $1 million to the WFP, kicking off WFP's challenge to America to help feed 10 million children for a year.[14]

Investments continue to support entrepreneurship and microfinance

The Omidyar Network, established by eBay founder Pierre Omidyar and his wife, announced major commitments to microfinance and supporting market development in emerging economies. The group's foundation will grant $9 million to Unitus for expanding microfinance projects into several new regions over the next three years.[15] Another commitment of up to $10 million granted to Endeavor will promote economic development through identifying and supporting high-impact entrepreneurs. Endeavor strives to give local entrepreneurs the tools and training to become high-impact innovators and is part of the growing trend of harnessing capitalism for international development.[16]

Charitable response to international disaster relief and conflict

During 2008, two major natural disasters in China and Myanmar elicited charitable support from U.S.-based donors. Although neither disaster reached the scale of the 2004 Asian tsunami, American charities raised over $72 million for the disasters.[17] In addition, donors responded to pleas for assistance resulting from civil war and ongoing famine in Sudan.

Robust response to China earthquake in Sichuan

On May 12, 2008, a powerful earthquake struck the Sichuan province of China, killing over 80,000 people and displacing 20 million from their homes.[18] The American Red Cross contributed $10 million to support the relief and recovery efforts of the Red Cross Society of China with corporations and their foundations pledging over $6.4 million.[19] In total, American donors gave over $85 million to relief efforts, of which $49 million was in cash and pledges, and more than $36 million in goods and services donated in kind.[20]

Donors respond to Myanmar cyclone despite government obstacles

Tropical cyclone Nargis struck Myanmar on May 2, 2008, causing the worst natural disaster in the country's history, affecting 2.4 million and killing approximately 130,000 people. In the first three weeks following the disaster, the country's governing military rulers blocked most outside aid and prohibited most foreign aid workers from entering the country. Despite initial resistance, aid expanded throughout 2008 and Americans donated $30.1 million through private charities.[21]

Conflicts around the globe spur donor efforts

Rising international tensions and ongoing conflicts in Georgia, the Gaza Strip, Afghanistan, Iraq, and Sudan prompted a response from U.S.-based donors.

■ Celebrities Ben Affleck and Mick Jagger announced the creation of a media campaign called "Gimme Shelter" to raise money for and to increase awareness of the conflict in the Democratic Republic of the Congo in association with the UN Refugee Agency, UNHCR. The campaign centers on a short film titled "Gimme Shelter," which is set to the Rolling Stones song and highlights the plight of 1.3 million displaced people in the Congo. It hopes to raise $23 million during 2009 for emergency humanitarian aid in the region.[22]

- Armed conflict erupted in the Georgian regions of South Ossetia and Abkhazia between August 5-12, 2008, following mounting tensions between Georgia and Russia. The conflict displaced up to 100,000 people and created 30,000 refugees. Many aid organizations responded to the emergency humanitarian crisis, including 22 members of InterAction.[23]

- Conflict intensified between Israel and militants in the Gaza Strip beginning on December 27 following an end to the ceasefire between Israel and Palestine's Hamas. The American Red Cross and others quickly began to support organizations responding to the growing crisis.[24]

- Deteriorating security conditions in Afghanistan during 2008 worsened the humanitarian situation in the country, especially for refugees and returnees.[25]

- U.S. and international humanitarian groups continued to operate in Iraq, yet fewer organizations returned after trends in rising violence subsided during 2007.[26]

- In 2008, Sudan continued to cope with conflict, displacement, and insecurity in the western region of Darfur and bordering regions of Chad. Several U.S. celebrities including Kobe Bryant,[27] Don Cheadle, George Clooney, Matt Damon, and Brad Pitt worked to bring attention and donations to ending the conflict.[28]

Clinton Global Initiative (CGI) expands commitments

At its fourth annual meeting in 2008, the CGI received 250 new pledges valued at $8 billion. Participants at the meeting were asked to make a "Commitment to Action" in CGI's focus areas: education, energy and climate change, and public health.[30] The CGI also expanded its global outreach through the first CGI Asia meeting held in Hong Kong. CGI Asia members made commitments with an estimated total value of $185 million.[31]

GOOD TO KNOW

Celebrity spokespeople and media coverage of conflict areas are two ways that residents of the United States become aware of urgent needs in other countries.

In the 2005 wave of the Center on Philanthropy Panel Study, 5 percent of American households reported giving to international aid or relief organizations. The average gift from donor households was $342. This compares with 29 percent who gave an average of $482 to help meet people's basic needs. This is the most recent data available as of May 2009.[29]

President Clinton also began Clinton Global Initiative University (CGIU), a project to encourage college students to take on global problems with concrete steps and commitments. CGIU's inaugural meeting was held at Tulane University in March 2008 and brought together students, academics, and social, political, and cultural leaders to discuss pressing issues and solutions.[32]

Studies on charitable support for international affairs organizations

A number of research studies that include examinations of charitable support for international affairs organizations were published in 2008. These studies examined contributions from high net-worth individuals, international development activities by U.S. organizations, corporate international giving priorities, and international foundation giving. The results of these studies are summarized below.

Donations to International Affairs by High-Net-Worth Individuals

According to the *2008 Bank of America Study of High Net-Worth Philanthropy*, written at the Center on Philanthropy at Indiana University, 29.5 percent of high-net-worth households (with an annual income of more than $200,000 or a net worth of more than $1 million) made a donation to international organizations in 2007. This is the lowest participation rate among the types of organizations in the study but compares favorably with the 5 percent of households in a general population study.[33]

The average gift size to international organizations from high-net-worth

households in 2007 was $4,062, and the median was $500. International organizations received the lowest share (1.5 percent) of the total giving by high-net-worth households in 2007. It is also noteworthy, that 11.1 percent of high-net-worth households with a secondary residence made a donation to international organizations, while only 1.6 percent of those without a secondary residence did so.

The study also differentiated between giving through personal assets and through foundations, funds, and trusts. In this case, the figures are the following:

- 27.3 percent of high-net-worth households gave to international organizations through their personal assets in 2007 and the average amount contributed was $2,436. The median was $500.

- 6.1 percent gave to international affairs through foundations, funds, or trusts. The average amount was $13,429 and the median was $1,000.[34]

Hudson Institute Index of Global Philanthropy

The Hudson Institute's Center on Global Prosperity released its third edition of *The Index of Global Philanthropy* in 2008 estimating the international development activities by U.S. organizations to outside countries. The index measures official development assistance, private philanthropy, remittances, and private capital flows, which totaled $193.1 billion dollars worth of engagement during 2006. Direct charitable investment, fitting with the *Giving USA*

Table 3
Private assistance flows (in billions of dollars) from U.S. donors to other countries

Source of Aid	2008	2007
Foundations	$4.0	$2.2
Corporations	$5.5	$5.1
Private Voluntary Organizations	$12.8	$16.2
Colleges and Universities	$3.7	$4.6
Religious Organizations	$8.8	$5.4
Total	**$34.8**	**$33.5**

Source: Index of Global Philanthropy 2008, p. 17; 2007, p.14

definition, totaled $34.8 billion dollars in U.S. private capital flows. Table 3 reports the breakdown of private sources of charitable dollars in the 2007 and 2008 editions.[35]

The total of $34.8 billion shows a slight increase from $33.5 billion, which was reported in the 2007 edition. The 2008 report uses some differing methodologies from the 2007 report. Notably, religious giving increased by almost two-thirds (63 percent) based on gathering data through the first random sample of giving by religious organizations from the University of Notre Dame's Center for the Study of Religion and Society. This survey of religious giving reported that 57 percent of religious organizations contributed to relief and development in other countries with an average contribution of $10,700. Private voluntary organization assistance was the largest category for both years and includes the value of volunteer time estimated at $2.2 billion for the 2007 edition.

Corporate international giving allocated primarily in Europe
The Conference Board's *2008 Corporate Contributions Report* included infor-

mation on the geographic allocation of corporate international giving during 2007 from 86 U.S. firms for the first time in its publication. Companies reported contributing the most to Europe, followed by Asia-Pacific (India and China not included) and Canada (See Figure 1).

Companies were also asked about the criteria they use to determine giving outside of the U.S. The top drivers for international allocation were the size of the company's workforce in the local market (selected by 54 percent of companies) and humanitarian needs (selected by 52 percent). Other reasons included the opportunity for business growth in the local market (34 percent), company revenue in the local market (31 percent), and the potential for local economic development (20 percent).[36]

International foundation giving reaches record levels
A report released in December 2008 by the Foundation Center and the Council on Foundations, *International Grantmaking IV: An Update on U.S. Foundation Trends*, reported that U.S. foundations gave a record $5.4 billion for international purposes in 2007,

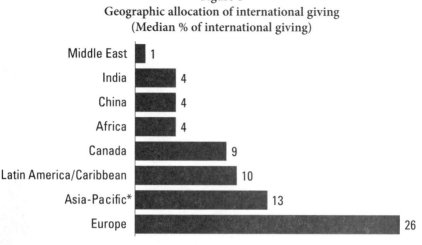

Figure 1
Geographic allocation of international giving
(Median % of international giving)

Middle East	1
India	4
China	4
Africa	4
Canada	9
Latin America/Caribbean	10
Asia-Pacific*	13
Europe	26

*Excludes China and India
Source: The Conference Board, The *2008 Corporate Contributions Report*

and giving in 2008 was likely to exceed that benchmark.

Trends show that international giving grew faster than overall giving between 2002 and 2007, after inflation, rising by more than 50 percent from $3.2 billion in 2002. In comparison, during the same period, foundation giving rose 22.3 percent; the Gates Foundation accounted for more than half of the increase in funding. Increases in international giving were also attributed to an increase in funding by new or newly large foundations, as well as the foundations' responses to natural and humanitarian disasters.

Over one third (36.8 percent) of international funders made grants directly to overseas recipients—mainly to global programs based in Western Europe (such as the Global Fund to Fight AIDS, Tuberculosis, and Malaria and the World Health Organization), and

to targeted programs focused on Sub-Saharan Africa. International health issues captured the largest share of international grant dollars in 2006, while funding for international development tripled in growth from 2002 to 2006.

Among the 20 leading grantmakers, most reported they expect their contributions to international causes will grow during the next two to three years, even if there is a prolonged downturn in the U.S. economy.[37]

Key findings from annual studies summarized

Table 2 presents three years of data from studies released annually about contributions to the international affairs organizations. Web site addresses are provided so readers can access the full reports.

Table 2

Key findings from other studies about giving to international affairs organizations

Million Dollar List, gifts from individuals $10 million and above (2006–2008) to international organizations (does not include gifts to foundations) Center on Philanthropy at Indiana University, www.philanthropy.iupui.edu			
	2006	2007	2008
Number of international affairs gifts	4	6	2
Largest gift to international affairs	$50 million from Warren E. Buffett to the Nuclear Threat Initiative, to jump-start the creation of a reserve fuel bank run by the International Atomic Energy Agency $50 million from George Soros to help eliminate poverty in African nations $50 million pledge from John and Jacque Weberg for a microfinance program at Opportunity International	$75 million to Hadassah: The Women's Zionist Organization of America, for a hospital in Israel, from William and Karen Davidson	$30 million to American Committee for the Weizmann Institute of Science from Lorry I. Lokey for international scientific education and research
International affairs gifts as a percentage of all individual gifts $10 million and above	1.1 percent	0.7 percent	1.2 percent

Foundation Giving Trends: Update on Funding Priorities Grants in the major subject category of international affairs, development, and peace Foundation Center, www.foundationcenter.org			
	2005	2006	2007
Average grant amount	$172,366	$270,990	$273,668
Median grant amount	$45,000	$50,000	$50,000
International subsector funding as a percentage of grant dollars (surveyed foundations, including corporate foundations)	3.6 percent	5.3 percent	4.5 percent

IRS tax-exempt organizations in international affairs subsector Charities and Other Tax-Exempt Organizations, 2003, 2004, and 2005 *Statistics of Income Bulletin*, www.irs.gov			
	2003	2004	2005
Number filing IRS Form 990	3,131	3,486	4,167
Charitable revenue reported*	$13.10 billion	$15.36 billion	$16.70 billion

*Charitable revenue includes gifts and foundation grants (which is comparable to what *Giving USA* tracks), as well as government grants and allocations from other nonprofit agencies, such as the United Way and United Jewish Communities (which are not included in *Giving USA* estimates for contributions).

1   Giving to the international affairs subsector includes contributions to organizations formed for purposes of providing international relief and development aid, promoting international understanding or exchange, engaging in policy issues related to national and international security, or advancing human rights internationally. Organizations in this subsector are classified in the National Taxonomy of Exempt Entities (NTEE) as being in Major Category Q.

2   Giving during recessions, *Giving USA Spotlight*, #3, 2008, available from www.givingusa.org.

3   The Center on Philanthropy at Indiana University, Philanthropic Giving Index, December 2008, www.philanthropy.iupui.edu.

4   The Center on Philanthropy at Indiana University, Philanthropic Giving Index, December 2007, www.philanthropy.iupui.edu.

5   *Business Wire* Founder Lorry I. Lokey Donates $50 Million to Weizmann Institute of Science in Israel, The American Committee for the Weizmann Institute of Science, Press release, Jan. 7, 2008, www.weizmann-usa.org.

6   Adelson Shrinks Giving to Birthright, the *Jewish Daily Forward*, Sept. 18, 2008, www.forward.com.

7   S. Lawrence and R. Mukai, *International Grantmaking IV: Highlights*, Foundation Center, page 5, www.foundationcenter.org; C. Cavicchio and J. Torok, *The 2008 Corporate Contributions Report*, The Conference Board, page 28, www.conference-board.org.

8   About the Microcredit Summit Campaign, Microcredit Summit Campaign, www.microcreditsummit.org.

9   $306 million commitment to agricultural development, Gates Foundation, Press release, Jan. 25, 2008, www.gatesfoundation.org.

10 Gates Foundation to boost farm aid 50% as food crisis deepens, *Bloomberg News*, April 24. 2008, www.bloomberg.com.

11 Rockefeller Foundation grants search, www.rockfound.org.

12 Purchase for Progress Initiative launched in New York, World Food Programme, Press release, September 24, 2008, www.wfp.org.

13 WFP welcomes historic commitment led by YUM! Brands to school feeding at CGI, World Food Programme, Press release, September 25, 2008, www.wfp.org.

14 Drew Barrymore announces US $1 million donation on Oprah, *Reuters*, March 3, 2008, www.reuters.com.

15 Omidyar Network and Unitus to help millions of the working poor participate in the global economy, Omidyar Network, Press release, April 23, 2008, www.omidyar.net.

16 Endeavor receives $10 million commitment from Omidyar Network to support high-impact entrepreneurship in emerging markets, *Business Wire*, July 31, 2008, www.businesswire.com.

17 C. Preston, U.S. charities raise more than $70-million for Asian disasters, *Chronicle of Philanthropy*, June 3, 2008, www.philanthropy.com.

18 IFRC, China Earthquake: Facts and Figures,

October 31, 2008, www.ifrc.org.

19 America Generously Responds to China Earthquake, American Red Cross, Press release, May 23, 2008, www.americanredcross.org.

20 The US-China Business Council, US company contributions for earthquake relief, June 25, 2008, www.uschina.org.

21 C. Adelman, The boom in private giving, *International Herald Tribune*, June, 4, 2008, www.iht.com.

22 Ben Affleck video unveiled for UNHCR "Gimme Shelter" campaign, *Reuters AlertNet*, December 17, 2008, www.alertnet.org.

23 Georgia: InterAction members respond to crisis in the Caucasus, InterAction, Press release, August 13, 2008, www.interaction.org.

24 Red Cross Partners Respond to Crisis in Gaza, American Red Cross, Press release, Dec. 31, 2008, www.redcross.org.

25 Refugees International, Afghanistan: Invest in people, July 10, 2008, www.refugeesinternational.org.

26 J. Hagengruber, In a desert camp, Iraqis find aid and zone of trust, *Christian Science Monitor*, November, 7, 2008, www.csmonitor.com.

27 H. Araton, Gingerly, the athlete turns activist, *The New York Times*, March 15, 2008, www.nytimes.com.

28 Oxfam, Chad/Sudan: Celebrity advocacy & aid organization donates $500,000 to Oxfam America, 11 Dec. 11, 2008, www.reliefweb.int.

29 The Center on Philanthropy at Indiana University, Philanthropy Panel Study,

www.philanthropy.iupui.edu.

30 Former President Clinton announces global impact of Clinton Global Initiative at conclusion of annual meeting, Clinton Global Initiative, Press release, Sept. 26, 2008, www.clintonglobalinitiative.org.

31 Former President Clinton concludes CGI Asia meeting and announces impact of commitment, Clinton Global Initiative, Press release, Dec. 3, 2008

32 J. Pope, Bill Clinton talks student activism, *USA Today*, March 13, 2008, www.usatoday.com.

33 The Center on Philanthropy at Indiana University, Philanthropy Panel Study, 2005 wave, www.philanthropy.iupui.edu.

34 The Center on Philanthropy at Indiana University, *Bank of America Study of High Net-Worth Philanthropy*, 2008, www.philanthropy.iupui.edu.

35 Center for Global Prosperity, *The Index of Global Philanthropy*, 2008, Hudson Institute, www.hudson.org.

36 The Conference Board, *The 2008 Corporate Contributions Report*, December 2008, www.conference-board.org.

37 The Foundation Center and the Council on Foundations, *International Grantmaking IV: An Update on U.S. Foundation Trends*, December 2008, www.cof.org. The 2007 estimates and the 2008 forecast were based on a survey of nearly 80 foundations that give the most to international causes, while trends in international giving through 2006 are based on grants awarded by approximately 1,000 of the wealthiest U.S. foundations.

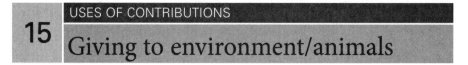

15 Giving to environment/animals

- Donations to environment/animals organizations fell to an estimated $6.58 billion in 2008.

- This is a decline of 5.5 percent (-9 percent adjusted for inflation).

- This subsector is 2 percent of total estimated giving.

- The environment/animals subsector includes zoos and aquariums; botanical gardens and horticultural programs; humane societies and other animal rescue organizations; wildlife and habitat preservation groups; and groups working for pollution abatement or control. It also includes programs for environmental education, outdoor survival, and beautification of open spaces.

Giving USA findings for giving to environment/animals organizations, 2008

The estimate for the change in giving to organizations in the environment/animals subsector is based on the historical relationship between giving to environment/animals charities and broader economic trends.[1] Specifically, the estimate looks at changes in personal income, changes in wealth as measured by the Standard & Poor's 500 stock index, and changes in giving in the recent past.

Giving USA will revise the estimates of giving to environment/animals organizations and all other subsectors as more data become available. The final figures will be based on data compiled from IRS Forms 990 by the National Center for Charitable Statistics.

Trends in giving to the environment/ animals subsector

Using *Giving USA* data, two different ways of measuring trends in giving to environment/animals organizations are presented. The first looks at giving to these organizations during recession years. The second shows the trend in giving to the environment/animals subsector over time, measured per household (including all environment/animals donations divided by all households).

In prior recession years from 1987 to 2006, giving to environment/animals organizations averaged an inflation-adjusted increase of 6.2 percent from the prior year. The range was from a growth of 5 percent in 1990 to a growth of over 8 percent in 2001. Note that data collection on giving to environment/animals organizations only began in 1987; therefore, only three recession years are included in this analysis up through 2006.[2]

Using a standardized measure of giving to environment/animals organizations allows us to compare contributions to this subsector over time. One standard measure is to estimate giving per household. To do this, the sum of contributions from all sources (not just households) is divided by the number of households in the country. Table 1 shows the results for giving to the

Table 1
Per household measure of giving to the environment/animals subsector
Includes contributions from all sources divided by number of households
(adjusted for inflation)

Year	Per household	# of households
1988	$23	91.12 million
1998	$45	102.53 million
2008	$56	116.78 million

Data: Giving to environment/animals organizations from *Giving USA* estimate divided by the number of households in that year from the U.S. Bureau of the Census' Current Population Survey.

environment/animals subsector per household since 1988. IRS Forms 990 are used as the basis for subsector estimates of contributions received.

Philanthropic Giving Index "present situation" for giving to the PEAI (public-society benefit, environment/animals, and international affairs) subsector drops to 54.9 in 2008 from 79.1 in 2007

In December 2008, the Philanthropic Giving Index (PGI), which measures the fundraising confidence of nonprofit fundraisers and is conducted semi-annually by the Center on Philanthropy, reported a "present situation" index of 54.9 (on a scale of 100) for a combination of organizations that includes those in three subsectors: public-society benefit; environment/animals; and international affairs (PEAI).[3] This is the lowest level of fundraising confidence expressed for the PEAI cluster since the PGI began in 1998. The late 2008 PGI reported that:

- PEAI fundraisers, along with those in human services, had the lowest PGI in December 2008, indicating that charities in these areas had the least amount of success in raising gifts and were the least optimistic

about fundraising in the coming six months (the expectations index) compared to other subsectors.

- Fundraisers in this group were among the least likely to report success with email fundraising, at just 12.5 percent. This compares with one-third of religious fundraisers and 43 percent of education fundraisers reporting success with this vehicle.

- However, more fundraisers in the PEAI cluster reported success with special events (93.8 percent) than did fundraisers in other subsectors. In most other types of charities, special events were less likely to be reported as successful when compared to major gifts. In contrast, 62.5 percent of the PEAI cluster reported success with major gifts.

Table 2 shows the fundraising success according to type reported by public-society benefit, environment/animals, and international affairs organization respondents (PEAI) in 2007 and 2008. Compared with 2007, PEAI organization respondents reported particularly pronounced declines in corporate gifts (from 52.9 percent reporting success in 2007 to 37.5 percent reporting success

Table 2
Percentage of public-society benefit, environment/animals,
and international affairs (PEAI) respondents reporting success
with fundraising vehicle, 2007–2008

	Direct mail	Telephone	Special events	Planned giving	Major gifts	Corporate	Foundation	Email	Internet
2007	58.8	25.0	70.6	76.5	76.5	52.9	76.5	12.5	29.4
2008	43.8	43.8	93.8	62.5	62.5	37.5	68.8	12.5	37.5

in 2008) and in planned giving and major gifts (both dropping from 76.5 percent success rates in 2007 to 62.5 percent in 2008).

GuideStar poll of giving in 2008

Each year since 2002, GuideStar.org has posted a late-year online poll asking users of its site to report changes in giving to their organizations compared to the prior year.[4] We present a summary of these findings here. Note that these findings are not nationally representative, nor are they drawn from a random sample. There were 375 respondents from environment and animals organizations in 2008, with results as follows:

- 40 percent of participants, who said their organization works in the environmental and animal domain, reported an increase in contributions received, compared with 2007.

- 22 percent of participants reported that contributions to their organizations stayed about the same, compared with the previous year.

- 34 percent of environmental and animal-related organizations reported a drop in giving in 2008 from 2007.

In 2007, among environment/animals recipients, 56 percent reported an increase in contributions from the prior year. The 40 percent seeing growth in 2008 is a notable difference.

Million-dollar-and-up gifts for the environment/animals subsector

The environment/animals subsector typically receives a relatively small percentage of the number of multimillion-dollar gifts and a small percentage of the total dollars that are publicly announced in the media and tracked on the Center on Philanthropy's Million Dollar List. In 2008, approximately $350 million (of more than $22.3 billion in gifts of $1 million or more) went to organizations categorized as in the environment/animals subsector. Of these, the largest were:

- The John D. and Catherine T. MacArthur Foundation announced a multi-year commitment of $50 million in grants to be awarded to conservation organizations working in eight "biodiversity hotspots" as part of the foundation's mission to preserve habitats and species that are particularly vulnerable to the effects of climate change.[5] This award is in addition to a June 2008 grant of $12 million to the Critical Ecosystem Partnership Fund.[6]

Sitting on the dock at Rodeheaver Boys Ranch, Melton dangles his feet over the clear, sparkling water of the scenic St. Johns River. Summer dreaming doesn't get much better than this ... unless a four-legged friend begs to play a game of 'catch the stick!' Pictured are Melton Griffis, 12, and Buster, the Ranch dog.

Organization represented: Rodeheaver Boys Ranch, Palatka, FL (www.rbr.org)

Photographer: Greg Lepera, St. Augustine, FL, for www.giftcounsel.com,
          Ponte Vedra Beach, FL

- The estate of Sulo and Aileen Maki included a $20 million gift to the Desert Research Institute to endow water-resources programs in southern Nevada.[7]

- Hyde Family Foundations of Memphis granted $20 million to the Shelby Farms Park Conservancy as a challenge grant to raise funds for a plan to transform 4,500 acres into an urban park.[8]

- Toyota Motor Corporation made a five-year pledge totaling $20 million to the National Audubon Society to launch a new nationwide conservation program.[9]

The largest announced gift from a living individual donor was for $10 million to the Nature Conservancy in Illinois from Dennis and Connie Keller to support a partnership between the Conservancy and the African Wildlife Foundation.[10]

Corporations, foundations, individuals and governments acting together to address environmental and conservation needs

2008 saw a continued philanthropic emphasis on climate change and its sister issues: renewable energy and energy efficiency. While the immediate crisis in the economy overshadowed the crisis in the environment, eco-philanthropy still resonated with philanthropists in the United States and elsewhere. Government agencies, corporations, foundations, and individuals all took action in 2008 to address issues of mutual concern. Some of the publicly reported events are summarized below.

Global recognition of and support for reversing climate change
President George W. Bush announced in April 2008 his support for a national strategy to reduce greenhouse gas emissions in the United States by 2025.[13] In his announcement, the president mentioned laws passed by Congress that mandate greater fuel efficiency in vehicles (35 miles per gallon by 2012) and increases in federal government expenditures for research about renewable fuels, nuclear power and "clean coal." Quoted in *The Christian Science Monitor*, Robert Stavins, an environmental economist at Harvard University, said, "Given the [Bush] administration's track record and its reputation on global climate-

GOOD TO KNOW

Conservation organizations working internationally recognize—and often directly address—human needs in areas where they work, although there are difficulties in reporting impact where some results (environmental) take years and others (some human needs) are very short-term.[11]

One scholar, Dilys Roe, traced the history of the conservation vs. poverty-alleviation debate. She suggested that efforts to reduce emissions from deforestation, as part of the climate change agenda, are likely to bring greater attention to the need to balance human needs and environmental needs.[12]

change policy to date, this is a step in the right direction." [14]

Former U.S. Vice President Al Gore, continuing on the momentum of his 2007 Nobel Peace Prize, launched a $300 million campaign through the Alliance for Climate Protection, which was designed to mobilize Americans to push for climate policy change.[15] Many of the gifts received are linked with international donors:

- GMO LLC, a Boston-based company led by Briton Jeremy Grantham, gave £12 million (equivalent to almost $24 million) to the London School of Economics and a similar gift to the Imperial College of London. The gifts will fund collaboration by the two institutions to develop policy-relevant research about climate change, its causes, and potential solutions.[16]

- HSBC (Hongkong and Shanghai Banking Corp.) committed $100 million to each of four organizations working on climate change issues: The Climate Group, Earthwatch Institute, Smithsonian Tropical

Research Institute, and the World Wildlife Fund (WWF).[17] The funding is intended to help create cleaner urban environments in five model cities: Hong Kong, London, Mumbai, New York, and Shanghai. Three of the funded organizations operate in the United States. The Climate Group is headquartered in London.

Renewable energy generates research funding
As with other types of issues that inspire research to tackle problems, donors turned to higher education and research institutes to generate knowledge about energy.

- Gerhard Andlinger contributed $100 million to Princeton University for the Gerhard R. Andlinger Center for Energy and the Environment. Major research areas at the center will include improving energy efficiency and conservation; developing sustainable energy sources; and improving the management of carbon, with a focus on moving new discoveries rapidly to the marketplace.[18]

- The Doris Duke Foundation awarded grants for energy-related projects to the Massachusetts Institute of

GOOD TO KNOW

Prior research about the arts, education, and religious organizations has found that when government funding is available, private contributions are reduced. Environmental organizations that receive government funding, in general, may find it helpful to remain diligent in communicating with donors about the creation and successes of programs and activities that do not receive government support. In addition, a match is often required to receive a government grant, so private support is critical even when government support is available. It is likely that donors will continue to be involved when they can see that their gifts will make a difference.

Technology (nearly $2 million), Harvard University ($1.46 million), and Carnegie Mellon University ($1.85 million).[19]

- The Cynthia & George Mitchell Foundation announced a $6 million initiative with the Energy Foundation to advance renewable energy technologies in Texas.[20]

Giving to offset personal carbon emission
A number of charities in the United States offer carbon offset opportunities. The most widely publicized, carbon-offset programs include Carbonfund.org, Conservation International, and the Nature Conservancy. At these organizations and at other Web sites, individuals can use carbon estimators to approximate the volume of carbon emissions that they use and then donate a monetarily equal amount to projects for renewable energy, reforestation, or other efforts that reduce carbon emissions or increase carbon dioxide absorption by plant..

Corporations fund improvements to energy efficiency

Google.org announced an ambitious multi-sector plan to wean the United States off fossil fuels by 2030.[21] Google.org, which is registered as a for-profit corporation rather than a foundation, directed millions of dollars in funding to companies focused on renewable energy technologies, in addition to awarding some grants to nonprofit organizations. Google also collaborates with major energy firms, such as General Electric (GE), to develop new technologies for transmission of electrical power. Using social networking

to gather public comment on its plan, Google.org released a revised version of the Clean Energy 2030 proposal in late November 2008, which incorporated comments from people in response to the first version.[22]

Working toward the fuel conservation goal, the X PRIZE Foundation and Progressive Insurance launched a $10 million competition to develop marketable cars with reliable mileage of at least 100 miles per gallon of gasoline.[23] To win, a team must design, build, and bring to market a hundred-miles-per-gallon energy-equivalent vehicle that meets market needs for price, size, capability, safety, and performance, with judging to occur in 2009.

Green homebuilding with focus on energy-efficiency supported by Home Depot

While not in the environment/animals subsector, Habitat for Humanity, with funding from the Home Depot Foundation, announced a Green Building Program. This five-year, $30 million national initiative will help Habitat affiliates build at least 5,000 energy-efficient homes—roughly 17 percent of all the single- and multi-family homes Habitat will build over that period.[24]

Water supply concerns drawing attention of corporate donors

Already existing problems with global water supply are expected to be exacerbated by climate change. As the average temperature increases, scientists predict that existing rainfall patterns will be amplified, with the polar and sub-polar regions receiving more rainfall and the tropical regions receiving less rainfall. This drop in rainfall is expected to cause hardship in already dry regions that depend on irrigation, such as Africa and the Mediterranean Basin.[25] Recognizing this pressing issue, many corporations have begun to partner with nonprofit organizations to provide relief and to improve water conservation:

- The National Audubon Society announced a five-year, $20 million grant from Toyota Motor Corp. to launch a new nationwide conservation program called TogetherGreen.[26] This is the largest single grant that the Audubon Society has ever received. Among other activities, TogetherGreen will fund innovation grants for grassroots projects to engage diverse communities in achieving measurable impact in water, land, and energy conservation.

- The Coca-Cola Company made water one of its funding priorities starting in 2005. In 2008, its corporate foundation announced $1 million in grants to promote clean and safe water in India, as well as Rwanda, Kenya, and South Africa.[27] The company also announced a global partnership with the World Wildlife Federation through 2012 to work together to reduce the company's carbon emissions and to improve water efficiency.[28]

- In another water-related activity, the Coca-Cola Foundation pledged $1 million to Ocean Conservancy to sponsor the International Coastal Cleanup, continuing its 13-year

partnership with the Ocean Conservancy for this annual event.[29]

- The PepsiCo Foundation announced a three-year, $6 million grant to the Earth Institute at Columbia University and a one-year, $2.5 million grant to the H2O Africa Foundation for initiatives to improve sustainable water practices across the globe. Studies have found that more than one billion people do not have access to safe drinking water, while every year approximately two million children die from water-related diseases in the developing world.[30]

Action plans funded for wild animals

The Doris Duke Charitable Foundation granted $13 million to a multi-organization partnership headed by the Nature Conservancy to accelerate the implementation of state wildlife action plans in Arizona, Colorado, Montana, New Mexico, and Wyoming.[31] Mandated by Congress and approved by the U.S. Fish and Wildlife Service, state wildlife action plans are comprehensive strategies that take into account the broad range of a state's wildlife, including game, non-game, and common and endangered species.

Congress extends tax incentive for donation of conservation easements

In mid-2008, Congress renewed a provision originally included in the 2006 Pension Protection Act that allows landowners who donate property for conservation purposes to benefit from a charitable deduction of 50 percent of adjusted gross income.[32]

Summary of studies released

Foundations and researchers study charitable giving to the environment/animals subsector. One report, released in 2008, challenged foundations to think of ecotourism as a legitimate conservation method; the second presents data about the environmental giving of high-net-worth households in the United States. Each is summarized below.

Grantmakers encouraged to support responsible ecotourism

The Environmental Grantmakers Association released an estimate that, in 2005, U.S. grantmakers awarded $6.4 million (less than one percent of all environmental grantmaking that year) for ecotourism and sustainable tourism programs.[33] To support activities consistent with environmental goals, foundations funding in this domain were encouraged to support the creation of standards and certification systems for the quality of ecotourism; to facilitate site-specific community involvement; to consider using program-related investments (PRI) for capital funding of small and medium-sized projects; and to implement low-impact travel practices, such as the use of public transportation, locally owned and operated lodging sites and the purchase of carbon offsets for work-related air travel.

High-net-worth philanthropists and giving for environment- and animal-related causes

According to the *2008 Bank of America Study of High Net-Worth Philanthropy*, which was written by the Center on Philanthropy, 50 percent of high-net-worth households (with an annual income of more than $200,000, or a net worth of more than $1 million) made a donation to environmental and animal care organizations in 2007.[34] The average gift size in 2007 was $3,171, the lowest average when compared to other types of nonprofit organizations. The median gift size was $400. In terms of total dollar amount, environmental and animal care organizations together had the second lowest share (2 percent) of all giving by high-net-worth households in 2007.

The study also asked about giving through personal assets and through foundations, funds, and trusts. Comparing the two sources of funds:

- 48 percent of high-net-worth households gave an average of $2,724 (median = $300) to environment/animals organizations from their personal assets in 2007.

- 9 percent gave to environment/animals organizations utilizing foundations, funds, or trusts. The average amount was $5,124 (median = $1,000).

Key findings from annual studies

Table 4 presents three years of data from studies released annually about contributions to organizations in the environment/animals subsector. Web site addresses are provided so readers can access the full reports.

GOOD TO KNOW

Among a national sample of high-net-worth donors, giving to the environment is a relatively small proportion of their total giving. However, donations to environment/animals charities are more likely to occur among households with an annual income of at least $100,000 than they are among households with an annual income less than $50,000.

Table 4
Key findings from other studies about giving to environment/animals organizations

Million Dollar List, gifts from individuals $10 million and above (2006–2008) to environment/animals organizations (does not include gifts to foundations) Center on Philanthropy at Indiana University, www.philanthropy.iupui.edu		
	2006	2007	2008
Number of gifts to organizations in the environment/animals subsector	10	7	2
Largest gift to an organization in the environment/animals subsector	$80 million from Henry M. and Wendy J. Paulson to the Bobolink Foundation in grants to education, environmental, and conservation groups	$20 million bequest from Kathryn Wasserman Davis to Scenic Hudson for riverside parks	$20 million bequest from Sulo and Aileen Maki to the Desert Research Institute in Nevada for water-resources programs
Environment/animals gifts as a percentage of all individual gifts of $10 million or above	3.0 percent	0.4 percent	0.3 percent

Foundation Giving Trends: Update on Funding Priorities Grants to environment/animals organizations Foundation Center, www.foundationcenter.org		
	2005	2006	2007
Average grant amount	$126,925	$132,642	148,908
Median grant amount	$30,000	$39,661	$35,000
Environment and animals funding as a percentage of grant dollars (surveyed foundations, including corporate foundations)	6.3 percent	6.0 percent	6.8 percent

IRS tax-exempt organizations in environment/animals category Charities and other tax-exempt organizations, 2003, 2004, 2005 *Statistics of Income Bulletin*, www.irs.gov			
	2003	2004	2005
Number	10,454	11,576	12,422
Charitable revenue*	$5.94 billion	$6.80 billion	$7.72 billion

*Charitable revenue includes gifts and foundation grants (which is comparable to what *Giving USA* tracks), as well as government grants and allocations from other nonprofit agencies, such as the United Way and United Jewish Communities (which are not included in *Giving USA* estimates for contributions).

1   The model used to estimate giving was tested in late fall 2007 and early 2008 by Partha Deb (Hunter College, NY) and found to be the most accurate method over time for predicting giving to human services. Professor Deb looked at other potential variables, such as the percentage of the population in different age categories or the percentage that is uninsured, and found that they did not improve the estimating procedure.

2   Giving during recessions, *Giving USA Spotlight*, #3, 2008, www.givingusa.org.

3   The Center on Philanthropy, *Philanthropic Giving Index*, December 2008, www.philanthropy.iupui.edu.

4   Seventh Annual GuideStar Nonprofit Survey: Charitable Organizations and the Economy, Oct. 6-20, 2008, Released in the fall, 2008, www.guidestar.org.

5   $50 Million to Protect Biodiversity Threatened by Climate Change, John D. and Catherine T. MacArthur Foundation, Press release, October 6, 2008, www.macfound.org.

6   John D. and Catherine T. MacArthur Foundation, Critical Ecosystem Partnership Fund Receives Support for Conserving Biodiversity Hotspots, June 28, 2008, www.macfound.org.

7   America's Top Donors, *The Chronicle of Philanthropy*, 2009, www.philanthropy.com.

8   Hyde Family Foundations Announces $20 Million for Shelby Farms Park, Shelby Farms Park, Press release, August 7, 2008, www.shelbyfarmspark.org.

9   Audubon and Toyota Announce Five-Year Alliance to Promote Conservation Action and Grow Leaders for Tomorrow, National Audubon Society, Press release, March 26, 2008, www.web1audobon.org.

10   $10 Million Gift Expands Convervation in Africa, the Nature Conservancy in Illinois, Press release, April 24, 2008, www.nature.org.

11   H. Tallis, P. Kareiva, M. Marvier, and A. Chang, An ecosystem services framework to support both practical conservation and economic development, *Proceedings of the National Academy of Sciences*, July 2008. The authors are scholars at Stanford University or Santa Clara University or staff researchers with the Nature Conservancy in Seattle or Santa Clara, California.

12   D. Roe, The origins and evolution of the conservation-poverty debate: A review of key literature, events, and policy processes, *Oryx*, October 2008, 42:491-503.

13   CQ Transcripts, Bush remarks on climate change, *The Washington Post*, April 16, 2008, www.washingtonpost.com.

14   P. Spotts, Bush's climate goals vague—but a start, *The Christian Science Monitor*, April 16, 2008, www.csmonitor.com.

15   J. Eilperin, Gore Launches Ambitious Advocacy Campaign on Climate, *The Washington Post*, March 31, 2008.

16   No author, Climate change donation for LSE, BBC News Channel, April 17, 2008, www.bbc.co.uk.

17   T. Torres, HSBC invests $400 million to fight climate change, *The Philippine Star*, www.philstar.com.

18   S. Schultz, Gift of $100 million to transform energy and environment research at Princeton, Princeton School of Engineering and Applied Science, July 1, 2008, www.princeton.edu.

19   Foundation Awards $6.6 Million to Accelerate Development of Clean Energy Technologies, Doris Duke Charitable Foundation, Press release, February 7, 2008, www.ddcf.org.

20   Mitchell Foundation Creates $6 Million Energy and Climate Change Program, *Philanthropy News Digest*, February 13, 2008, www.foundationcenter.org.

21   J. Greenblat and D. Reicher, Clean Energy 2030, Google.org, October 1, 2008, http://blog.google.org/2008/10/clean-energy-2030.html.

22   Google.org, Clean Energy 2030: Google's Proposal for Reducing U.S. Dependence on Fossil Fuels, 2009, http://knol.google.com/k/-/-/15x31uzlqeo5n/1#.

23   X PRIZE Foundation & Progressive Insurance Join Forces to Officially Announce the $10 Million Progressive Automotive X PRIZE, X PRIZE Foundation, Press release, March 20, 2008, www.progressiveautoxprize.org.

24   Habitat for Humanity International and the Home Depot Foundation Announce National Green Building Effort, Habitat for Humanity International, Press release, March 20, 2008, www.habitat.org.

25   E. Kolbert, Changing Rains, *National Geographic Magazine*, May 2009.

26   Audubon and Toyota Announce Five-Year Alliance to Promote Conservation Action and Grow Leaders for Tomorrow, National Audubon Society, Press release, March 26, 2008, www.web1audobon.org.

27   Coca-Cola Foundation gives to water projects, *Atlanta Business Chronicle*, December 19, 2008, www.bizjournals.com/Atlanta.

28   CNW group, WWF-Canada and Coca-Cola in Canada partner on freshwater conservation and climate protection, October 30, 2008, CNW Group, www.newswire.ca.

29   The Coca-Cola Foundation Pledges $1 Million to Ocean Conservancy to Help Eradicate Ocean Litter, Redorbit.com, Sept. 3, 2008, www.redorbit.com.

30   PepsiCo Announces Initiatives with the Earth Institute and H20 Africa to Drive Sustainable Water Practices Efforts to Improve Rural Water in Africa, China, India and Brazil, PepsiCo, Press release, January 22, 2008, www.pepsico.com.

31   $13 Million Grant to Accelerate the Conservation of Wildlife Habitat in the West, Doris Duke Charitable Foundation, Press release, March 18, 2008, www.ddcf.org.

32   E. Schwinn, Congress extends tax break for land-conservation gift, *The Chronicle of Philanthropy*, June 12, 2008, www.philanthropy.com.

33   G. Biggs, Ecotourism as a Conservation Strategy for Funders, Environmental Grantmakers Association, January 2008, www.ega.org.

34   Center on Philanthropy, *Bank of America 2008 Study of High Net-Worth Philanthropy*, www.philanthropy.iupui.edu.

16 Legal and legislative issues

Summary of legal and legislative issues

The heightened scrutiny of tax-exempt organizations as reported in *Giving USA 2008* did not wane during 2008, particularly as the United States entered one of its worst financial downturns in history. Congress, agency regulators, and the courts all took actions that were relevant to tax-exempt organizations. Most notably, the Internal Revenue Service (IRS) continued implementation of provisions relating to charitable organizations that were part of the Pension Protection Act (PPA) of 2006, and Congress extended some provisions related to charitable donations that were set to expire. While federal activities concentrated on efforts to monitor nonprofit organizations, state courts and legislatures addressed important topics, including a continued examination of compliance with state tax exemption laws, donor disclosure through public records laws, and the recognition of a new financial entity, the L3C.

Federal Activity

The effects of the PPA continued to be felt in 2008. The PPA contained a number of provisions for charity reporting requirements that were implemented or extended in 2008. During 2008, several other federal initiatives related to tax-exempt charities were also announced, including new nonprofit investment rules, scrutiny of large endowments at colleges and universities, the return

of the "commensurate" test, and plans for future scrutiny of nonprofits.

Continued implementation of the Pension Protection Act

The Pension Protection Act of 2006 triggered a redesign of Form 990, the annual return filed by many tax exempt groups. For many organizations, the revised form requires more detailed information about income and community benefit. The other significant change to annual filing requirements is the addition of a new electronic short form that must be completed by small organizations with revenues of less than $25,000. Under the new rules, small organizations previously exempted from regular filings must now file annual notice with the IRS.

The New Form 990: On December 20, 2007, the IRS released the final version of Form 990. The IRS claims the revisions are intended to improve transparency among exempt organizations, increase compliance, increase accountability, and reduce the filing burden on organizations completing the form.[1,2]

The new form consists of an 11-page "core-form" section completed by all filers.[3] Further, there are 16 different schedules that address a number of issues including: political activity, lobbying, fundraising, charity gaming activities, foreign activities, grant-making, compensation, loans, valuation of noncash contributions, and relationships and transactions with other

Between 2009 and 2011, organizations with different budget sizes will be filing IRS Forms 990 that will not all be the same. This may cause confusion among donors looking at forms and researchers seeking to compile data about the nonprofit sector.

organizations. The schedules are not uniformly applicable. Some schedules target particular types of organizations, such as hospitals and private schools, and will not apply to many organizations. Many of the important aspects of the new form were discussed in *Giving USA 2008*.

The new Form 990 will be used first in 2009 (to reflect the 2008 tax year). To ease concern over the new form, the IRS established graduated transition periods. For 2009, only organizations with gross receipts over $1 million or total assets greater than $2.5 million will be required to file the new Form 990 for the 2008 tax year. In 2010, groups with gross receipts of more than $500,000 or total assets of more than $1.25 million will be required to use the new Form 990. All other 990 filers will use the new form in 2011 to report on the 2010 tax year.

Due to the redesign of Form 990, the IRS and the Treasury Department issued new regulations regarding the approval process for organizations seeking tax-exempt status as public charities.[4] Because additional information will now be reported on the Form 990, the "advance rulings" that granted a five-year initial public charity status, but then required a demonstration of the necessary public support, have been eliminated. The IRS plans

to develop other procedures to monitor the public charity status of 501(c)(3) organizations.

E-Postcard: Before the Pension Protection Act, organizations with gross receipts of less than $25,000 were not required to make any filing with the Internal Revenue Service.[5] Beginning in 2008, for the 2007 tax year, many small exempt organizations are now required to file an electronic "e-postcard" (Form 990N) with the IRS. The card is due by the fifteenth day of the fifth month after the close of the organization's tax year. Electronic filing is the only option. By September 2008, almost 200,000 organizations had filed their e-Postcards.[6] Though there are some exceptions, organizations are not required to file if they are:

- Included in a group return;
- Private foundations required to file a Form 990PF;
- Section 509(a)(3) supporting organizations required to file a Form 990 or 990EZ;
- Section 527 (political) organizations required to file a Form 990 or 990-EZ; or
- Churches or their integrated auxiliaries, conventions, or associations.

Failure to File: The Pension Protection Act requires the IRS to revoke the

Many more charities face a filing requirement than previously, including those asked to submit an "e-postcard" to attest to their continued operation and low revenue (less than $25,000).

Failure to file the required document with the IRS could potentially result in revocation of an organization's tax-exempt charitable status, and donors to that organization would no longer be able to legally deduct gifts to that entity on their federal tax returns.

exemption of any group that fails to meet its filing obligations for three consecutive years. This provision applies to groups required to file under the pre-Pension Act rules, as well as those small organizations now required to submit e-filings. It was recommended by the Advisory Committee on Tax Exempt and Governmental Entities that the IRS implement a voluntary compliance program to help bring non-filers into compliance before the automatic revocation process begins, and in 2009, the IRS expects to implement an Exempt Organizations Voluntary Compliance Program to address the concern.[7] This program is not yet in place, however, so organizations should be vigilant in knowing and following filing requirements and monitoring for any further developments.

Guidelines on Donor-Advised Funds: Due to changes resulting from the PPA, the IRS provided a new guide sheet in July 2008 to assist in the processing of Form 1023 applications for recognition of exemption under 501(c)(3) submitted by sponsoring organizations that maintain donor-advised funds.[8] Particularly, the guide sheet asks questions related to the level of control the donor has over the fund; any policies and procedures that

require a minimum distribution from the fund account on an annual basis; the selection process and identity of investment advisors; and how the sponsoring organization reviews donor advice. The guide sheet is intended to assist organizations with compliance and does not change any prior regulations.

Extension of the Conservation-Easement Deduction: The PPA established a temporary expansion of the federal tax breaks for donating land development rights, also known as conservation easements; these were set to expire in December 2007. In 2008, Congress extended the tax break through the end of 2009.[9] Landowners who take advantage of this tax break will be able to:[10]

- Increase their charitable deduction from 30 percent to 50 percent of their adjusted gross income (AGI) in the year of their gift (qualified farmers may deduct up to 100 percent of AGI); and

- Carry over any unused deduction for up to 15 years, instead of only five years.

New nonprofit investment rules for donor-restricted endowment funds
The Federal Accounting Standards Board (FASB) issued Staff Position

(FSP) No. FAS 117-1 to provide guidance regarding the Uniform Prudent Management of Investment Funds Act (UPMIFA) approved by the Uniform Law Commission in 2006.[11] As of March 2009, UPMIFA had been enacted in five states and was being considered by state legislatures in many others.[12] UPMIFA is a modernized version of the Uniform Management of Institutional Funds Act of 1972 (UMIFA), the model act on which almost every state and the District of Columbia have based their primary laws governing the investment and management of donor-restricted endowment funds by not-for-profit organizations.

FSP No. FAS 117-1 has two objectives: 1) provide guidance on the net asset classification of donor-restricted endowment funds for not-for-profit organizations subject to an enacted version of UPMIFA; and 2) provide increased disclosures about an organization's endowment funds (both donor-restricted endowment funds and board-designated endowment funds) whether or not the organization is subject to UPMIFA.

Further, nonprofits with board-designated or donor-restricted endowment funds, whether or not subject to an enacted version of UPMIFA, must make additional disclosures in their financial statements under FAS 117-1.[13] Illustrative examples of the required disclosures can be found in Appendix C of FAS 117-1[14].

Higher education under greater scrutiny

As discussed in *Giving USA 2008*, the IRS intended to focus compliance and enforcement efforts on higher education in 2008. In furtherance of that intention, the IRS distributed 400 compliance questionnaires to a cross-section of small, midsized, and large private and public four-year colleges and universities. The questionnaire focused on relationships between related and unrelated entities, unrelated business income, endowments, and executive compensation practices.[15] The information from the questionnaires will help the IRS better understand how colleges and universities[16]:

- Report revenues and expenses from taxable trade or business activities on Form 990-T;

- Classify activities as exempt or taxable;

- Calculate and report income or losses on Form 990-T;

GOOD TO KNOW

An important result of the changes UPMIFA brings is that the portion of donor-restricted endowment funds that is not classified as permanently restricted net assets must now be classified as temporarily restricted net assets (time restricted) until appropriated for expenditure by the organization.

Under UPMIFA, nonprofits must update their financial statements by reclassifying certain amounts previously reported as unrestricted to temporarily restricted net assets to the extent they have not already been appropriated for expenditure.

- Allocate revenues and expenses between exempt and taxable activities;
- Invest and use endowment funds; and
- Determine types and amounts of executive compensation.

The results of the questionnaire are to be released some time in 2009.

In addition to the IRS questionnaire, Senators Baucus and Grassley, the leaders of the Senate Finance Committee, sent a letter in January 2008 to the 136 universities and colleges in the United States with endowments over $500 million, inquiring about endowment growth and student aid spending. A primary intent of the letter is to gather information so they can better understand how the tax benefits for higher education endowments are improving education and making undergraduate education more affordable for low and middle income families today.[17]

The return of the "commensurate test"

In an April 2008 speech, Steven Miller, commissioner of the IRS's tax-exempt and government-entities division, announced the IRS would use a controversial measure—a so-called commensurate test—to determine whether charities were using their

money in an acceptable way.[18] Given that there is very little case law on the commensurate test, it remains to be seen exactly how it will be interpreted and implemented.

Not long after the reintroduction of the commensurate test was announced, the National Foundation of America, based in Tennessee, was denied tax exemption in part because it did not carry on a charitable program "commensurate in scope" with its financial resources.[19] Some nonprofit leaders and legal experts worry that the commensurate test will force organizations to demonstrate sufficient expenditures on charitable programs under the threat of losing their tax exemption. Others feel the test is a legitimate tool to determine whether organizations are actually providing the charitable work for which they receive their tax exemption.

IRS announces plans for reviewing nonprofits in 2009

The IRS announced a number of new compliance initiatives for 2009, including the implementation of a long-range study to learn more about sources and uses of funds in the charitable sector and their impact on the accomplishment of charitable purposes.[20] Other new initiatives include the scrutiny of the valuation methods used for non-cash gifts given to tax-exempt

GOOD TO KNOW

The "commensurate test" looks at whether the tax exempt organization is performing charitable activities commensurate in scope with its financial resources. The test is part of an ongoing IRS commitment to put more effort into monitoring the efficiency and effectiveness of charitable organizations.

organizations, as well as that then contribute the items to a broad effort to educate nonprofit staff members on governance issues, such as determining whether an organization qualifies as a charity.

State Activity

As discussed in *Giving USA 2008*, the assumption that nonprofit organizations could reasonably assume that satisfying the criteria for exemption under the federal tax code also meant that they could pass the test for state tax exemptions is no longer safe. With many states incurring substantial budget shortfalls under the pressures of dwindling tax revenues and weakening economic conditions, state courts and officials continue to scrutinize the activities of tax-exempt organizations, particularly nonprofit hospitals, more closely to ensure the organizations are fulfilling a charitable purpose. Further, other state actions impacting nonprofits included the weakening of donor anonymity through open records laws and the emergence of a new type of organizational status that may have big implications for private foundations.

Property tax exemptions for nonprofit hospitals come under question

Across the country, states began to monitor more closely and scrutinize tax-exempt organizations to ensure that they meet the requirements necessary to obtain and/or maintain their tax-exempt status. This is particularly true for nonprofit hospitals—institutions that receive substantial tax breaks due to the high value of their property. While a number of examples exist,

attention is focused on an Illinois Appellate Court case to provide an example of how courts are addressing this issue.

Provena Covenant Medical Center v. Department of Revenue

In August 2008, the Illinois Fourth District Court of Appeals ruled that the Champaign County Board of Review and Illinois Department of Revenue did not err in denying tax exemption to Provena Covenant Medical Center (Provena). This ruling reversed the lower court's decision that Provena was tax-exempt.[21] Provena claimed that it was a health care ministry of the Roman Catholic Church and argued that it was tax-exempt either as a charitable organization or a religious organization. The court did not accept either of these arguments. First, the court addressed Provena's claimed status as a charitable organization. The court tried to distinguish the activities of Provena from a for-profit hospital, but stated, "it is unclear to what extent Provena exercises 'general benevolence' as opposed to doing what a for-profit hospital does: selling medical services."[22] The court also determined that "[b]ecause Provena's charity care program in 2002 [the initial tax year in question] considered only the patient's income relative to the federal poverty guidelines without considering the amount of the medical bill or the patient's other liabilities and [Provena] devoted only 0.7 percent of its revenue to charity care, the Director could regard the program merely as a pretense of charity, a *pro forma* procedure that was not calculated to make a serious evaluation of need."[23]

GOOD TO KNOW

The Provena case is an important overview of how one state court interprets what it means to be charitable. The court's treatment of the religious nature of the hospital has wide-ranging implications for nonprofit hospitals, especially those affiliated with or governed by religious organizations.

The ruling in this case by the Supreme Court of Illinois will have a significant impact on nonprofit hospitals throughout the country as other states review with a critical eye the charitable activities of nonprofit hospitals.

In fact, Provena had revenues of $113 million in 2002 and its charitable activities cost only $831,724 – Provena's property tax exemption was worth over $1.1 million.

The court also addressed Provena's claimed status as a religious organization. Under Illinois law, in order to be granted property tax exemption for religious purposes, the property needs to be used exclusively for religious purposes.[24] The court determined that "if the operation of the property is businesslike and more characteristic of a place of commerce than a facility used primarily for religious purposes, the property is not exempt from taxation."[25] As such, the court determined Provena "more resembled a business with religious overtones than property used primarily for religious purposes."[26]

Provena has appealed this decision to the Supreme Court of Illinois and a ruling is pending as of this writing. The tax exempt status of Provena is not a small matter, as over $6 million in taxes has accrued since Provena was initially denied its tax exemption in 2002.[27]

Donor anonymity is weakened in Kentucky

Donors to public institutions in Kentucky are no longer able to give anonymously after the Supreme Court of Kentucky, in *Cape Publications, Inc. v. University of Louisville Foundation, Inc.*[28], ruled that donations to public institutions are subject to Kentucky's Open Records Act. In reaching this conclusion, the Court first agreed with the lower court's determination that the University of Louisville Foundation was essentially one and the same as the University, thus rendering it a public institution and subject to the Open Records Act. The Court then determined that all non-anonymous donors had a very minimal expectation of privacy regarding their donations and the public had a legitimate interest in who donated and how much. The Court did maintain anonymity for those donors who had previously requested it, but only because the Foundation's status as a public institution had not yet been established when the gifts were made. The Court warned that future gifts to public institutions "are subject to disclosure regardless of any requests for anonymity."[29]

An L3C (low-profit limited liability company) is intended to be an organization that realizes some profit, but its primary purpose is to do social good. It is essentially a hybrid legal structure, merging the social advantages of a non-profit entity with the financial advantages of the limited liability company. By March 2009, four states recognized L3C entities and more were considering legislation to recognize them.

States creating new L3C corporate status

In April 2008, Vermont became the first state to recognize a new type of financial entity, the low-profit limited liability company, or L3C.[30] The L3C entity was also adopted in Michigan in January 2009,[31] in Wyoming in February 2009,[32] and in Utah in March 2009.[33] The L3C is intended to be a conduit for private foundations to make program-related investments (PRIs) in order to assist in meeting their 5 percent payout requirement.[34]

Proponents of L3Cs suggest these entities will allow for an increase in commercial investment in charitable ventures as PRIs essentially function like a low rate loan that is repaid over time. The implementation of PRIs under the L3C model enables charitable ventures to be infused with initial capital by attracting private sector investment. Additionally, since PRIs function like loans, these private foundations also gain a financial return that can be reinvested in other programs. However, the IRS still can determine whether a PRI invested in an L3C is allowed and has not yet announced a particular stand on L3Cs and their impact on foundation payout requirements. As of this writing, eight additional states have introduced and are considering legislation to recognize L3Cs.[35]

Summary

The nonprofit sector has seen increasing scrutiny in recent years. This has occurred in part as a result of public and governmental reactions to real or perceived abuse of the provisions that exempt charitable organizations from income tax and in some jurisdictions, from property and sales tax. The changing regulatory and legal environment also reflects a broader push to make tax-advantaged organizations more accountable to the public, more transparent to their stakeholders and others, and more responsive to government and public expectations.

Of particular concern for fundraising are the tensions between public accountability and the rights of donors. In 2008, court decisions or legislative actions had the potential to change the nature of the organization's relationship with donors. These include efforts by regulators to determine whether or not an institution is sufficiently charitable (based on scholarships provided, charity care from a hospital, or on other grounds). This also includes expectations that the public has a right to know the names of donors to public institutions of higher education. These issues, and others, are likely to continue to spark debate in the nonprofit sector for many more years.

1   See Internal Revenue Document 2007-204. The redesigned Form 990 and more information regarding the changes made to the form, including instructions, may be found on the IRS Web site at www.irs.gov/charities/article/0,,id=176613,00.html.

2   See Letter from the IRS Exempt Organizations Director at http://ftp.irs.ustreas.gov/pub/irs-tege/finalannualrptworkplan11_25_08.pdf.

3   C. Hepp, Dramatic IRS shift for nonprofits. Complex new forms focus less on finances, more on how groups operate and prevent corruption, *The Philadelphia Inquirer*, February 17, 2009.

4   See Letter from EO Director p. 24 (note 2); for the full language of the new regulations, see www.irs.gov/pub/irs-tege/tempregs_arpe_fedreg090908.pdf.

5   Additional information about the e-postcard can be obtained from the IRS Web site at www.irs.gov/charities/article/0,,id=169250,00.html.

6   See Letter from EO Director p. 18 (note 2).

7   See Letter from EO Director p. 19 (note 2).

8   For the full text of the guide sheet and additional related materials, see www.irs.gov/charities/charitable/article/0,,id=185378,00.html.

9   A. Ebeling, Landowners and charities farm tax break, June 11, 2008, at www.forbes.com.

10 C. Gilliland and N. Nichols, Conservation Easements Revisited, Real Estate Center at Texas A & M University, Jan. 2009.

11 Full text of the FASB Staff Position is available at: www.fasb.org/pdf/fsp_fas117-1.pdf.

12 See www.nccusl.org/Update/ActSearchResults.aspx?ActId=134.

13 M. Piszko, New nonprofit investment rules about to hit, *The NonProfit Times*, December 29, 2008, www.nptimes.com.

14 Same as Note 11.

15 See IRS press release at www.irs.gov/irs/article/0,,id=187328,00.html; see also Letter from EO Director p. 21 (note 2).

16 See www.irs.gov/charities/article/0,,id=186865,00.html; see the following for a sample questionnaire: www.irs.gov/pub/irs-tege/sample_cucp_questionnaire.pdf.

17 For a copy of the U.S. Senate Finance Committee news release containing the text of the letter, see www.nacua.org/documents/BaucusGrassleyLetterReEndowments.pdf.

18 D. Blum and G. Williams, Putting charity to the test: IRS considers controversial measure for charitable activity, *The Chronicle of Philanthropy*, May 15, 2008, www.philanthropy.com.

19 G. Williams, IRS denies tax-exempt status to group that spends too little money on charitable programs, *The Chronicle of Philanthropy*, May 13, 2008, www.philanthropy.com.

20 See Letter from EO Director pp. 20-21 (note 2); see also E. Kelderman, IRS discloses 2009 plans for nonprofit review, *The Chronicle of Philanthropy*, December 11, 2008, www.philanthropy.com.

21 *Provena Covenant Medical Center v. Department of Revenue*, 894 N.E.2d 452 (Ill. Ct. App. 2008).

22 Same as Note 21, p. 462.

23 Same as Note 21, p. 469.

24 Same as Note 21, p. 479; See also 35 ILCS 200/15-40(a)(1).

25 Same as Note 21, p. 480.

26 Same as Note 21, p. 480.

27 See also, D. Pressey, Provena Covenant Medical Center loses tax exemption again, *The News-Gazette* (Champaign-Urbana, IL), Aug. 29, 2008.

28 *Cape Publications, Inc. v. University of Louisville Foundation, Inc.*, 260 S.W.3d 818 (Ky. 2008).

29 Ibid. at 824.

30 Vermont House Bill 0775.

31 Michigan Senate Bill 1445.

32 Wyoming House Bill 182.

33 Utah Senate Bill 148.

34 J. Kelly, A Push for Investments Instead of Grants, *Youth Today*, Sept. 1, 2008, www.youthtoday.org.

35 The eight additional states are: Arkansas, Illinois, Missouri, Montana, North Carolina, North Dakota, Oregon, and Tennessee. For more information regarding what stage L3C legislation is at in each state, please see www.americansforcommunitydevelopment.org/legislativewatch.html.

17 | Gifts of $10 million or more in 2008

The Center on Philanthropy at Indiana University issues a quarterly list of announced gifts of $1 million or more. From this list, *Giving USA* has compiled a list of gifts or pledges of $10 million or more made by individuals (not corporations or foundations) announced in 2008. The amounts reported here are those that appear in newspapers or other media outlets; they have not been verified with the recipient institution.

This is not a complete listing of all gifts in the United States of $10 million or more because many such gifts are not reported in the press. It also does not represent actual transfers made to institutions in 2007. Many of the gifts are pledges or estate gifts that will be paid over time. Gifts in kind are reported at values announced in the media.

Gifts are organized in descending order by size and then alphabetically by donor's last name. The size categories are $1 billion and above; $500 million to $999.99 million; $250 million to $499.99 million, $100 million to $249.99 million, $50 million to $99.99 million, $25 million to $49.99 million, and $10 million to $24.99 million.

$1 billion and above

Dollar Amount	Donor	Recipient
$4,500,000,000	James LeVoy Sorenson (Estate)	Sorenson Legacy Foundation
$1,000,000,000	Peter G. Peterson	Peter G. Peterson Foundation

$500 million to $999.99 million

Dollar Amount	Donor	Recipient
No Data		

$250 million to $499.99 million

Dollar Amount	Donor	Recipient
$360,000,000	Harold Alfond (Estate)	Harold Alfond Foundation
$350,000,000	William P. Carey	W. P. Carey Foundation
$300,000,000	David Booth	University of Chicago

$100 million to $249.99 million

Dollar Amount	Donor	Recipient
$225,000,000	Dorothy Patterson (Estate)	Patterson Foundation
$200,000,000	Emily Rauh Pulitzer	Harvard Art Museum
$150,000,000	Helen Kimmel	New York University
$136,000,000	Frank Doble (Estate)	Tufts University
$136,000,000	Frank Doble (Estate)	Lesley University
$125,000,000	Hansjorg Wyss	Harvard University
$110,000,000	Anonymous	New York University
$100,000,000	Gerhard (Gerry) Andlinger	Princeton University
$100,000,000	Philip and Penny Knight	Oregon Health & Science University
$100,000,000	David Koch	New York State Theater
$100,000,000	Kenneth and Elaine Langone	New York University Medical Center
$100,000,000	T. Boone Pickens	Oklahoma State University

$100 million to $249.99 million (continued)

Dollar Amount	Donor	Recipient
$100,000,000	David Rockefeller	Harvard University
$100,000,000	Stephen A. and Christine Schwarzman	New York Public Library

$50 million to $99.99 million

Dollar Amount	Donor	Recipient
$80,000,000	Fritz and Dolores Russ (Estate)	Ohio University
$75,000,000	Lorry I. Lokey	Stanford University
$75,000,000	Robert and Catherine McDevitt (Estate)	Georgetown University
$70,000,000	Frank and Jane Batten (Sr.)	Culver Academies
$65,000,000	Ric Weiland (Estate)	Pride Foundation
$63,000,000	T. Boone Pickens	Oklahoma State University
$60,000,000	Anonymous	Carnegie Corporation of New York
$60,000,000	Guy E. Beatty, Jr.	College of Charleston
$60,000,000	Ric Weiland (Estate)	Stanford University
$58,000,000	Roger Cramer Holden (Estate)	Amherst College
$57,200,000	Malone (III) and Amy Mitchell	Oklahoma State University
$55,000,000	Ernest and Sarah Butler	University of Texas at Austin
$55,000,000	Stewart and Lynda Resnik	Los Angeles County Museum of Art
$50,000,000	Anonymous	Boston College
$50,000,000	Anonymous	Wycliffe Bible Translators
$50,000,000	Anonymous	St. Thomas University
$50,000,000	Steven and Alexandra Cohen	Morgan Stanley Children's Hospital of New York-Presbyterian
$50,000,000	Jerome and Ann Fisher	University of Pennsylvania
$50,000,000	Felix E. Martin, Jr. (Estate)	Felix E. Martin, Jr. Foundation
$50,000,000	Robert and Catherine McDevitt (Estate)	Le Moyne College
$50,000,000	Michael Moritz and Harriet Heyman	Christ Church, Oxford
$50,000,000	Ross Perot, Jr., Katherine Perot, Carolyn Rathjen, Suzanne McGee, and Nancy Mulford (all siblings)	Museum of Nature & Science
$50,000,000	Harold and Annette Simmons	University of Texas Southwestern Medical Center
$50,000,000	Harold and Annette Simmons and Family	Parkland Foundation

$25 million to $49.99 million

Dollar Amount	Donor	Recipient
$45,000,000	Stanley and Fiona Druckenmiller	New York University Medical Center
$45,000,000	Emily Rauh Pulitzer	Harvard Art Museum
$40,000,000	Andy Grove	Michael J. Fox Foundation for Parkinson's Research
$40,000,000	John and Cynthia Fry Gunn	San Francisco Opera
$35,000,000	Michael S. "Mickey" and Janie Maurer	Indiana University
$35,000,000	Andrew and Ann Tisch	Cornell University
$35,000,000	Ric Weiland (Estate)	Various Organizations
$34,200,000	Donald and Dorothy Stabler (Estate)	Lehigh University
$30,000,000	Anonymous	Carnegie Corporation
$30,000,000	Adrienne Arsht	Adrienne Arsht Center for the Performing Arts of Miami-Dade County

$25 million to $49.99 million (continued)

Dollar Amount	Donor	Recipient
$30,000,000	David Bolger	Valley Hospital
$30,000,000	Patricia Corbett (Estate)	University of Cincinnati College-Conservatory of Music, the Society for the Preservation of Music Hall, the Cincinnati Symphony Orchestra, Cincinnati Opera, Northern Kentucky University, Cincinnati Musical Festival Association (the May Festival) and Cincinnati Children's Theatre
$30,000,000	Edmund Hajim	University of Rochester
$30,000,000	Jen-Hsun Huang	Stanford University
$30,000,000	Lorry I. Lokey	American Committee for the Weizmann Institute of Science
$30,000,000	Robert and Catherine McDevitt (Estate)	Diocese of Syracuse
$30,000,000	Steven Mihaylo	California State University, Fullerton
$30,000,000	T. Denny Sanford	Sanford Consortium for Regenerative Medicine
$27,000,000	H. F. (Gerry) and Marguerite B. Lenfest	Philadelphia Museum of Art
$27,000,000	Carl J. and Ruth Shapiro	Dana-Farber/Brigham and Women's Cancer Center
$25,000,000	Anonymous	Marquette University
$25,000,000	David and Patricia Atkinson	University Medical Center at Princeton
$25,000,000	Verna (Dr.) Dauterive	University of Southern California
$25,000,000	Stephen and Diana Goldberg	Children's National Medical Center
$25,000,000	David and Ruth Gottesman	Yeshiva University
$25,000,000	Dennis and Constance Templeton Keller	Princeton University
$25,000,000	Sidney Kimmel	Kimmel Center
$25,000,000	H. F. (Gerry) and Marguerite B. Lenfest	Curtis Institute of Music
$25,000,000	Joe R. and Teresa Lozano Long	University of Texas Health Science Center at San Antonio
$25,000,000	Joe and Rika Mansueto	University of Chicago
$25,000,000	Joseph H. Moss	Children's Healthcare of Atlanta
$25,000,000	Peter T. Paul	University of New Hampshire
$25,000,000	Ronald O. Perelman	NewYork-Presbyterian Hospital
$25,000,000	Ronald O. Perelman	Weill Cornell Medical College
$25,000,000	David Rockefeller	Stone Barns Center for Food and Agriculture
$25,000,000	Henry M. and Lee Rowan	Williamson Free School of Mechanical Trades
$25,000,000	Ben and Luanne Russell	Children's Hospital of Alabama
$25,000,000	Clarence Scharbauer, Jr.	Midland Memorial Hospital
$25,000,000	R. Michael and Mary Shanahan	Harvey Mudd College
$25,000,000	Oscar Tang and Argie Ligeros (spouse)	Phillips Academy Andover

$10 million to $24.99 million

Dollar Amount	Donor	Recipient
$23,000,000	Dwight Goldthorpe (Estate)	Amherst College
$22,600,000	Ron and Nancy Harrington, Steve and Jill McLaughlin, and Ron and Lydia Harrington	University Hospitals of Cleveland
$22,000,000	Alfred Taubman	University of Michigan
$20,000,000	Anonymous	College of St. Catherine
$20,000,000	Anonymous	University of Cincinnati
$20,000,000	Anonymous	University of Wisconsin-Madison
$20,000,000	Anonymous	Archdiocese of New York

$10 million to $24.99 million (continued)

Dollar Amount	Donor	Recipient
$20,000,000	Frank Batten, Sr.	City of Norfolk
$20,000,000	Annette Bloch	University of Kansas
$20,000,000	Ann Carell and Family	Vanderbilt University
$20,000,000	Frank Eck (Estate)	University of Notre Dame
$20,000,000	William Eckhardt	University of Chicago
$20,000,000	Bruce and Martha Karsh	Duke University
$20,000,000	John and Pat Klingenstein	Teachers College, Columbia University
$20,000,000	H. Fitzgerald "Gerry" and Marguerite Lenfest	Williamson Free School of Mechanical Trades
$20,000,000	Sulo and Aileen Maki (Estate)	Desert Research Institute
$20,000,000	John Albert Marque (Estate)	Greater New Orleans Foundation
$20,000,000	Henry M. and Lee Rowan	Williamson Free School of Mechanical Trades
$20,000,000	John and Regina Scully	Stanford University
$20,000,000	Ralph Stayer	University of Notre Dame
$20,000,000	H. Campbell "Cal" Stuckeman	Pennsylvania State University
$18,000,000	Ronald and Maxine Linde	California Institute of Technology
$17,000,000	Anonymous	Spelman College
$17,000,000	H. F. (Gerry) and Marguerite B. Lenfest	Washington and Lee University
$16,000,000	Will and Beverly O'Hara	University of Texas McCombs School of Business
$15,000,000	Robert and Frances Biolchini	University of Notre Dame
$15,000,000	Dolph Briscoe, Jr.	University of Texas at Austin
$15,000,000	Christopher Browne	University of Pennsylvania
$15,000,000	D. Travis and Anne Engen	Smithsonian National Air and Space Museum
$15,000,000	William Fry	Indiana University
$15,000,000	Bob Herd	Texas Tech University
$15,000,000	Joseph Jamail	University of Texas at Austin
$15,000,000	H. F. (Gerry) and Marguerite B. Lenfest	Barnes Foundation
$15,000,000	H. F. (Gerry) and Marguerite B. Lenfest	Columbia University School of Law
$15,000,000	Earle Mack	Drexel University
$15,000,000	John Menard, Jr.	Mayo Clinic
$15,000,000	Roger and Victoria Sant	Smithsonian Institution
$15,000,000	Donald Soffer	Brandeis University
$15,000,000	Nicholas and Jenny Taubman	Art Museum of Western Virginia
$15,000,000	P. Roy and Diana Vagelos	Barnard College
$14,700,000	Michael and Ann Armstrong	Miami University (Ohio)
$13,670,000	Beverly Lewis and Family	University of Oregon
$13,500,000	Shelby Moore Cullom Davis	Macalester College
$13,000,000	Anonymous	Rutgers University
$12,800,000	James and Donna Barksdale	University of Mississippi
$12,500,000	Anonymous	Saint Francis Hospital and Medical Center
$12,500,000	Aubrey and Kathleen McClendon	University of Oklahoma
$12,000,000	Anonymous (Estate)	University of Pittsburgh at Johnstown
$12,000,000	Mary and Alex Mackenzie (Estate)	Community Foundation of Broward
$12,000,000	John and Antreen Pfau, Elly Pfau, Madelaine Pfau and Charles Jones	California State University San Bernardino
$12,000,000	S. Donald Sussman and Family	Skidmore College
$11,000,000	Betty Wold Johnson	New Jersey Performing Arts Center
$11,000,000	Clifton Stewart (Estate)	University of Southern California Keck School of Medicine

$10 million to $24.99 million (continued)

Dollar Amount	Donor	Recipient
$10,900,000	H. F. (Gerry) and Marguerite B. Lenfest	Natural Lands Trust, Mastery Charter Schools, Library of Congress, Salvation Army, and Swarthmore College
$10,000,000	Anonymous	University of Dayton
$10,000,000	Anonymous	Pittsburg State University
$10,000,000	Anonymous	Canterbury School
$10,000,000	Anonymous	Claremont Museum of Art
$10,000,000	Anonymous	University of South Florida
$10,000,000	Anonymous	Museum of Fine Arts (Boston)
$10,000,000	Anonymous	Star Academy
$10,000,000	Edward and Jeannie Arnold	Boy Scouts of America National Foundation
$10,000,000	Todd and Linda Broin	Sanford USD Medical Center
$10,000,000	Robert and Joan Campbell	Fordham University
$10,000,000	Wilford Cardon and Family	Banner Health
$10,000,000	A. James Clark	Johns Hopkins University
$10,000,000	James and Ruth Clark	Cape Cod Healthcare Foundation
$10,000,000	David A. and Mary Ann Cofrin	University of Florida
$10,000,000	Kathryn Hach Darrow	Iowa State University
$10,000,000	Jim Easton	University of California at Los Angeles
$10,000,000	Don and Ellen Edmondson	University of Arkansas
$10,000,000	Lawrence and Eris Field	City University of New York Bernard M. Baruch College
$10,000,000	Laurence and Lori Fink	University of California Los Angeles
$10,000,000	William Flanagan	Wentworth Institute of Technology
$10,000,000	Richard and Sandra Forsythe	Miami University (Ohio)
$10,000,000	Eugene and Mary Frey	University of St. Thomas
$10,000,000	B. Thomas Golisano	Niagara University
$10,000,000	Harry Halloran, Jr.	University of St. Thomas
$10,000,000	Nancy Hamon	Dallas Center for the Performing Arts
$10,000,000	Romuald Hejna (Estate)	University of Illinois at Chicago
$10,000,000	Rafael Herrera and Family	Miami Children's Hospital Foundation
$10,000,000	Dave House	Michigan Technological University
$10,000,000	Roy Huffington	Southern Methodist University
$10,000,000	Harold Ivie	Oklahoma State University Foundation
$10,000,000	Irwin and Joan Jacobs	Salk Institute for Biological Studies
$10,000,000	Jeremy and Margaret Jacobs and Family	University at Buffalo
$10,000,000	Ed and Bernice Johnson (Estate)	Belmont University
$10,000,000	Julia Kahrl, Benjamin and Karen Smith Kahrl	Pathfinder International
$10,000,000	Cyrus (Dr.) and Myrtle Katzen	George Washington University
$10,000,000	Dennis and Constance Templeton Keller	The Nature Conservancy in Illinois
$10,000,000	Rajen Kilachand	Pathfinder International
$10,000,000	Gertrude Lamden	San Diego State University
$10,000,000	Henry and Marsha Laufer	Stony Brook University
$10,000,000	H. F. (Gerry) and Marguerite B. Lenfest	Various organizations including HMS School for Children with Cerebral Palsy, Pennsylvania Horticultural Society, Philadelphia Orchestra, American Friends of Israel Museum, Catholic Mission Board, and Teach for America
$10,000,000	Benjamin (Jr.) Leon	Florida International University
$10,000,000	William Lyles and Family	California State University, Fresno

$10 million to $24.99 million (continued)

Dollar Amount	Donor	Recipient
$10,000,000	Richard and Peggy Notebaert	University of Notre Dame
$10,000,000	Peter Peckham Family	Rady Children's Hospital San Diego
$10,000,000	T. Boone Pickens	Museum of Nature & Science (Dallas)
$10,000,000	Michael "Mickey" Ross	City College of New York
$10,000,000	Kenneth Schack and Family	New York University
$10,000,000	Earl and Brenda Shapiro and Family	University of Chicago's Laboratory Schools
$10,000,000	Helena Theurer	Hackensack University Medical Center
$10,000,000	Peter and Ann Tombros	Pennsylvania State University
$10,000,000	Bob and Mary Van Diest	Hamilton Hospital
$10,000,000	Scott Walker	Thunderbird School of Global Management
$10,000,000	Ronald and Eileen Weiser	University of Michigan

For more information about these and other gifts, see The Center on Philanthropy at Indiana University Web site, www.philanthropy.iupui.edu.

Sources used for the Million Dollar List maintained by the Center on Philanthropy include *The Chronicle of Philanthropy*, *Chronicle of Higher Education*, *Philanthropy News Digest*, and newspaper articles, tracked by the Center.

18

Data tables for charts in *Giving USA*: The Numbers

Giving by source, 1968–2008
(in billions of current dollars)

	Total	Percent change	Corpora- tions	Percent change	Founda- tions	Percent change	Bequests	Percent change	Individuals	Percent change
1968	18.85	10.7	0.90	9.8	1.60	14.3	1.60	14.3	14.75	10.0
1969	20.66	9.6	0.93	3.3	1.80	12.5	2.00	25.0	15.93	8.0
1970	21.04	1.8	0.82	-11.8	1.90	5.6	2.13	6.5	16.19	1.6
1971	23.44	11.4	0.85	4.2	1.95	2.6	3.00	40.8	17.64	9.0
1972	24.44	4.3	0.97	14.1	2.00	2.6	2.10	-30.0	19.37	9.8
1973	25.59	4.7	1.06	9.3	2.00	0.0	2.00	-4.8	20.53	6.0
1974	26.88	5.0	1.10	3.8	2.11	5.5	2.07	3.5	21.60	5.2
1975	28.56	6.3	1.15	4.5	1.65	-21.8	2.23	7.7	23.53	8.9
1976	31.85	11.5	1.33	15.7	1.90	15.2	2.30	3.1	26.32	11.9
1977	35.21	10.5	1.54	15.8	2.00	5.3	2.12	-7.8	29.55	12.3
1978	38.57	9.5	1.70	10.4	2.17	8.5	2.60	22.6	32.10	8.6
1979	43.11	11.8	2.05	20.6	2.24	3.2	2.23	-14.2	36.59	14.0
1980	48.63	12.8	2.25	9.8	2.81	25.4	2.86	28.3	40.71	11.3
1981	55.28	13.7	2.64	17.3	3.07	9.3	3.58	25.2	45.99	13.0
1982	59.11	6.9	3.11	17.8	3.16	2.9	5.21	45.5	47.63	3.6
1983	63.21	6.9	3.67	18.0	3.60	13.9	3.88	-25.5	52.06	9.3
1984	68.58	8.5	4.13	12.5	3.95	9.7	4.04	4.1	56.46	8.5
1985	71.69	4.5	4.63	12.1	4.90	24.1	4.77	18.1	57.39	1.6
1986	83.25	16.1	5.03	8.6	5.43	10.8	5.70	19.5	67.09	16.9
1987	82.20	-1.3	5.21	3.6	5.88	8.3	6.58	15.4	64.53	-3.8
1988	88.04	7.1	5.34	2.5	6.15	4.6	6.57	-0.2	69.98	8.4
1989	98.30	11.7	5.46	2.2	6.55	6.5	6.84	4.1	79.45	13.5
1990	100.52	2.3	5.46	0.0	7.23	10.4	6.79	-0.7	81.04	2.0
1991	104.92	4.4	5.25	-3.8	7.72	6.8	7.68	13.1	84.27	4.0
1992	111.79	6.5	5.91	12.6	8.64	11.9	9.54	24.2	87.70	4.1
1993	116.86	4.5	6.47	9.5	9.53	10.3	8.86	-7.1	92.00	4.9
1994	120.29	2.9	6.98	7.9	9.66	1.4	11.13	25.6	92.52	0.6
1995	123.68	2.8	7.35	5.3	10.56	9.3	10.41	-6.5	95.36	3.1
1996	139.10	12.5	7.51	2.2	12.00	13.6	12.03	15.6	107.56	12.8
1997	162.99	17.2	8.62	14.8	13.92	16.0	16.25	35.1	124.20	15.5
1998	176.80	8.5	8.46	-1.9	17.01	22.2	12.98	-20.1	138.35	11.4
1999	202.74	14.7	10.23	20.9	20.51	20.6	17.37	33.8	154.63	11.8
2000	229.71	13.3	10.74	5.0	24.58	19.8	19.88	14.5	174.51	12.9
2001	232.03	1.0	11.66	8.6	27.22	10.7	19.80	-0.4	173.35	-0.7
2002	233.11	0.5	10.79	-7.5	26.98	-0.9	20.90	5.6	174.44	0.6
2003	238.05	2.1	11.06	2.5	26.84	-0.5	18.19	-13.0	181.96	4.3
2004	259.59	9.0	11.36	2.7	28.41	5.8	18.46	1.5	201.36	10.7
2005	293.20	12.9	16.59	46.0	32.41	14.1	23.45	27.0	220.75	9.6
2006	295.33	0.7	14.89	-10.2	34.91	7.7	21.65	-7.7	223.88	1.4
2007	314.07	6.3	15.18	1.9	40.00	14.6	23.31	7.7	235.58	5.2
2008	307.65	-2.0	14.50	-4.5	41.21	3.0	22.66	-2.8	229.28	-2.7

Source for foundation giving: The Foundation Center

Notes: All figures are rounded. *Giving USA* changed its rounding procedure from the 2003 edition forward. All estimates are rounded to two places then operations performed. In the past, operations were performed first and the results were rounded.

Giving by source, 1968–2008
(in billions of inflation-adjusted dollars)

	Total	Percent change	Corpora-tions	Percent change	Founda-tions	Percent change	Bequests	Percent change	Individuals	Percent change
1968	116.64	6.2	5.57	5.3	9.90	9.6	9.90	9.6	91.27	5.6
1969	121.17	3.9	5.45	-2.2	10.56	6.7	11.73	18.5	93.43	2.4
1970	116.75	-3.6	4.55	-16.5	10.54	-0.2	11.82	0.8	89.84	-3.8
1971	124.62	6.7	4.52	-0.7	10.37	-1.6	15.95	34.9	93.78	4.4
1972	125.91	1.0	5.00	10.6	10.30	-0.7	10.82	-32.2	99.79	6.4
1973	124.10	-1.4	5.14	2.8	9.70	-5.8	9.70	-10.4	99.56	-0.2
1974	117.37	-5.4	4.80	-6.6	9.21	-5.1	9.04	-6.8	94.32	-5.3
1975	114.28	-2.6	4.60	-4.2	6.60	-28.3	8.92	-1.3	94.16	-0.2
1976	120.50	5.4	5.03	9.3	7.19	8.9	8.70	-2.5	99.58	5.8
1977	125.07	3.8	5.47	8.7	7.10	-1.3	7.53	-13.4	104.97	5.4
1978	127.38	1.8	5.61	2.6	7.17	1.0	8.59	14.1	106.01	1.0
1979	127.84	0.4	6.08	8.4	6.64	-7.4	6.61	-23.1	108.51	2.4
1980	127.07	-0.6	5.88	-3.3	7.34	10.5	7.47	13.0	106.38	-2.0
1981	130.93	3.0	6.25	6.3	7.27	-1.0	8.48	13.5	108.93	2.4
1982	131.88	0.7	6.94	11.0	7.05	-3.0	11.62	37.0	106.27	-2.4
1983	136.64	3.6	7.93	14.3	7.78	10.4	8.39	-27.8	112.54	5.9
1984	142.10	4.0	8.56	7.9	8.18	5.1	8.37	-0.2	116.99	4.0
1985	143.43	0.9	9.26	8.2	9.80	19.8	9.54	14.0	114.83	-1.8
1986	163.53	14.0	9.88	6.7	10.67	8.9	11.20	17.4	131.78	14.8
1987	155.79	-4.7	9.87	-0.1	11.14	4.4	12.47	11.3	122.31	-7.2
1988	160.22	2.8	9.72	-1.5	11.19	0.4	11.96	-4.1	127.35	4.1
1989	170.69	6.5	9.48	-2.5	11.37	1.6	11.88	-0.7	137.96	8.3
1990	165.57	-3.0	8.99	-5.2	11.91	4.7	11.18	-5.9	133.49	-3.2
1991	165.85	0.2	8.30	-7.7	12.20	2.4	12.14	8.6	133.21	-0.2
1992	171.56	3.4	9.07	9.3	13.26	8.7	14.64	20.6	134.59	1.0
1993	174.13	1.5	9.64	6.3	14.20	7.1	13.20	-9.8	137.09	1.9
1994	174.76	0.4	10.14	5.2	14.03	-1.2	16.17	22.5	134.42	-1.9
1995	174.74	0.0	10.38	2.4	14.92	6.3	14.71	-9.0	134.73	0.2
1996	190.90	9.2	10.31	-0.7	16.47	10.4	16.51	12.2	147.61	9.6
1997	218.63	14.5	11.56	12.1	18.67	13.4	21.80	32.0	166.60	12.9
1998	233.52	6.8	11.17	-3.4	22.47	20.4	17.14	-21.4	182.74	9.7
1999	262.01	12.2	13.22	18.4	26.51	18.0	22.45	31.0	199.83	9.4
2000	287.21	9.6	13.43	1.6	30.73	15.9	24.86	10.7	218.19	9.2
2001	282.06	-1.8	14.17	5.5	33.09	7.7	24.07	-3.2	210.73	-3.4
2002	278.97	-1.1	12.91	-8.9	32.29	-2.4	25.01	3.9	208.76	-0.9
2003	278.55	-0.2	12.94	0.2	31.41	-2.7	21.28	-14.9	212.92	2.0
2004	295.87	6.2	12.95	0.1	32.38	3.1	21.04	-1.1	229.50	7.8
2005	323.23	9.2	18.29	41.2	35.73	10.3	25.85	22.9	243.36	6.0
2006	315.39	-2.4	15.90	-13.1	37.28	4.3	23.12	-10.6	239.09	-1.8
2007	326.14	3.4	15.76	-0.9	41.54	11.4	24.21	4.7	244.63	2.3
2008	307.65	-5.7	14.50	-8.0	41.21	-0.8	22.66	-6.4	229.28	-6.3

Source for foundation giving: The Foundation Center
Notes: All figures are rounded. *Giving USA* changed its rounding procedure from the 2003 edition forward. All estimates are rounded to two places then operations performed. In the past, operations were performed first and the results were rounded. Inflation adjustment uses the Consumer Price Index calculator available at www.bls.gov. 2008 = 100.

Contributions by type of recipient organization, 1968–2008
(in billions of current dollars)

	Total	Pct chg	Religion	Pct chg	Education	Pct chg	Human services	Pct chg	Health	Pct chg	Public-society benefit	Pct chg
1968	18.85	10.7	8.42	11.1	2.38	11.7	2.31	11.6	2.08	8.9	0.43	4.9
1969	20.66	9.6	9.02	7.1	2.54	6.7	2.71	17.3	2.31	11.1	0.56	30.2
1970	21.04	1.8	9.34	3.5	2.60	2.4	2.92	7.7	2.40	3.9	0.46	-17.9
1971	23.44	11.4	10.07	7.8	2.75	5.8	3.01	3.1	2.61	8.8	0.68	47.8
1972	24.44	4.3	10.10	0.3	2.98	8.4	3.16	5.0	2.80	7.3	0.82	20.6
1973	25.59	4.7	10.53	4.3	3.33	11.7	3.07	-2.8	3.10	10.7	0.62	-24.4
1974	26.88	5.0	11.84	12.4	3.38	1.5	3.90	27.0	3.53	13.9	0.89	43.5
1975	28.56	6.3	12.81	8.2	3.19	-5.6	3.92	0.5	3.66	3.7	1.22	37.1
1976	31.85	11.5	14.18	10.7	3.59	12.5	4.03	2.8	3.74	2.2	1.48	21.3
1977	35.21	10.5	16.98	19.7	3.89	8.4	4.10	1.7	3.93	5.1	1.29	-12.8
1978	38.57	9.5	18.35	8.1	4.32	11.1	4.22	2.9	4.10	4.3	1.50	16.3
1979	43.11	11.8	20.17	9.9	4.70	8.8	4.31	2.1	4.28	4.4	1.82	21.3
1980	48.63	12.8	22.23	10.2	5.07	7.9	4.45	3.2	4.48	4.7	2.28	25.3
1981	55.28	13.7	25.05	12.7	5.93	17.0	4.59	3.1	4.63	3.3	2.13	-6.6
1982	59.11	6.9	28.06	12.0	6.14	3.5	4.76	3.7	4.87	5.2	2.42	13.6
1983	63.21	6.9	31.84	13.5	6.71	9.3	4.90	2.9	4.93	1.2	2.48	2.5
1984	68.58	8.5	35.55	11.7	7.27	8.3	5.03	2.7	5.32	7.9	2.88	16.1
1985	71.69	4.5	38.21	7.5	8.05	10.7	5.16	2.6	5.63	5.8	3.20	11.1
1986	83.25	16.1	41.68	9.1	9.38	16.5	5.30	2.7	5.97	6.0	3.78	18.1
1987	82.20	-1.3	43.51	4.4	9.78	4.3	5.42	2.3	6.12	2.5	4.26	12.7
1988	88.04	7.1	45.15	3.8	10.12	3.5	5.60	3.3	6.28	2.6	5.14	20.7
1989	98.30	11.7	47.77	5.8	11.13	10.0	6.27	12.0	6.52	3.8	6.94	35.0
1990	100.52	2.3	49.79	4.2	11.68	4.9	6.46	3.0	7.35	12.7	7.36	6.1
1991	104.92	4.4	50.00	0.4	12.36	5.8	7.46	15.5	7.75	5.4	8.31	12.9
1992	111.79	6.5	50.95	1.9	13.00	5.2	8.44	13.1	8.46	9.2	8.51	2.4
1993	116.86	4.5	52.89	3.8	14.23	9.5	8.74	3.6	8.71	3.0	8.68	2.0
1994	120.29	2.9	56.43	6.7	14.08	-1.1	8.93	2.2	9.17	5.3	9.96	14.7
1995	123.68	2.8	58.07	2.9	15.63	11.0	9.74	9.1	13.93	51.9	11.25	13.0
1996	139.10	12.5	61.90	6.6	18.46	18.1	10.42	4.0	14.15	10.4	11.33	6.6
1997	162.99	17.2	64.69	4.5	20.35	10.2	12.62	4.1	12.76	1.0	12.94	10.8
1998	176.80	8.5	68.25	5.5	23.84	17.1	15.55	23.2	13.24	3.8	13.95	7.8
1999	202.74	14.7	71.25	4.4	27.22	8.5	17.86	14.9	15.22	6.3	13.02	-6.7
2000	229.71	13.3	76.95	8.0	29.65	8.9	20.02	12.1	16.43	8.0	15.36	18.0
2001	232.03	1.0	79.87	3.8	32.73	10.4	21.76	8.7	18.25	11.1	16.52	7.6
2002	233.11	0.5	82.91	3.8	29.96	-8.5	24.40	12.1	17.76	-2.7	17.97	8.8
2003	238.05	2.1	84.57	2.0	29.77	-0.6	23.47	-3.8	20.54	15.7	16.42	-8.6
2004	259.59	9.0	87.95	4.0	33.75	13.4	24.42	4.0	20.15	-1.9	18.82	14.6
2005	293.20	12.9	93.03	5.8	37.31	10.5	26.10	6.9	22.49	11.6	21.29	13.1
2006	295.33	0.7	97.52	4.8	40.73	9.2	27.35	4.8	21.97	-2.3	21.41	0.6
2007	314.07	6.3	101.32	3.9	43.32	6.4	29.64	8.4	23.15	5.4	22.65	5.8
2008	307.65	-2.0	106.89	5.5	40.94	-5.5	25.88	-12.7	21.64	-6.5	23.88	5.4

Notes: All figures are rounded. *Giving USA* changed its rounding procedure in the 2003 edition. All estimates are rounded to two places then operations performed. In earlier editions, calculations were performed before rounding and results were rounded to two places.

	Arts, culture, humanities	Pct chg	Inter- national affairs	Pct chg	Environ- ment/ animals	Pct chg	Gifts to foun- dations	Pct chg	Gifts to indi- viduals	Unallo- Unallocated
1968	0.60	7.1								2.63
1969	0.72	20.0								2.80
1970	0.66	-8.3								2.66
1971	1.01	53.0								3.31
1972	1.10	8.9								3.48
1973	1.26	14.5								3.68
1974	1.46	15.9								1.88
1975	1.49	2.1								2.27
1976	1.54	3.4								3.29
1977	1.84	19.5								3.18
1978	1.87	1.6					1.61			2.60
1979	1.98	5.9					2.21	37.3		3.64
1980	2.12	7.1					1.98	-10.4		6.02
1981	2.28	7.5					2.39	20.7		8.28
1982	2.71	18.9					4.00	67.4		6.15
1983	2.46	-9.2					2.71	-32.3		7.18
1984	2.56	4.1					3.36	24.0		6.61
1985	2.75	7.4					4.73	40.8		3.96
1986	3.00	9.1					4.96	4.9		9.18
1987	3.15	5.0	0.81		1.08		5.16	4.0		2.91
1988	3.31	5.1	0.89	9.9	1.14	11.4	3.93	-23.8		6.48
1989	3.74	13.0	1.71	92.1	1.40	-14.0	4.41	12.2		8.41
1990	3.98	6.4	2.24	31.0	1.55	30.9	3.83	-13.2		6.28
1991	4.29	7.8	2.12	-5.4	1.70	10.7	4.46	16.4		6.47
1992	4.52	5.4	2.38	12.3	1.72	6.5	5.01	12.3		8.80
1993	4.86	7.5	2.23	-6.3	1.96	2.2	6.26	25.0		8.30
1994	4.75	-2.3	2.71	21.5	2.04	11.0	6.33	1.1		5.89
1995	5.67	19.4	3.01	11.1	2.29	12.5	8.46	33.6		-4.37
1996	6.38	12.5	3.57	18.6	2.62	1.6	12.63	49.3		-2.36
1997	7.34	-2.8	4.21	17.9	3.09	7.4	13.96	10.5		11.03
1998	9.87	34.5	5.08	20.7	3.51	13.6	19.92	42.7		3.59
1999	9.24	-6.4	6.58	29.5	4.24	20.8	28.76	44.4		9.35
2000	10.48	13.4	7.20	9.4	4.75	12.0	24.71	-14.1		24.16
2001	11.41	5.6	8.31	13.0	5.29	4.0	25.67	3.9		12.22
2002	10.83	-5.1	8.70	4.7	5.29	0.0	19.16	-25.4		16.13
2003	10.83	0.0	9.84	13.1	5.44	2.8	21.62	12.8		15.55
2004	11.78	8.8	11.55	17.4	5.50	1.1	20.32	-6.0	1.74	23.61
2005	11.76	-0.2	15.18	31.4	5.99	8.9	27.46	35.1	3.11	29.48
2006	12.68	7.8	11.39	-25.0	6.28	4.8	30.60	11.4	3.83	21.57
2007	13.67	7.8	13.22	16.1	6.96	10.8	40.43	32.1	3.37	16.34
2008	12.79	-6.4	13.30	0.6	6.58	-5.5	32.65	-19.2	3.71	19.39

Notes: Gifts to foundations from 1992–2007 represent total gifts reported to the Foundation Center minus gifts to corporate foundations, the assets transferred to health care foundations for the years 1992–1998, and Warren Buffett's gifts in 2006 and 2007 to the Gates Foundation. These were subtracted from the Foundation Center's report of gifts to foundations. Gifts to foundations for 2008 are here estimated jointly by *Giving USA* and the Foundation Center. This figure will be released in early 2010. Funds given to nonprofits not reported by an organization in a subsector are included in "Unallocated Gifts." See the pie chart for a definition of Unallocated.

Contributions by type of recipient organization, 1968–2008
(in billions of inflation-adjusted dollars)

	Total	Pct chg	Religion	Pct chg	Education	Pct chg	Human services	Pct chg	Health	Pct chg	Public-society benefit	Pct chg
1968	116.65	6.2	52.10	6.6	14.73	7.3	14.29	7.0	12.87	4.5	2.66	0.8
1969	121.17	3.9	52.90	1.5	14.90	1.2	15.89	11.2	13.55	5.3	3.28	23.3
1970	116.77	-3.6	51.83	-2.0	14.43	-3.2	16.20	2.0	13.32	-1.7	2.55	-22.3
1971	124.61	6.7	53.54	3.3	14.62	1.3	16.00	-1.2	13.88	4.2	3.62	42.0
1972	125.91	1.0	52.04	-2.8	15.35	5.0	16.28	1.8	14.43	4.0	4.22	16.6
1973	124.10	-1.4	51.07	-1.9	16.15	5.2	14.89	-8.5	15.03	4.2	3.01	-28.7
1974	117.38	-5.4	51.70	1.2	14.76	-8.6	17.03	14.4	15.41	2.5	3.89	29.2
1975	114.29	-2.6	51.26	-0.9	12.77	-13.5	15.69	-7.9	14.65	-4.9	4.88	25.4
1976	120.51	5.4	53.65	4.7	13.58	6.3	15.25	-2.8	14.15	-3.4	5.60	14.8
1977	125.08	3.8	60.32	12.4	13.82	1.8	14.56	-4.5	13.96	-1.3	4.58	-18.2
1978	127.38	1.8	60.60	0.5	14.27	3.3	13.94	-4.3	13.54	-3.0	4.95	8.1
1979	127.85	0.4	59.82	-1.3	13.94	-2.3	12.78	-8.3	12.69	-6.3	5.40	9.1
1980	127.07	-0.6	58.09	-2.9	13.25	-4.9	11.63	-9.0	11.71	-7.7	5.96	10.4
1981	130.93	3.0	59.33	2.1	14.05	6.0	10.87	-6.5	10.97	-6.3	5.05	-15.3
1982	131.88	0.7	62.61	5.5	13.70	-2.5	10.62	-2.3	10.87	-0.9	5.40	6.9
1983	136.64	3.6	68.83	9.9	14.50	5.8	10.59	-0.3	10.66	-1.9	5.36	-0.7
1984	142.11	4.0	73.66	7.0	15.06	3.9	10.42	-1.6	11.02	3.4	5.97	11.4
1985	143.44	0.9	76.45	3.8	16.11	7.0	10.32	-1.0	11.26	2.2	6.40	7.2
1986	163.52	14.0	81.87	7.1	18.42	14.3	10.41	0.9	11.73	4.2	7.42	15.9
1987	155.80	-4.7	82.47	0.7	18.54	0.7	10.27	-1.3	11.60	-1.1	8.07	8.8
1988	160.22	2.8	82.17	-0.4	18.42	-0.6	10.19	-0.8	11.43	-1.5	9.35	15.9
1989	170.69	6.5	82.95	0.9	19.33	4.9	10.89	6.9	11.32	-1.0	12.05	28.9
1990	165.57	-3.0	82.01	-1.1	19.24	-0.5	10.64	-2.3	12.11	7.0	12.12	0.6
1991	165.86	0.2	79.04	-3.6	19.54	1.6	11.79	10.8	12.25	1.2	13.14	8.4
1992	171.56	3.4	78.19	-1.1	19.95	2.1	12.95	9.8	12.98	6.0	13.06	-0.6
1993	174.13	1.5	78.81	0.8	21.20	6.3	13.02	0.5	12.98	0.0	12.93	-1.0
1994	174.76	0.4	81.98	4.0	20.46	-3.5	12.97	-0.4	13.32	2.6	14.47	11.9
1995	174.74	0.0	82.04	0.1	22.08	7.9	13.76	6.1	19.68	47.7	15.89	9.8
1996	190.89	9.2	84.95	3.5	25.33	14.7	14.30	3.9	19.42	-1.3	15.55	-2.1
1997	218.63	14.5	86.77	2.1	27.30	7.8	16.93	18.4	17.12	-11.8	17.36	11.6
1998	233.52	6.8	90.15	3.9	31.49	15.3	20.54	21.3	17.49	2.2	18.43	6.2
1999	262.01	12.2	92.08	2.1	35.18	11.7	23.08	12.4	19.67	12.5	16.83	-8.7
2000	287.21	9.6	96.21	4.5	37.07	5.4	25.03	8.4	20.54	4.4	19.20	14.1
2001	282.07	-1.8	97.09	0.9	39.79	7.3	26.45	5.7	22.19	8.0	20.08	4.6
2002	278.97	-1.1	99.22	2.2	35.85	-9.9	29.20	10.4	21.25	-4.2	21.51	7.1
2003	278.55	-0.2	98.96	-0.3	34.84	-2.8	27.46	-6.0	24.03	13.1	19.21	-10.7
2004	295.87	6.2	100.24	1.3	38.47	10.4	27.83	1.3	22.97	-4.4	21.45	11.7
2005	323.21	9.2	102.56	2.3	41.13	6.9	28.77	3.4	24.79	7.9	23.47	9.4
2006	315.39	-2.4	104.14	1.5	43.50	5.8	29.21	1.5	23.46	-5.4	22.86	-2.6
2007	326.14	3.4	105.21	1.0	44.98	3.4	30.78	5.4	24.04	2.5	23.52	2.9
2008	307.65	-5.7	106.89	1.6	40.94	-9.0	25.88	-15.9	21.64	-10.0	23.88	1.5

Notes: *Giving USA* uses the Consumer Price Index to adjust for inflation. All figures are rounded. Source for foundation giving: The Foundation Center. *Giving USA* changed its rounding procedure in 2003. All estimates are rounded to two places then operations performed. In the past, operations were performed first and the results were rounded.

	Arts, culture, humanities	Pct chg	International affairs	Pct chg	Environment/ animals	Pct chg	Gifts to foundations	Pct chg	Gifts to individuals	Unallocated
1968	3.71	2.8								16.27
1969	4.22	13.7								16.42
1970	3.66	-13.3								14.76
1971	5.37	46.7								17.60
1972	5.67	5.6								17.93
1973	6.11	7.8								17.85
1974	6.38	4.4								8.21
1975	5.96	-6.6								9.08
1976	5.83	-2.2								12.45
1977	6.54	12.2								11.30
1978	6.18	-5.5					5.32			8.59
1979	5.87	-5.0					6.55	23.1		10.79
1980	5.54	-5.6					5.17	-21.1		15.73
1981	5.40	-2.5					5.66	9.5		19.61
1982	6.05	12.0					8.92	57.6		13.72
1983	5.32	-12.1					5.86	-34.3		15.52
1984	5.30	-0.4					6.96	18.8		13.70
1985	5.50	3.8					9.46	35.9		7.92
1986	5.89	7.1					9.74	3.0		18.03
1987	5.97	1.4	1.54		2.05		9.78	0.4		5.52
1988	6.02	0.8	1.62	5.2	2.07	1.0	7.15	-26.9		11.79
1989	6.49	7.8	2.97	83.3	2.43	17.4	7.66	7.1		14.60
1990	6.56	1.1	3.69	24.2	2.55	4.9	6.31	-17.6		10.34
1991	6.78	3.4	3.35	-9.2	2.69	5.5	7.05	11.7		10.23
1992	6.94	2.4	3.65	9.0	2.64	-1.9	7.69	9.1		13.51
1993	7.24	4.3	3.32	-9.0	2.92	10.6	9.33	21.3		12.37
1994	6.90	-4.7	3.94	18.7	2.96	1.4	9.20	-1.4		8.56
1995	8.01	16.1	4.25	7.9	3.24	9.5	11.95	29.9		-6.17
1996	8.76	9.4	4.90	15.3	3.60	11.1	17.33	45.0		-3.24
1997	9.85	12.4	5.65	15.3	4.14	15.0	18.73	8.1		14.80
1998	13.04	32.4	6.71	18.8	4.64	12.1	26.31	40.5		4.74
1999	11.94	-8.4	8.50	26.7	5.48	18.1	37.17	41.3		12.08
2000	13.10	9.7	9.00	5.9	5.94	8.4	30.90	-16.9		30.21
2001	13.87	5.9	10.10	12.2	6.43	8.2	31.21	1.0		14.86
2002	12.96	-6.6	10.41	3.1	6.33	-1.6	22.93	-26.5		19.30
2003	12.67	-2.2	11.51	10.6	6.37	0.6	25.30	10.3		18.20
2004	13.43	6.0	13.16	14.3	6.27	-1.6	23.16	-8.5	1.98	26.91
2005	12.96	-3.5	16.73	27.1	6.60	5.3	30.27	30.7	3.43	32.50
2006	13.54	4.5	12.16	-27.3	6.71	1.7	32.68	8.0	4.09	23.04
2007	14.20	4.9	13.73	12.9	7.23	7.7	41.98	28.5	3.50	16.97
2008	12.79	-9.9	13.30	-3.1	6.58	-9.0	32.65	-22.2	3.71	19.39

Giving as a percentage of gross domestic product (GDP), 1968–2008
(in billions of inflation-adjusted dollars)

Year	Total giving	GDP	Giving as a percentage of GDP
1968	116.65	5,631.19	2.1
1969	121.17	5,774.78	2.1
1970	116.77	5,763.04	2.0
1971	124.61	5,992.03	2.1
1972	125.91	6,379.70	2.0
1973	124.10	6,705.63	1.9
1974	117.38	6,550.22	1.8
1975	114.29	6,555.82	1.7
1976	120.51	6,906.17	1.7
1977	125.08	7,214.56	1.7
1978	127.38	7,578.27	1.7
1979	127.85	7,601.72	1.7
1980	127.07	7,283.29	1.7
1981	130.93	7,409.76	1.8
1982	131.88	7,262.38	1.8
1983	136.64	7,645.27	1.8
1984	142.11	8,150.02	1.7
1985	143.44	8,443.98	1.7
1986	163.52	8,766.06	1.9
1987	155.80	8,983.13	1.7
1988	160.22	9,288.08	1.7
1989	170.69	9,523.18	1.8
1990	165.57	9,558.72	1.7
1991	165.86	9,478.19	1.7
1992	171.56	9,726.37	1.8
1993	174.13	9,920.13	1.8
1994	174.76	10,274.88	1.7
1995	174.74	10,451.68	1.7
1996	190.89	10,727.19	1.8
1997	218.63	11,139.24	2.0
1998	233.52	11,554.82	2.0
1999	262.01	11,977.77	2.2
2000	287.21	12,274.32	2.3
2001	282.07	12,312.18	2.3
2002	278.97	12,529.44	2.2
2003	278.55	12,825.65	2.2
2004	295.87	13,318.78	2.2
2005	323.21	13,694.08	2.4
2006	315.39	14,073.47	2.2
2007	326.14	14,338.01	2.3
2008	307.65	14,264.60	2.2

Notes: Percentages include computer rounding. *Giving USA 2009* uses the data for Gross Domestic Product available from the Bureau of Economic Analysis, release of March 26, 2009. Inflation adjustment uses the Consumer Price Index calculator available at www.bls.gov. 2008=$100.

Individual giving as a percentage of disposable personal income, "essential" expenditures, and "luxury" expenditures 1968–2008
(in billions of inflation-adjusted dollars)

Year	Individual giving	Disposable personal income	Essential personal expenditures	Luxury personal expenditures	Giving, as a percentage of Disposable personal income	Essential personal expenditures	Luxury personal expenditures
1968	91.27	3867.57	1489.48	459.1584	2.4	6.1	19.9
1969	93.43	3953.08	1526.69	471.5543	2.4	6.1	19.8
1970	89.84	4082.69	1545.50	495.0055	2.2	5.8	18.2
1971	93.78	4262.63	1579.48	507.7087	2.2	5.9	18.5
1972	99.79	4477.59	1657.91	539.9279	2.2	6.0	18.5
1973	99.56	4744.42	1734.72	565.9554	2.1	5.7	17.6
1974	94.32	4679.48	1755.90	564.6288	2.0	5.4	16.7
1975	94.16	4751.50	1773.11	577.4310	2.0	5.3	16.3
1976	99.58	4928.11	1830.87	607.6428	2.0	5.4	16.4
1977	104.97	5100.18	1887.74	623.0906	2.1	5.6	16.8
1978	106.01	5311.43	1941.22	644.9802	2.0	5.5	16.4
1979	108.51	5318.80	1966.79	647.0937	2.0	5.5	16.8
1980	106.29	5245.43	1954.83	630.5483	2.0	5.4	16.9
1981	108.93	5319.99	1959.73	632.1649	2.0	5.6	17.2
1982	106.27	5402.05	1952.48	637.4386	2.0	5.4	16.7
1983	112.54	5638.56	2008.00	675.0973	2.0	5.6	16.7
1984	116.99	6033.98	2063.61	705.7605	1.9	5.7	16.6
1985	114.83	6221.09	2129.25	727.6911	1.8	5.4	15.8
1986	131.78	6452.76	2168.73	763.8971	2.0	6.1	17.3
1987	122.31	6554.78	2210.77	798.5216	1.9	5.5	15.3
1988	127.35	6822.02	2259.51	839.8544	1.9	5.6	15.2
1989	137.96	6983.33	2308.73	864.5598	2.0	6.0	16.0
1990	133.49	7059.46	2324.16	893.7572	1.9	5.7	14.9
1991	133.21	7057.07	2312.84	889.3456	1.9	5.8	15.0
1992	134.59	7291.90	2325.81	917.1271	1.8	5.8	14.7
1993	137.09	7319.18	2347.49	939.2043	1.9	5.8	14.6
1994	134.42	7484.82	2405.35	954.8162	1.8	5.6	14.1
1995	134.73	7640.86	2429.22	971.0370	1.8	5.5	13.9
1996	147.61	7806.37	2477.43	989.8449	1.9	6.0	14.9
1997	166.60	8033.27	2521.40	1017.706	2.1	6.6	16.4
1998	182.76	8449.01	2573.45	1067.371	2.2	7.1	17.1
1999	199.83	8652.11	2669.68	1121.737	2.3	7.5	17.8
2000	218.19	8994.75	2770.07	1169.167	2.4	7.9	18.7
2001	210.73	9101.39	2825.67	1178.215	2.3	7.5	17.9
2002	208.76	9370.63	2849.81	1207.516	2.2	7.3	17.3
2003	212.92	9551.25	2916.10	1234.613	2.2	7.3	17.2
2004	229.50	9893.89	3021.31	1286.642	2.3	7.6	17.8
2005	243.36	9990.08	3138.57	1311.212	2.4	7.8	18.6
2006	239.09	10295.49	3236.65	1357.326	2.3	7.4	17.6
2007	244.63	10561.27	3318.90	1391.796	2.3	7.4	17.6
2008	229.28	10642.10	no data	no data	2.2		

Notes: Percentages include computer rounding. *Giving USA 2009* uses the data for disposable personal income and personal expenditures from the Bureau of Economic Analysis as downloaded March 26, 2009. The personal income information is from Table 2.1. Expenditure information is from Table 2.4.5. "Essential" expenditures include clothing, energy (gasoline and heating fuels), food (excluding restaurants), housing, and housing operation (utilities). "Luxury" expenditures include restaurants, alcohol, tobacco, jewelry and watches, recreation, and international travel. Inflation adjustment uses the Consumer Price Index calculator available at www.bls.gov. 2008=$100.

Corporate giving as a percentage of pretax corporate profits, 1968–2008
(in billions of inflation-adjusted dollars)

Year	Corporate giving	Corporate pretax profits	Giving as a percentage of pretax profits
1968	5.57	572.02	1.0
1969	5.45	535.90	1.0
1970	4.55	449.46	1.0
1971	4.52	493.69	0.9
1972	5.00	555.44	0.9
1973	5.14	653.97	0.8
1974	4.80	645.24	0.7
1975	4.60	582.40	0.8
1976	5.03	679.92	0.7
1977	5.47	747.47	0.7
1978	5.61	812.87	0.7
1979	6.08	806.41	0.8
1980	5.88	662.39	0.9
1981	6.25	577.31	1.1
1982	6.94	442.98	1.6
1983	7.93	505.62	1.6
1984	8.56	556.59	1.5
1985	9.26	515.08	1.8
1986	9.88	483.13	2.0
1987	9.87	601.98	1.6
1988	9.72	702.59	1.4
1989	9.48	666.34	1.4
1990	8.99	674.56	1.3
1991	8.30	668.65	1.2
1992	9.07	707.60	1.3
1993	9.64	770.52	1.3
1994	10.14	838.39	1.2
1995	10.38	952.67	1.1
1996	10.31	1,005.95	1.0
1997	11.56	1,070.63	1.1
1998	11.17	948.71	1.2
1999	13.22	1,002.68	1.3
2000	13.43	966.99	1.4
2001	14.17	860.58	1.6
2002	12.91	919.62	1.4
2003	12.94	1,062.58	1.2
2004	12.95	1,403.24	0.9
2005	18.29	1,596.19	1.1
2006	15.90	2,000.97	0.8
2007	15.76	1,958.77	0.8
2008	14.50	1,597.30	0.9

Notes: Percentages include computer rounding. *Giving USA 2009* uses the data for corporate pretax profits from the Bureau of Economic Analysis, National Income and Product Accounts, Table 6.17, as downloaded on March 26, 2009 for values for 1968 to 2007. The value for 2008 is from the BEA press release dated March 26, 2009. Inflation adjustment uses the Consumer Price Index calculator available at www.bls.gov. 2008=$100.

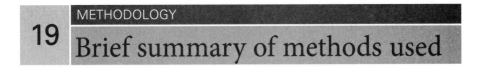

19 Brief summary of methods used

Overview of methodology for 2008 estimates

Giving USA presents estimates for the four primary sources of giving and for nine principal types of recipients of contributions. These are preliminary estimates for 2008, which use the best information available as of March and April 2009. They will be revised in 2010 and in 2011 as more data are available. Revisions of *Giving USA*'s estimates for 2006 and earlier are reflected in the data tables in this volume.

The *Giving USA* estimates apply methods developed by scholars of giving and are reviewed and approved by the members of the *Giving USA* Advisory Council on Methodology. Members of that group include research directors from a number of other organizations involved in studying the nonprofit sector. They are listed in this volume.

The rest of this chapter provides an overview of the methods used to develop the estimates for 2008, organized to present the sources of giving first, followed by the types of recipients. Separate methodology papers are available for estimating giving by individuals and corporations, and for estimating giving to religion.

Estimate of giving by individuals

For giving in 2008, we used the final IRS data about itemized deductions for charitable contributions claimed on individual income tax returns for 2006. To this total are added estimated changes in itemized charitable contributions for 2007 and 2008, plus estimates of giving by households that do not itemize. The nonitemizer household estimate is based on the Center on Philanthropy Panel Study (COPPS), which asks more than 7,800 households about their charitable giving. The Center on Wealth and Philanthropy at Boston College and the Center on Philanthropy at Indiana University did the analysis of 2004 COPPS data to develop an estimate of giving by nonitemizing households. That estimate is adjusted for changes in household giving as household income changes and for the changing number of non-itemizing households to create an estimate for charitable giving in each year since 2005.

Table 1 shows the components of the estimates of individual giving for 2006, 2007, and 2008.

The estimated change in individual giving is developed using government data about changes in personal income and tax rates, and the change in the Standard & Poor's 500 Index. The amount of estimated change is based on the long-term historical relationship between these economic variables and changes in itemized deductions for charitable contributions. This method was developed and tested by economists Partha Deb, Mark Wilhelm, and Patrick Rooney.[1]

Estimate of giving by bequest

The method of estimating contributions by bequest follows procedures

Table 1
Estimate of individual giving, 2006 through 2008
($ in billions)

2006

Itemized deductions for charitable contributions, IRS	186.646
Estimated giving by non-itemizers, COPPS	37.233
Total estimated individual giving	223.879

2007

2006 itemized deductions for charitable contributions, IRS	186.646
Estimated change in giving by itemizers, 2006	7.740
Estimate for giving by non-itemizers, COPPS	41.186
Total estimated individual giving	235.572

2008

2006 itemized deductions for charitable contributions, IRS	186.646
Estimated change in giving by itemizers, 2007	7.740
Estimated change in giving by itemizers, 2008	− 7.690
Estimate for giving by non-itemizers, COPPS	42.582
Total estimated individual giving	229.278

Data sources: IRS=Internal Revenue Service; GUSA=*Giving USA*; and COPPS=Center on Philanthropy Panel Study

introduced in *Giving USA 2005*. The procedure uses data collected by the Council for Aid to Education (CAE) about bequests received at institutions of higher education to develop an estimate of the amount bequeathed to all charities by estates that file estate tax returns. To that estimate is added a value representing charitable bequests made by estates below the federal estate tax filing threshold.

For charitable bequests in 2008, the estimate of giving by bequest is based on the reported $2.654 billion reported in the survey for 2007-2008. Over time, the CAE value has been 13.7 percent of all reported bequests on estate tax returns. For the 2008 estimate in *Giving USA*, the CAE amount is divided by 0.137 to get $19.42 billion (all calculations are rounded). To that is added a supplement representing very large estate gifts that are likely to have

Table 2
Bequests announced in 2006 and included in the
Giving USA estimate for 2008

Decedent	Billion $
Joan Palevsky	0.200
Frederic and Eleanor Schwartz	0.053
Randall Terry	0.025
Total	$0.278

Table 3
Bequest estimate, 2008
($ in billions)

Council for Aid to Education (CAE) findings, bequest receipts, higher educational institutions, 2007–2008	2.65
CAE result divided by 0.137 to yield estimate of all giving by estates that file estate tax returns, *GUSA*	19.42
Supplemental 'mega-bequests,' *GUSA*, 2006 amounts likely to be on 2008 estate tax returns	0.28
Estimate, giving by estates below $2 million, 2008, GUSA	2.96
Total estimated giving by charitable bequest	22.66

Data sources: CAE=Council for Aid to Education; GUSA=Giving USA

been filed on estate tax returns in 2008. These estates are identified by examining announced gifts reported in 2006, as it typically takes about two years for an estate to file an estate tax return.

Added to the value resulting from the CAE estimate and the large estates is an estimate of contributions made by estates that are below the federal estate tax filing threshold of $2.0 million in 2008. The method used to estimate giving by estates below the filing threshold for federal estate tax is deliberately conservative and is likely to underestimate total charitable bequests given in any year. In the absence of firm data about bequests from estates with gross estate value below $2 million, *Giving USA* has adopted this conservative approach that sets a lower boundary on the estimate. The estimate for contributions made by estates below the federal estate tax filing threshold relies on some known information and some estimates. The known information includes:

- Number of deaths of adults aged 55 and above;

- An average net worth for adults in that age group; and

- The average percentage of net estate value left to charity by adults in this age group.

Table 3 shows the several components of the bequest estimate for 2008.

Estimate of giving by foundations

The estimate of giving by foundations uses the figures released by the Foundation Center for giving by independent, community, and operating foundations in 2008.[2] The estimated total for giving to foundations does not include payments by Warren Buffett to the Bill & Melinda Gates Foundation. Those donations are intended to be granted to their ultimate charitable beneficiaries within a few years and will be tracked as awards are announced. The Foundation Center also estimates giving by corporate foundations. That component is moved from the Foundation Center's estimate of giving by all types of foundations and put in the *Giving USA* estimate of giving by corporations.

Estimate of giving by corporations

The estimate of giving by corporations is based on the most recent final data available for itemized contributions claimed by companies on federal tax returns, which is modified to:

1) Add changes in corporate giving found in an estimating procedure used by *Giving USA* for the two most recent years;

2) Deduct corporate contributions to corporate foundations, as estimated by *Giving USA* for the most recent year based on findings about the prior year released by the Foundation Center; and

3) Add the Foundation Center's estimate of giving by corporate foundations.[3]

For giving in 2008, the final IRS data about contributions itemized by corporations are available for 2006. Table 4 illustrates components of the estimate of corporate giving for 2006, 2007, and 2008. A more technical explanation of the *Giving USA* estimating procedure for corporate giving appears in a paper written in 2004 by W. Chin, M. Brown, and P. Rooney that is available at www.philanthropy.iupui.edu.

Table 4
Corporate giving estimate, 2006–2008
($ in billions)

2006

Itemized deductions for corporate charitable contributions, IRS	14.79
Minus gifts to foundations in 2006, FC	− 4.00
Plus corporate foundation grants made	+ 4.10
Total estimated corporate giving	14.89

2007

2006 itemized deductions for charitable contributions, IRS	14.79
Estimated change in corporate giving, 2007	+ 0.41
Sub-total before adjustments for foundations, disasters	15.20
Less gifts to foundations in 2007, FC	− 4.42
Plus corporate foundation grants made, FC	+ 4.40
Total estimated corporate giving	15.18

2008

2006 itemized deductions for charitable contributions, IRS	14.79
Estimated change in corporate giving, 2007	+ 0.41
Estimated change in corporate giving, 2008	− 0.83
Sub-total before adjustments for foundations	14.37
Less gifts to foundations in 2008, *GUSA*	− 4.30
Plus corporate foundation grants made, FC	+ 4.43
Total estimated corporate giving	14.50

Data sources: IRS=Internal Revenue Service; *GUSA=Giving USA*; FC=Foundation Center

Estimates of giving to types of recipient organizations

Giving USA relies on data provided by other research organizations for some components of the estimates of giving by type of recipient. Giving USA has, with this edition, developed estimates using modeling procedures similar to the ones used since 2002 for giving by individuals. The following sections describe briefly the data sources and methods used in developing estimates for each subsector.

Estimate of giving to religion

The estimate of giving to religion relies on data from several sources:

■ A baseline estimate from 1986 of $50 billion in giving to religion that was developed separately by three different organizations.[4]

■ A percentage change in giving to religion developed when summing contributions data released by the National Council of Churches of Christ of the USA, an estimate of giving to the Roman Catholic Church

based on surveys analyzed from 2002 through 2006,[5] and amounts report by members of the Evangelical Council for Financial Accountability.

Because the denominational contributions data are typically released a year or more after *Giving USA* releases its initial estimates for giving by subsector, the current year's estimate of giving to religion is a *Giving USA* estimate based on the past three years of changes. *Giving USA* averaged the inflation-adjusted percentage changes found in giving to religion from 2005 through 2007.[6] Adjusted for inflation, the multiple-year average is an increase of 1.6 percent. Converted to remove the inflation adjustment, that is an estimated increase of 5.5 percent in giving to religion in 2008. Table 5 delineates the steps used in estimating giving to religion.

Estimates of giving by subsector

The estimates for subsectors for 2005 other than religion and foundations are based on IRS Forms 990 analyzed

Table 5
Components of the estimate of giving to religion, 2008
($ in billions)

Inflation-adjusted estimate for 2007, to equivalent of 2008 dollars, *GUSA* + change from NCCC, ECFA, *GUSA*		105.21
Estimated percentage change, 2008, *GUSA**	1.8%	
Dollar change, 2008 using rate of previous change (inflation-adjusted dollars)		+ 1.68
Total, 2008 in 2008 dollars		106.89

*Inflation-adjusted rate, averaged over 2005–2007 was 1.8 percent change. With inflation in 2008 at 3.8 percent, this equates to a 5.7 percent change with rounding, in current dollars (without inflation adjustment).
Data sources: NCCC=National Council of Churches of Christ; ECFA=Evangelical Council for Financial Accountability; *GUSA=Giving USA.*

by the National Center for Charitable Statistics for *Giving USA*.

The estimates for 2006 apply the rate of change found in the survey conducted by *Giving USA* in spring 2007 to the revised 2005 estimates.

The estimates for 2007 and those released in this volume use a method developed in 2008 to be consistent with other estimating procedures used for *Giving USA*. *Giving USA* will use results from the National Center for Charitable Statistics when it analyzes IRS Forms 990 to revise the estimates for 2006 through 2008.

New method for estimating giving to subsectors

The 2007 and 2008 estimates for giving by subsector use a method developed specifically for *Giving USA*. The estimates derive from a modeling procedure similar to the one used since 2002 for individual giving. The model predicts the dollar amount (in billions) of change in giving to each subsector for 2008. That dollar amount of change is added to the estimate for 2007 to yield the total estimated giving to a subsector for 2008.

The subsector estimating model is applied for estimating giving to education, environment/animals, human services, health, international affairs, and public-society benefit. For each subsector in turn, the model uses inflation-adjusted changes in:

- Standard & Poor's 500 stock index;
- Personal income;
- Total giving two years ago (lagged); and

- Contributions to the same subsector one year earlier (lagged).

The model was developed and tested by Partha Deb, an economist at Hunter College in New York City and a specialist in time-series forecasting. It was implemented with *Giving USA 2008*.

Estimate of giving to foundations

The Foundation Center and *Giving USA* estimate contributions to foundations of $32.65 billion for 2008. Approximately 30 percent of giving to foundations in any one year is from estates that file income tax returns, based on *Giving USA*'s comparison of estate tax return information about charitable bequests and the Foundation Center's reports of giving to foundations. Typically, major estate gifts to foundations arrive at the foundations over time as the estate is settled. The estimate for 2008 is 13 percent of estimated individual and bequest contributions for 2008. This is the average share of individual and bequest giving that went to foundations from 2005 through 2007, based on *Giving USA* estimates for charitable giving and Foundation Center reported values for gifts to grantmaking foundations (excluding corporate foundations).

Giving USA 2009 survey for human services organizations

Giving USA surveyed organizations in one subsector, human services, about their fundraising results for 2008. This survey was conducted online, with an invitation sent to more than 5,954 organizations. The sample was prepared with assistance from the National

Center for Charitable Statistics (NCCS). It combined all organizations identified as having charitable revenue of $10 million or more and a random sample of organizations with charitable revenue below $10 million. Organizations were identified for the sample and if no email information was available through the list from NCCS, they were not sent the survey.

The initial sample was 13,709 organizations. Emails were identified for 5,954, and after undeliverable messages, a total of 3,211 were successfully sent. A total of 228 responses were received. This is 7.1 percent of invitations confirmed as delivered and 1.7 percent of the initial list (which included organizations for which no email address could be found). The survey was not used in developing estimates for *Giving USA*. Results include information about the percentage of funding from various types of donors, the types of fundraising methods used, receipt of charitable bequests and planned gift commitments in 2008, and more.

What is excluded from *Giving USA* estimates

Giving USA researchers develop estimates of the amount of philanthropic giving to charitable organizations in the United States, including gifts to houses of worship and their national headquarters. *Giving USA* does not estimate all forms of revenue to nonprofit organizations. Among the types of revenue not included in *Giving USA* are allocations from other charitable organizations, such as United Way or a communal fund;

fees for services; payments that are not tax-deductible as gifts because the donor receives services of value in exchange; gross proceeds from special events; and membership dues.

Why can't all giving be allocated to a recipient?

Each year, a portion of total charitable receipts reported by *Giving USA* is labeled as unallocated, meaning that *Giving USA* cannot attribute all giving to a subsector. Unallocated giving occurs for various reasons, which include:

- **All *Giving USA* figures are estimates.** Tax data are used to estimate the sources of giving.

- **Estimates done in different ways should NOT match.** It is not expected that the estimate of sources of giving will exactly match the estimate of uses of these gifts. Government agencies, such as those that release Gross Domestic Product figures, also acknowledge differences between estimates developed using one method and those developed using a different method.[7]

- **Nonprofits formed since 2006 are not included in the IRS Forms 990 values.** *Giving USA* bases its estimates on IRS Forms 990. In order to have a complete record that represents the nonprofit sector, a year is selected for which most of the required IRS Forms 990 are already received. Since 2006, more organizations have formed but IRS Forms 990 have not been tabulated according to subsector. Nevertheless, they are accounted in *Giving USA* overall and included in the count.

- **Gifts made to government agencies are charitable contributions but are not tracked in *Giving USA*'s survey of charitable organizations.** *Giving USA* does not track charitable gifts received at government agencies, such as school districts, parks and recreation departments, civic improvement programs, state institutions of higher education, and public libraries. There is no single national list of the public organizations that receive gifts. They cannot be identified and surveyed. The amount donated in recent years to school districts, especially by foundations, has grown significantly. *Giving USA* uses publicly reported large gifts ($1 million or more) to public schools to supplement the estimate of giving to public schools. Other donations, likely to be very frequent in households with children in school, are not included, however.

- **Foundation grants paid to organizations in other countries that are not registered as charities in the United States appear on the "sources" side but are not tracked by type of recipient.** The Foundation Center estimates $1.9 billion in grants paid to recipients in other countries in 2007.

- **A gift in the calendar year will not appear in a fiscal year report by a charity filing an IRS Form 990.** A gift for the calendar year might not appear in a fiscal report by a charity, and *Giving USA* uses the data charities report as the basis for the estimates. For example, gifts to higher education institutions in December 2007 are likely to appear as part of the education estimate for 2008 since most higher education institutions use a fiscal year for reporting.

- **Some donors make arrangements for significant deferred charitable gifts without telling the nonprofit.** For instance, a donor can create a trust through a financial institution and take the allowed deduction subject to IRS rules for valuing such gifts. Unless the donor informs the nonprofit organization that will ultimately receive some of the trust's proceeds, the nonprofit is unaware of the gift and does not report it as revenue.

- **A donor might claim a different amount for a deduction than a charity records as a receipt.** This discrepancy can occur for an in-kind gift, in which the donor claims market value of an item, and the charity reports as charitable revenue the amount received from the sale of the item or some other value based on a different scale than the one the donor used.

Why *Giving USA* makes revisions
Because *Giving USA*'s results are a series of estimates, they are revised as additional information becomes available. Government agencies such as the Internal Revenue Service, the Bureau of Economic Analysis, and many others routinely issue preliminary estimates that are revised as more data are obtained and analyzed.

A discussion of the revisions made to prior years' *Giving USA* estimates is available at www.givingusa.org, with the user name and password appearing on the first page.

---

1   P. Deb, M. Wilhelm, M. Rooney, and M. Brown, Estimating charitable giving, Nonprofit and Voluntary Sector Quarterly, December 2003.

2   S. Lawrence and R. Mukai, *Foundation Growth and Giving Estimates: Current Outlook: 2009 Edition*, The Foundation Center, 2008, www.foundationcenter.org.

3   ibid.

4   An examination of *Giving USA*'s estimate of giving to religion, compared with estimates developed using two other methods, appears in the paper "Reconciling estimates of religious giving," written in 2005 by J. C. Harris, M. Brown, and P. Rooney. The three methods yield estimates within 5 percent of one another, offering some reassurance that using 1986 findings as a baseline is at least as good as some other approaches.

5   Joseph Claude Harris estimated Catholic giving for *Giving USA* for the years 2002 to 2006 using data from a survey of Catholic parishes.

6   This is a change in methodology implemented in *Giving USA 2008*. The change was recommended by the Advisory Council on the grounds that the past three years are better predictors of current behavior.

7   C. Ehemann and B. Moulton, Balancing the GDP account, working paper, Bureau of Economic Analysis, May 2001, www.bea.gov, under "papers and presentations."

Some of the definitions are from the National Center for Charitable Statistics http://nccs.urban.org/glossary.htm.

Average: In statistics, the *mean*. This figure is calculated by summing the values from each respondent or reporting organization and then dividing by the number of respondents. An average can be a good representation of a trend if the organizations in the group report amounts that are relatively close together. It can misrepresent a trend if the difference between the highest amount reported and the lowest amount reported is very large. In that instance, a median might be a better point of comparison. *See also* **Median**.

Charitable revenue: Philanthropic gifts received by a charity organization. *Giving USA* asks organizations that participate in its survey to report cash received or the cash value of in-kind gifts. Where possible, we ask that unpaid pledges be excluded from the total reported charitable revenue.

Charity or charitable organization: In this book, charitable organization denotes an entity recognized as tax-exempt under section 501(c)(3) of the Internal Revenue Code. Charitable organizations are exempt from federal income taxes because of their religious, educational, scientific, and public purposes. They are eligible to receive tax-deductible gifts. *See also* **Public charity**, **Private foundation**.

Direct public support: As used on IRS Form 990, direct public support appears on line 1a and represents charitable revenue (gifts and grants).

Gift: Transfer of cash or other asset by an individual, corporation, estate or foundation. Gifts do not include government grants or contracts, allocations from nonprofit organizations, such as United Ways or communal funds, or distributions from donor-advised funds.

Indirect public support: As used on IRS Form 990, indirect public support appears on line 1b and includes transfers from one nonprofit organization to another. This includes allocations from federated campaigns, distributions from donor-advised funds, and contributions from a religious organization to another nonprofit, among other transfers.

IRS Form 990: An annual return filed with the Internal Revenue Service by nonprofit, tax-exempt organizations (even those that are not charities) with gross receipts for the year of $25,000 or more. May be submitted on a 990-EZ (when receipts are from $25,000 to $100,000 and assets are less than $250,000). Private foundations use a variation of the form, the Form 990-PF, with additional information required.

Large organization: *Giving USA* defines large organizations as those that had charitable revenue of $20 million or more.

Mean: *See* **Average**.

Median: In a summary of data, the median is the middle response. When the responses are organized sequentially, one-half of the responses given are lower than the median, and one-half are higher. Typically, when the amounts reported in a survey are close together, the median and the mean (average) will be close together. If the answers are very different from one another, the average and the median can be very different. Median values are less sensitive to the effects of outliers than are mean values. *See also* **Average**.

Medium-sized organization: *Giving USA* defines medium-sized organizations as those with total charitable revenue between $1 million and $4.99 million.

Moderately sized organization: *Giving USA* presents information about moderately sized organizations, those with charitable revenue between $5 million and $19.99 million.

National Taxonomy of Exempt Entities: A definitive classification system for nonprofit organizations that are recognized as tax-exempt under section 501(c)(3) of the Internal Revenue Code. See the online resources available at the site listed at the front of this book for a listing of the 26 major groups (named by letters of the alphabet) and examples of organizations within each group. Major groups have been clustered into 10 subsectors as follows. *See also* **Subsector**.

Subsector	Major groups included
Arts, culture, and humanities	A
Education	B
Environment/animals	C, D
Health	E, F, G, H
Human services	I, J, K, L, M, N, O, P
International affairs	Q
Public-society benefit	R, S, T, U, V, W
Religion	X
Mutual/membership benefit*	Y
Unknown, unclassified	Z

*This subsector is not tracked by *Giving USA*

Nonprofit organization: An organization whose net revenue is not distributed to individuals or other stakeholders, but is used to further the organization's mission. The organization is not owned by but is governed by a board of trustees. Not all nonprofit organizations are charities.

Nonprofit sector: A sector of the economy, apart from the government, for which profit is not a motive. Organizations may be exempt from federal, state, and local taxes. Includes houses of worship; charitable organizations formed under section 501(c)(3) of the Internal Revenue Code; and organizations formed under other sections of the Code, such as advocacy organizations, membership organizations, and others.

NTEE: *See* **National Taxonomy of Exempt Entities**.

Planned gift: The Association of Fundraising Professionals says a planned gift is structured and integrates personal, financial, and estate-planning goals with the donor's lifetime or testamentary (will) giving. Many planned gift vehicles are used, including bequests, charitable trusts, and charitable annuities.

Private foundation: Private foundation status is granted to an organization formed for a charitable purpose under section 501(c)(3) of the Internal Revenue Code that does not receive one-third or more of its support from public donations. Most, but not all, private foundations give grants to public charities. *See also* **Charity or charitable organization**, **Public charity**.

Public charity: An organization that qualifies for status as a public charity under Section 509 (a) of the Internal Revenue Code. A public charity includes tax-exempt organizations formed for certain purposes (a church; an educational organization, including public schools; a hospital or medical research facility; or an endowment operated for the benefit of a higher education institution). An organization formed for other purposes can also be a public charity if it receives a substantial part of its support from the general public. Support from a governmental unit is considered public support by proxy via taxes. Complete information about public charities can be found in IRS Publication 557. Note that some, but not all, charitable organizations formed under section 501(c)(3) are public charities. *See also* **Charity or charitable organization**, **Private foundation**.

Public support: As used by the Internal Revenue Service on IRS Form 990, line 1d, public support is the sum of line 1a or "direct public support," generally charitable gifts or grants; line 1b or "indirect public support," generally transfers from other nonprofits; and line 1c or government grants.

Reporting organization: A charitable organization that files an IRS Form 990.

Sector: The portion of the national economy that fits certain criteria for ownership and distribution of surplus. Examples include the business sector, the government sector, and the nonprofit sector. *See also* **Subsector**.

Small organization: *Giving USA* identifies small organizations as those with less than $1 million in charitable revenue.

Subsector: There are several nonprofit subsectors based on organizational purposes. *See also* **National Taxonomy of Exempt Entities, Sector**.

Tax-deductible: A contribution to an organization is deductible for income tax purposes if the organization is a church or is registered with and recognized by the IRS as a tax-exempt, nonprofit charity.

Tax-exempt: An organization may be exempt because it is a church or because of registration within a state or with the Internal Revenue Service. State exemptions may cover sales tax, property tax, and/or state income tax. Approved registration with the IRS will exempt an organization from federal income tax. Organizations that have more than $5,000 in gross revenues annually are legally responsible for registering with the IRS.

A-Arts, culture, humanities activities
- arts & culture (multipurpose activities)
- media & communications
- visual arts
- museums
- performing arts
- humanities
- historical societies & related historical activities

B-Educational institutions & related activities
- elementary & secondary education (preschool-grade 12)
- vocational/technical schools
- higher education
- graduate/professional schools
- adult/continuing education
- libraries
- student services & organizations

C-Environment quality, protection
- pollution abatement & control
- natural resources conservation & protection
- botanic/horticulture activities
- environmental beautification & open spaces
- environmental education & outdoor survival

D-Animal-related activities
- animal protection & welfare
- humane society
- wildlife preservation & protection
- veterinary services
- zoos & aquariums
- specialty animals & other services

E-Health-general & rehabilitative
- hospitals, nursing homes & primary medical care
- health treatment, primarily outpatient
- reproductive health care
- rehabilitative medical services
- health support services
- emergency medical services
- public health & wellness education
- health care financing/insurance programs

F-Mental health, crisis intervention
- addiction prevention & treatment
- mental health treatment & services
- crisis intervention
- psychiatric/mental health-primary care
- half-way houses (mental health)/transitional care

G-Disease/disorder/medical disciplines (multipurpose)
- birth defects & genetic diseases
- cancer
- diseases of specific organs
- nerve, muscle & bone diseases
- allergy-related diseases
- specific named diseases
- medical disciplines/specialties

H-Medical research
- identical hierarchy to diseases/disorders/medical disciplines in major field "G"
- example: G30 represents American Cancer Society; H30 represents cancer research

I-Public protection: crime/courts/legal services
- police & law enforcement agencies
- correctional facilities & prisoner services
- crime prevention
- rehabilitation of offenders
- administration of justice/courts
- protection against/prevention of neglect, abuse, exploitation
- legal services

J-Employment/jobs
- vocational guidance & training (such as on-the-job programs)
- employment procurement assistance
- vocational rehabilitation
- employment assistance for the handicapped
- labor union/organizations
- labor-management relations

K-Food, nutrition, agriculture
- agricultural services aimed at food procurement
- food service/free food distribution
- nutrition promotion
- farmland preservation

L-Housing/shelter
- housing development/construction
- housing search assistance
- low-cost temporary shelters such as youth hostels
- homeless, temporary shelter
- housing owners/renters organizations
- housing support services

M-Public safety/disaster preparedness & relief
- disaster prevention, such as flood control
- disaster relief (US domestic)
- safety education
- civil defense & preparedness programs

N-Recreation, leisure, sports, athletics
- camps
- physical fitness & community recreation
- sports training
- recreation/pleasure or social clubs
- amateur sports
- Olympics & Special Olympics

O-Youth Development
- youth centers (such as boys/girls clubs)
- scouting
- big brothers/sisters
- agricultural development (such as 4-H)
- business development, Junior Achievement
- citizenship programs
- religious leadership development

P-Human service-other/multipurpose
- multipurpose service organizations
- children & youth services
- family services
- personal social services
- emergency assistance (food, clothing)
- residential/custodial care
- centers promoting independence of specific groups, such as senior or women's centers

Q-International
- exchange programs
- international development
- international relief services (foreign disaster relief)
- peace & security
- foreign policy research & analyses (U.S. domestic)
- international human rights

R-Civil rights/civil liberties
- equal opportunity & access
- voter education/registration
- civil liberties

S-Community improvement/development
- community/neighborhood development
- community coalitions
- economic development, urban and rural
- business services
- community service clubs (such as Junior League)

T-Philanthropy & voluntarism
- philanthropy association/society
- private foundations, funds (e.g., women's funds), and community foundations
- community funds and federated giving
- voluntarism promotion

U-Science
- scientific research & promotion
- physical/earth sciences
- engineering/technology
- biological sciences

V-Social sciences
- social science research/studies
- interdisciplinary studies, such as black studies, women's studies, urban studies, etc.

W-Public affairs/society benefit
- public policy research, general
- government & public administration
- transportation systems
- public utilities
- consumer rights/education

X-Religion/spiritual development
- Christian churches, missionary societies and related religious bodies
- Jewish synagogues
- other specific religions

Y-Mutual membership benefit organizations
- insurance providers & services (other than health)
- pension/retirement funds
- fraternal beneficiary funds
- cemeteries & burial services

Z99-unknown, unclassifiable

Source: *The Foundation Grants Index,* The Foundation Center
Note: In 1994, community funds and federated giving programs were moved from letter **S** to letter **T**. They are still in the same broad category, called "public-society benefit."

Member firms

Giving Institute, the founding organization of Giving USA Foundation™, consists of member firms that embrace the highest ethical standards and maintain a strict code of fair practices. If you are looking for counsel or resources visit givinginstitute.org.

A.L. Brourman Associates, Inc.
Advantage Consulting
Alexander Haas
The Alford Group Inc.
American City Bureau, Inc.
Arnoult & Associates Inc.
Blackburn Associates, Inc.
CCS Fund Raising
Campbell & Company
Carlton & Company
The Collins Group, Inc.
Compton Fundraising Consultants, Ltd.
The Covenant Group
The Curtis Group
Danforth Development
Durkin Associates
The EHL Consulting Group, Inc.
eTapestry
Fund Inc®
Global Advancement, LLC
Grenzebach Glier & Associates, Inc.
Hodge, Cramer & Associates, Inc.
IDC
Jeffrey Byrne & Associates, Inc.
Ketchum, a Pursuant Company
Marts & Lundy, Inc.
Miller Group Worldwide, LLC
The Oram Group, Inc.
Raybin Associates, Inc.
Ruotolo Associates Inc.
The Sharpe Group
Smith Beers Yunker & Company, Inc.
StaleyRobeson®
Woodburn, Kyle & Company

2009 Board of Directors

Giving Institute officers

Nancy L. Raybin, Raybin Associates, Inc., *Chair*
Thomas W. Mesaros, CFRE, The Alford Group Inc., *1st Vice Chair*
David H. King, CFRE, Alexander Haas, *2nd Vice Chair*
Jeffrey D. Byrne, Jeffrey Byrne & Associates, Inc., *Treasurer*
Aggie Sweeney, The Collins Group, Inc., *Secretary*
George C. Ruotolo, Jr., CFRE, Ruotolo Associates Inc., *Immediate Past Chair*

Giving Institute directors

Anthony Alonso, Advantage Consulting
Leo P. Arnoult, CFRE, Arnoult & Associates Inc.
John M. Biggins, American City Bureau, Inc.
David W. Blackburn, Blackburn Associates, Inc.
Audrey Brourman, CFRE, A.L. Brourman & Associates, Inc.
Kristina Carlson, CFRE, eMPT, Ketchum, a Pursuant Company
L. Gregg Carlson, IDC
William L. Carlton, ACFRE, Carlton & Company
Michelle D. Cramer, CFRE, Hodge, Cramer & Associates, Inc.
W. Keith Curtis, The Curtis Group
William A. Durkin, Jr., Durkin Associates
Robert I. Evans, The EHL Consulting Group, Inc.
Donald M. Fellows, Marts & Lundy, Inc.
Peter J. Fissinger, CFRE, Campbell & Company
Rita J. Galowich, Fund Inc®
John J. Glier, Grenzebach Glier & Associates, Inc.
Henry (Hank) Goldstein, CFRE, The Oram Group, Inc.
Frederic (Rick) J. Happy, CCS Fund Raising
Sarah J. Howard, CFRE, Compton Fundraising Consultants, Ltd.
Edwine (Dana) Danforth Kimberly, CFRE, Danforth Development
Robert K. Lewis, Jr., CFRE, Global Advancement, LLC
Jay B. Love, eTapestry
John H. Miller, The Miller Group Worldwide, LLC
Leonard J. Moisan, Ph.D., The Covenant Group
Robert F. Sharpe, Jr., The Sharpe Group
Joseph L. Staley, CFRE, StaleyRobeson®
Peter Woodburn, Woodburn, Kyle & Company
James D. Yunker, Ed.D., Smith Beers Yunker & Company, Inc.

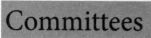
Committees

Editorial Review Board

James D. Yunker, Ed.D., *Chair*
Smith Beers Yunker & Company, Inc.

Sue S. Acri, CFRE
Ketchum, a Pursuant Company

L. Pendleton Armistead, Ed.D.
The Clements Group

Leo P. Arnoult, CFRE
Arnoult & Associates, Inc.

David Blackburn
Blackburn Associates

Gary L. Cardaronella
Cardaronella Stirling Associates

William L. Carlton, ACFRE
Carlton & Company

Matthew Cottle, CFRE
Jeffrey Byrne & Associates, Inc.

Robert I. Evans
The EHL Consulting Group, Inc.

Edith H. Falk
Campbell & Company

Kimberly Hawkins
Raybin Associates, Inc.

Scott R. Lange
Marts & Lundy, Inc.

Wendy S. McGrady
The Curtis Group

Leonard J. Moisan, Ph.D.
The Covenant Group

Elizabeth S. Morford, CFRE
Development Resources Unlimited

Donna L. Wiley, Ph.D.
Grenzebach Glier & Associates, Inc.

Resource Development Committee

Leo P. Arnoult, CFRE, *Co-Chair*
Arnoult & Associates

Edith H. Falk, *Co-Chair*
Campbell & Company

L. Gregg Carlson
IDC

Jennifer Furla
Jeffrey Byrne & Associates, Inc.

Henry (Hank) Goldstein, CFRE
The Oram Group, Inc.

Richard T. Jolly
Marts & Lundy, Inc.

Robert K. Lewis Jr., CFRE
Global Advancement, LLC

Del Martin, CFRE
Alexander Haas

Cover Photograph Contest Committee

Leslie Biggins Mollsen, *Chair*
American City Bureau, Inc.

Charlie Cummings
Giving USA Foundation™

Barry Dodd
Alexander Haas

Del Martin, CFRE
Alexander Haas

The Advisory Council on Methodology

Richard S. Belous, Ph.D.
Vice President, Research,
United Way National Headquarters

Eleanor Brown, Ph.D.
James Irvine Professor of Economics,
Pomona College

Carolyn C. Cavicchio
Senior Research Associate for
Global Corporate Citizenship,
The Conference Board Center for
Corporate Citizenship and Sustainability

Randy Cohen
Vice President of Policy & Research,
Americans for the Arts

Kirsten Grønbjerg, Ph.D.
Efroymson Chair in Philanthropy and
Professor of Public and Environmental
Affairs, Indiana University, The Center
on Philanthropy at Indiana University

Theodore R. Hart, CFRE
Hart Philanthropic Services Group

John J. Havens, Ph.D.
Senior Associate Director and Senior
Research Associate, Center on Wealth
and Philanthropy, Boston College

Nadine T. Jalandoni
Director, Research Services
INDEPENDENT SECTOR

Ann E. Kaplan
Director, Voluntary Support of Education,
Council for Aid to Education

John M. Kennedy, Ph.D.
Director, Indiana University Center for
Survey Research, Indiana University

Judith Kroll
Director of Research and Information,
Council on Foundations

Steven Lawrence
Senior Director of Research,
The Foundation Center

Eileen W. Lindner, Ph.D.
Editor, *Yearbook of American and
Canadian Churches*, National Council
Churches of Christ, USA

Robert B. McClelland, Ph.D.
Senior Research Economist,
U.S. Bureau of Labor Statistics

Lawrence T. McGill, Ph.D.
Senior Vice President for Research
The Foundation Center

Charles H. Moore, Executive Director,
Committee Encouraging Corporate
Philanthropy

Thomas A. Pollak
Program Director, National Center for
Charitable Statistics, The Urban Institute

Kathy L. Renzetti
Vice President - Membership,
Communications, Government Relations
Association for Healthcare Philanthropy

Lester M. Salamon, Ph.D.
Director, Center for Civil Society
Studies, The Johns Hopkins University

Paul G. Schervish, Ph.D.
Director, Center on Wealth and
Philanthropy, Boston College

Frank P. Stafford, Ph.D., Director,
Institute for Social Research,
University of Michigan

Richard S. Steinberg, Ph.D.
Professor of Economics, Indiana University-
Purdue University Indianapolis

Christopher Thompson, Ph.D.
Vice President of Research and Information
Services, Council for Advancement and
Support of Education

For Giving USA Foundation™

James D. Yunker, Ed.D. *Chair*
President, Smith Beers Yunker & Company

Leo P. Arnoult, CFRE
President, Arnoult & Associates, Inc.

David Bergeson, Ph.D., CAE (*ex officio*)
Executive Director,
Giving USA Foundation™

Del Martin, CFRE
Founding Partner, Alexander Haas

Nancy Raybin
Managing Partner, Raybin Associates, Inc.

Robert F. Sharpe, Jr.
President, The Sharpe Group

For the Center on Philanthropy at Indiana University

Reema T. Bhakta
Research Development Specialist

Melissa S. Brown
Managing Editor, *Giving USA*

Heidi K. Frederick
Assistant Director of Research

Una O. Osili, PhD.
Interim Director of Research

Patrick M. Rooney, Ph.D.
Executive Director

Staff

Reema T. Bhakta, Research Development Specialist
Melissa S. Brown, Managing Editor, *Giving USA*
Adriene L. Davis, Communications Manager
Heidi K. Frederick, Assistant Director of Research
Una O. Osili, Ph.D. Interim Director of Research
Patrick M. Rooney, Ph.D., Executive Director
Ke Wu, Applied Statistician
Assistants: Hao Han, Cynthia Hyatte, Teresa Jones, Sung-Ju Kim, Megan McDermott, Melanie Miller, Ani Muradyan, Kirk Ralston, Sangdong Tak

Chapter authors

Unless otherwise listed, chapters are by Melissa S. Brown.

Giving by Corporations	Xiaonan Kou
Giving to Religion	James R. Kienker
Giving to Education	Angela D. Seaworth
Giving to Human Services	Heidi K. Frederick and Megan McDermott
Giving to Public-Society Benefit	Rebecca Nannery
Giving to Arts	Scott D. Jones
Giving to International Affairs	Deborah A. Hirt
Legal-Legislative Overview	David A. Fleischhacker
$10 Million and Over List	David A. Fleischhacker

Index

Professional Code of Ethics

Member firms, in seeking at all times to provide candid and rigorous counsel, and the highest quality of services to every client, adhere to the following ethical standards:

- Member firms pledge to honor the confidentiality of client prospect and donor lists, their business affairs, and the right to privacy enjoyed by every institution, volunteer and donor.

- Members firms charge clients based upon the professional services provided. Their fees are never based upon charitable gifts raised or a percentage of contributions.

- Member firms disclose to clients and prospective clients any professional, personal, or client relationships that might be construed as conflicts of interest.

- Member firms seek at all times to ensure that their clients will deploy gifts for the purposes for which they were given.

- Member firms do not guarantee fundraising results, promise access to the donors of current or previous client institutions, or otherwise engage in marketing methods that are misleading to prospective clients, to the public or to individual donors.

- Member firms do not accept or maintain custody of gifts, or of gift funds that have been contributed to client institutions.

- Member firms do not make undisclosed payments or provide special consideration to volunteers, officers, directors, trustees, employees, beneficiaries or advisors to a not-for-profit organization as compensation for influencing the selection of the firm or its services.

- Member firms do not make exaggerated or erroneous claims relative to the past achievements of their firms, of their staff professionals, or of their client institutions.

Standards of Practice

A Statement of Best Practices Adopted By Its Members

- Members pledge to respect the mission and values of each client organization, and the central importance of each of its stakeholders.

- Members pledge to provide only those services that will advance the mission of each client organization, and which will support the values they espouse.

- Members, and their firms, will readily share the professional credentials and experience of each of their staff professionals.

- Member firms will always endeavor to put into place written service agreements with each of their client organizations.

- Member firms will be transparent and fair with respect to how they bill fees and expenses.

- Member firms will provide credible references for their previous client work, and ensure ready access to those client references.

- Members affirm their commitment to the appropriate recognition and stewardship of each gift, irrespective of its size or source.

- Member firms counsel their clients on the value of institutional stakeholders, and their professional staff, taking the lead in the solicitation of every gift.

- Members are committed to the shared standards of Best Practice for global philanthropy and Civil Society, wherever they come to exist.

 **G̃IVINGUSA** Order Your Copy of *Giving USA 2009* Today!

F O U N D A T I O N

First Name_____ Last Name _____

Organization _____

Address 1 _____

Address 2 _____

City_____ State _____ ZIP_____ Country _____

Phone _____Fax _____ E-mail (required)_____

Prepayment is required in U.S. Dollars payable to Giving USA Foundation™

Payment Type ❑ Check ❑ Visa ❑ MasterCard ❑ American Express ❑ Discover

Credit Card Number _____Exp. Date_____

Credit Card Billing Address (if different than above) _____

Signature_____

Code	Publication	Price	Qty	Total
5017-246	*Giving USA 2009* **Platinum Subscription! Best Value!** *Giving USA 2009*—The Annual Report on Philanthropy for the Year 2008 (Delivered in hard copy and searchable electronic format) *Giving USA Spotlight* e-Newsletter—4 issues *Giving USA 2009* Presentation on CD	$270		
5018-246	*Giving USA 2009* **Gold Subscription** *Giving USA 2009*—The Annual Report on Philanthropy for the Year 2008 *(Delivered in hard-copy format)* *Giving USA Spotlight* e-Newsletter—4 issues *Giving USA 2009* Presentation on CD	$210		
5019-246	*Giving USA 2009* **Silver Subscription** *Giving USA 2009*—The Annual Report on Philanthropy for the Year 2008 (Delivered in searchable electronic format) *Giving USA Spotlight* e-Newsletter—4 issues *Giving USA 2009* Presentation on CD	$200		
5020-246	*Giving USA 2009* **Bronze Subscription** *Giving USA 2009*—The Annual Report on Philanthropy for the Year 2008 (Delivered in hard-copy format) *Giving USA Spotlight* e-Newsletter—4 issues	$165		
8012-243	*Giving USA Spotlight* Issue 1—Annual Survey of State Laws Governing Charitable Solicitations as of January 1, 2009	$45		
8016-243	*Giving USA Spotlight* Issue 1—Annual Survey of State Laws Governing Charitable Solicitations as of January 1, 2010	$45		
1008-245	*Giving USA 2009* **Presentation on CD** Full-color, ready-made computer presentation with charts and talking points	$135		
5016-243	*Giving USA 2009 Spotlight* **e-Newsletter** 4 issues, including Annual Survey of State Laws	$90		
2023-241	**BOOK ONLY:** *Giving USA 2009* The Annual Report on Philanthropy for the Year 2008 *(hard copy)*	$75		
8014-248	**e-BOOK:** *Giving USA 2009* The Annual Report on Philanthropy for the Year 2008 (delivered in searchable electronic format)	$75		
	Donation to Giving USA Foundation			

***Shipping and handling**: In the U.S. add $9.95 for orders up to $100

$13.95 for orders up to $149

$18.95 for orders of $150+

Outside of U.S. add $25 for airmail delivery

Do not include shipping on electronic products (*Spotlight* e-newsletter and e-book).

Subtotal	$
***Shipping and handling**	$
If delivered in Illinois, 9.75% tax	$
TOTAL	$

Order By Mail	**Order By Phone**	**Order By Fax**	**Order Online**
Giving USA Foundation PO Box 3781 Oak Brook, IL 60522-3781	(credit card orders) 800/462-2372 847/375-4709	888/374-7258 International Fax: +1 847/375-6487	Visit our Web store at givingusa.org

In the event of a miscalculation, I authorize Giving USA Foundation™ to charge to the above-named credit card an amount reasonably deemed by Giving USA Foundation to be accurate and appropriate. NOTICE: It is the policy of Giving USA Foundation to charge credit cards when orders are received. Our 2009 products will be shipped beginning July 1, 2009.

BOOK09

Order Your Copy of *Giving USA 2009* Today!

First Name_____ Last Name _____

Organization _____

Address 1 _____

Address 2 _____

City_____ State _____ ZIP_____ Country _____

Phone _____Fax _____ E-mail (required)_____

Prepayment is required in U.S. Dollars payable to Giving USA Foundation™

Payment Type ❑ Check ❑ Visa ❑ MasterCard ❑ American Express ❑ Discover

Credit Card Number _____Exp. Date_____

Credit Card Billing Address (if different than above) _____

Signature_____

Code	Publication	Price	Qty	Total
5017-246	*Giving USA 2009* **Platinum Subscription! Best Value!** *Giving USA 2009*—The Annual Report on Philanthropy for the Year 2008 (Delivered in hard copy and searchable electronic format) *Giving USA Spotlight* e-Newsletter—4 issues *Giving USA 2009* Presentation on CD	$270		
5018-246	*Giving USA 2009* **Gold Subscription** *Giving USA 2009*—The Annual Report on Philanthropy for the Year 2008 (Delivered in hard-copy format) *Giving USA Spotlight* e-Newsletter—4 issues *Giving USA 2009* Presentation on CD	$210		
5019-246	*Giving USA 2009* **Silver Subscription** *Giving USA 2009*—The Annual Report on Philanthropy for the Year 2008 (Delivered in searchable electronic format) *Giving USA Spotlight* e-Newsletter—4 issues *Giving USA 2009* Presentation on CD	$200		
5020-246	*Giving USA 2009* **Bronze Subscription** *Giving USA 2009*—The Annual Report on Philanthropy for the Year 2008 (Delivered in hard-copy format) *Giving USA Spotlight* e-Newsletter—4 issues	$165		
8012-243	*Giving USA Spotlight* Issue 1—Annual Survey of State Laws Governing Charitable Solicitations as of January 1, 2009	$45		
8016-243	*Giving USA Spotlight* Issue 1—Annual Survey of State Laws Governing Charitable Solicitations as of January 1, 2010	$45		
1008-245	*Giving USA 2009* **Presentation on CD** Full-color, ready-made computer presentation with charts and talking points	$135		
5016-243	*Giving USA 2009 Spotlight* **e-Newsletter** 4 issues, including Annual Survey of State Laws	$90		
2023-241	**BOOK ONLY:** *Giving USA 2009* The Annual Report on Philanthropy for the Year 2008 *(hard copy)*	$75		
8014-248	**e-BOOK:** *Giving USA 2009* The Annual Report on Philanthropy for the Year 2008 (delivered in searchable electronic format)	$75		
	Donation to Giving USA Foundation			

*Shipping and handling: In the U.S. add $9.95 for orders up to $100 $13.95 for orders up to $149 $18.95 for orders of $150+ Outside of U.S. add $25 for airmail delivery **Do not include shipping on electronic products** (*Spotlight* **e-newsletter and e-book**).	**Subtotal**	$
	*Shipping and handling	$
	If delivered in Illinois, 9.75% tax	$
	TOTAL	$

Order By Mail	**Order By Phone**	**Order By Fax**	**Order Online**
Giving USA Foundation PO Box 3781 Oak Brook, IL 60522-3781	(credit card orders) 800/462-2372 847/375-4709	888/374-7258 International Fax: +1 847/375-6487	Visit our Web store at givingusa.org

In the event of a miscalculation, I authorize Giving USA Foundation™ to charge to the above-named credit card an amount reasonably deemed by Giving USA Foundation to be accurate and appropriate. NOTICE: It is the policy of Giving USA Foundation to charge credit cards when orders are received. Our 2009 products will be shipped beginning July 1, 2009.

BOOK09